Global Media Spectacle

SUNY series in Global Media Studies
Yahya R. Kamalipour and Kuldip R. Rampal, editors

Global Media Spectacle

News War over Hong Kong

Chin-Chuan Lee
Joseph Man Chan
Zhongdang Pan
Clement Y.K. So

STATE UNIVERSITY OF NEW YORK PRESS

Published by
State University of New York Press, Albany

Cover photograph: Hong Kong citizens watch live broadcast of the handover
events on June 30, 1997. Courtesy of the *Ming Pao Daily News*.

For information, address State University of New York Press,
90 State Street, Suite 700, Albany, NY 12207

Production by Diane Ganeles
Marketing by Patrick Durocher

Library of Congress Cataloging-in-Publication Data

Global media spectacle:news war over Hong Kong / Chin-Chuan Lee . . .
[et al.]
      p. cm. — (SUNY series in global media studies)
   Includes bibliographical references and index.
   ISBN 0-7914-5471-1 (alk. paper) — ISBN 0-7914-5472-X (pbk. : alk.
paper)
   1. Reporters and reporting.   2. Hong Kong (China)—History—Transfer
of Sovereignty from Great Britain, 1997.   I. Li, Jinquan, 1946– .
II. Series.
PN4781.G56 2002
070.4'3—dc21

                                                                    2001054156

                        10 9 8 7 6 5 4 3 2 1

To our families, with love and gratitude

Contents

Figures and Tables

Preface

If journalists are said to write the first draft of history, what kind of a history will they be writing in the age of globalized media? Does this history appear to be littered with contrived images and dramas, hyped media events, and ideologically soaked catchy phrases? All global news is local. How do the media—operating as a "twenty-four-hour ideological repair shop" (van Ginneken, 1998:32)—mold international news in accordance with national interest, domestic politics, and the prevailing cultural values? Sighting this scene of international newsmaking from a hub of the world capitalist system, we are awed at how much the process of constructing mediated narratives cum historical discourses is Western-dominated both organizationally and ideologically.

The ubiquitous mediated communication of secondhand reality has kept alive the powerful images of joy and despair, destruction and triumph, authority, and emotion from the Tiananmen Square, the Berlin Wall, the Gulf War, and the Moscow coup. But as students of international communication we know surprisingly little about how the world media and journalists plan, operate, compete, and produce during these historical episodes. We know of no systematic, broad comparative account of the dynamics of international newsmaking since Wilbur Schramm (1959) published *One Day in the World's Press*, an analysis of press coverage of the Suez Canal. This sustained neglect for four decades has been particularly extraordinary in view of the proliferation of journals and publications in media studies, and of the amazing growth in the number of theoretical treatises on the ideological underpinning of newswork in relation to social power and national interest. The heat of the New World Information and Communication Order debate, once highly visible and charged in the fora of international politics, threw little light on this issue. Even the current vogue in the glamour of media globalization has barely skirted around it.

By good fortune, we were at the right place at the right time. In 1997 we were on the spot to witness an important chapter of history—the transfer of

xi

sovereignty of Hong Kong—unfolding and, further, to observe the field of action by thousands of top international journalists at close range. We saw how journalists wrote the first drafts of history from their vantage points. The result, being presented to you after long years of labor, is, we hope, a theoretically informed and empirically grounded analysis of the international newsmaking process. How did our project begin? Our institutional memory has faded: two claim the idea came from a bus ride in Montreal, the other attributes it to a challenge from a Dutch colleague, and the fourth member decides not to contest the archeological truth. What is important, however, is that we did agree to follow the admirable tradition of C. Wright Mills in trying to integrate personal interest with public issues. We were intent on taking advantage of the world media that were to congregate in one place—an alien, exotic, but most likely routine-breaking place—to cover a momentous event of global significance.

We are a team of diverse backgrounds and compatible interests who actively engage one another's minds. Lee, a native of Taiwan, on a three-year leave from the University of Minnesota to be a chair professor at the Chinese University of Hong Kong, is interested in political and international communication, political economy of the media, and the interface between social theories and media studies. Chan, then chairing the department, was born in China but grew up in Hong Kong, with interest in international and political communication as well as the impact of information technology. Pan, arriving from his previous post at the University of Pennsylvania to join the team, is a native of China and is interested in framing analysis and political communication. So returned from Canada to his native land of Hong Kong to resume his teaching position, just in time to "catch the big show"; his interest includes media sociology and the sociology of knowledge. All educated in the United States, with prior journalistic backgrounds, we met in Hong Kong. The magnitude of this project might be unimaginable for any team less diverse or less committed than ours.

In this volume, we shall try to demonstrate how nation-states fight an international discursive battle via the media to compete for legitimacy and recognition. We shall explore the causes, processes, consequences, and limits of such discursive contestation. To these goals, we strive for a "thick description" (Geertz, 1973) of contestation and alliance, themes and variations, convergence and divergence between and within various blocks of nations. We take pains to collate a mountain of media texts with the "meaning world" of journalists. These theoretical points could not have been adequately made had it not been for the scope of empirical data that our project encompasses. Comparative studies being easier said than done, we are uniquely blessed to canvas the broad landscape of eight different "national" media systems: the People's Republic of China, Hong Kong, Taiwan, the United States, Britain, Canada, Australia, and Japan. We wish to paint a general picture of broad (yet nonreductive) outlines with nuanced analysis and a lot of rich details. Having poked into a world of life stories behind these media accounts for three long years, we are feeling bittersweet loss and relief at delivering this intellectual baby.

While incorporating the strength of area studies, we have above all aimed to keep pace—and dialogue—with theoretical and methodological advances in several fields of humanities and social sciences. We began by trying to conceptualize the project theoretically in terms of what Daniel Dayan and Elihu Katz (1992) call "media events" and methodologically in terms of what William Gamson (1988) calls a constructionist approach to discourse analysis. Interwoven into this theoretical and methodological matrix are a network of theoretical visions culled together from media sociology (including media occupation, profession, and organization), international communication (the geography, ideology, linguistics, and semiology of international news), cultural studies (social construction of meanings, ideological contestation, and Orientalism), and various strains of social theories (nationalism and globalization). This process involves developing layers of arguments through journeying back and forth between social theories, media theories, and the "real world"—all guided by a comparative light.

No sooner had we set out to interview journalists than we sensed pent-up anxiety about the gulf between what they had preconceived and what they were witnessing. Such revelation continually impressed on us to discard, modify, sharpen, and improvise many hypotheses, and we have in the end strayed quite far away from the original trajectory and terrain. We are therefore grateful to the seventy-six international journalists who shared their professional insights with us in a series of grueling interviews while in the thick of fighting their own "news war." They are in this sense distant coauthors of this book. But as interpreters of their interpretations we are ultimately responsible for the viewpoints expressed. In the course of interviewing these journalists, they were eager to have our take too. This experience gave us a unique position to penetrate their minds and see what really "troubles" them.

We have spent countless hours together mulling over the outlines and details that led to mutual fusing of perspectives, the incremental development of ideas, themes, and arguments, as well as the making sense of embedded empirical meanings. We debated in the little noodle corner, in the mountaintop office overlooking the magnificent Tolo Harbor, in the crowded subway, on the noisy phone, over the delicious Peking duck and Cantonese cuisine (all too infrequently), and via the corridor of global cyberspace. Ideas have germinated and taken shape with our travel in today's global air transport to Beijing, London, Jerusalem, Acapulco, Minneapolis, and Washington, D.C. While the project is a whole piece, writing involves inevitable division of labor. Lee drafted chapters 1, 5, and 9. Chan drafted chapters 3 and 6. So drafted chapters 2 and 8 as well as prepared the index and photos. Pan drafted chapters 4, 7, the epilogue, and Appendix IV;

he also prepared the methodological note and the quantitative data. Chan was the project coordinator. In the last stage, Lee was entrusted to critique and edit the entire manuscript; in various cases, this involved extensive rewriting. Three years of asking, arguing, laughing, and griping together have accomplished a profound level of borrowed learning, the impact of which will be quite obvious in each of our future work.

Acknowledgments

Without the generous assistance of many friends and colleagues we could have not assembled the complete texts of 32 newspapers, four news magazines, as well as news and special programs from 14 television channels, scattered from Beijing to London, from New York to Tokyo, from Sydney to Toronto, and from Hong Kong to Taipei. Deserving our gratitude are Qiu Xiangzhong (London), Dr. Zhao Bin (Cardiff), Eugene Louie (San Jose), Zhan Jun (Washington, D.C.), Dr. Judy Polumbaum (Iowa City), Dr. Chen Shimin (Taipei), Dr. Lo Venhui (Taipei), Professor Pang Kafat (Taipei), Dr. Yang Chang (Vancouver), Wang Bing (Tokyo), Professor Huang Shengmin (Tokyo), Zhong Jing (Beijing), and Yin Jing (Beijing). C. K. Lau, a *South China Morning Post* columnist, collected the Australian materials for us. The British Council library in Hong Kong donated copies of British newspapers. Doris Tsang shuttled between various newsrooms to fetch textual materials under the simmering sun. Lam Kong efficiently taped Hong Kong television. Mak Yiu-on provided CTN tapes. Our hats off to all of them.

This huge database was managed under the remarkably gracious and meticulous purview of Winnie Kwok, who prodded us on, gently scolded us when deserved, gave us a pat on the back when not so deserved, and pushed us through many moments of despair. To her we owe our deepest debt and admiration. Professor Huang Shengmin, whose one-month sojourn in Hong Kong as a visiting scholar was spent exclusively on no other bigger fun than decoding the meaning of Japanese media texts, deserves a hearty thank you. An anonymous Japanese researcher read a draft on Japan. A group of dedicated graduate students including Julia Chu, Francis Lee, Zhang Yong, and Li Yanhong undertook the content analysis. Julia Chu also contributed to library research and data management. Francis Lee analyzed the data of content analysis. Zhang Yong assisted in the preparation of Appendix I. Dr. Ma Ngor transcribed some of the interview tapes. Mandy Leung assisted in library research and in checking the citations. Mak Wing Kau helped in compiling the name and subject indices. We thank them.

This work, as part of the "Mass Media and Political Transition" project, received generous support with funds from the Universities Research Grants Committee of Hong Kong. Professors Jeremy Tunstall, Everette Dennis, Lowell Dittmer, and Lynn White III offered critical support at the early stage. We are also indebted to the Shaw College, the United College, and the Chinese University of Hong Kong for providing supplemental small grants. Throughout, we have had the intellectual blessing and encouragement of Professor Elihu Katz. Professor James Curran honored us with an invitation to contribute a chapter (Lee et al., 2000) to *Mass Media and Society*. Professor Akiba Cohen moderated a theme session devoted to our project at the International Communication Association convention in Jerusalem. Professors Cees Hamelink, Jon F. Nussbaum, and Dave Dembers have offered timely reassurance to our work in their capacities as editors of various journals (Pan et al., 1999, 2001; Lee et al., 2001).

Chapter 1

Global Event, National Prisms

What the fireworks of international news illuminate or leave in the dark
is the historic panorama beyond them.

—Jaap van Ginneken (1998: 126)

Political language is designed to make lies sound truthful and murder
respectable, and to give an appearance of solidity to pure wind.

—George Orwell (1954: 177)

A thin massive event: a small pellet of fish food being attacked by 8,000
piranhas.

—Chris Wood, a Canadian journalist,
on covering the handover of Hong Kong

It is often claimed that media discourse represents "a site of symbolic
struggle," but what are the processes, significance, and limits of that struggle?
As a global "media event" (Dayan and Katz, 1992), the transfer of Hong Kong
from British to Chinese sovereignty on July 1, 1997 provides such a site and moment for opposing *national* media communities to express, and thus reinforce,
their enduring values and dominant ideologies. More than 8,000 journalists and
778 media organizations from around the world reportedly congregated in this
bustling city to witness an event of presumed global significance.[1] The political
periphery of Hong Kong stands in sharp contrast to its status as a core hub of
global capitalism. Yet journalists are far more interested in China than in Hong
Kong. They are interested in China not so much as an ideologically benign site
of geography, as it is a rising economic power, a security risk, and an ideological foe in the post-Cold War era. They participate in the embedded ideological
struggle among various modern *-isms*: East versus West, capitalism versus socialism, democracy versus authoritarianism. As *New York Times* columnist
Thomas Friedman puts it vividly, Hong Kong's return to China is "not just a

1

slice of the West being given back to the East," but also "a slice of the future being given back to the past" (December 15, 1996). What marks for China national triumph over colonialism is, in the eyes of most western journalists, "a menacing, authoritarian Chinese government, its hands still stained by the blood of Tiananmen Square, riding roughshod over freewheeling, Westernized Hong Kong" (Chinoy, 1999: 394). The world media had worried about brutal Communist China turning Hong Kong into Tiananmen II. When that scary scenario did not come to pass, their interest in Hong Kong quickly faded away after the handover.[2] In view of Hong Kong's relative stability, the world media cast all but a casual glance at the neighboring Macau (a big casino showcasing capitalist vices) when it returned from Portugal to China two years later.

In the shadow of cultural and technological globalization (Braman and Sreberny-Mohammadi, 1996; Featherstone, 1995; Featherstone and Lash, 1995; Tomlinson, 1999; Waters, 1995), we wish to show in this volume that international newsmaking remains inherently ethnocentric, nationalistic, and even state-centered. Globalization may have brought the world "closer" in many ways. But global news continues to acquire paradoxically domestic, local, and above all *national* significance. The same event may be given distinct media representations by various nations, through the prisms of their dominant ideologies as defined by power structures, cultural repertoires, and politico-economic interests. Journalists try to illuminate complex and ambiguous political realities in remote foreign places through the process of "domestication" (Cohen et al., 1996). If international news is a state-centered enterprise, Hong Kong's sovereignty transfer explicitly foregrounds this nation-state problematic.

News is about the unexpected, the extraordinary, and the abnormal, but it can only be understood in terms of the expected, the ordinary, and the normal. As an event must be understood in relation to a whole stream of previous causes, collating selected facts into certain relationships is based on embedded cultural and national perspectives. van Ginneken (1998: 126) puts it so well: "What the fireworks of international news illuminate or leave in the dark is the historic panorama beyond them." In general, these media frames coincide with, echo, and support elite consensus within the established order. Moreover, the state, as a repository of "national interest," is a major contestant in international news discourse. As the media foreground the sovereignty reversion of Hong Kong as historical ruptures, lurking in the background are the ideological continuities of their nations toward China. Major western media do not recognize their quasi-consensual ideology but naturalize it as common sense. They emphasize the facts, but disguise the underlying ideology.

Nevertheless, the ceding of the "capitalist jewel" to a Communist regime, against the grand narratives of "the end of history" (Fukuyama, 1992) and "the clash of civilizations" (Huntington, 1993), is a rallying cry for national media resources to reinforce their core values and reaffirm the power structure. International journalism is in this sense an ideological war, a discursive contestation, or a symbolic struggle. From the perspective of comparative sociology of newsmaking, we wish to show how international journalists take part in a post-Cold War ideological discourse through making sense of a "media spectacle" (Edelman, 1988). The handover of Hong Kong is a media event that undergoes a transformation—thus robbed of conflict, suspense, and theatrical appeal. This does not prevent the world media, cum various national cultural arms, from plunging into discursive struggles to promote the legitimacy of their national regimes. The media utilize a set of rhetorical strategies from the entertainment-based media logic (Altheide and Snow, 1979) to articulate their ideological themes. The collusion of national interests and foreign policy goals on the one hand and the media interests in enthralling large audiences on the other brings the world media together to stage a global media spectacle in collaboration with their domestic authorities. It is illuminating to note that these international journalists come all the way to interview a small (probably no more than fifty) and highly overlapping set of people, mostly from the elite but with some token "ordinary folks" to put a "typical" face on the news. But different national narratives enable journalists to insert the present into a highly ideological perspective on the past and the future. In most foreign policy issues, media differences across the ideological divide *within* a nation tend to be dwarfed by media differences *between* nations. Such national perspectives interact with the sociological arrangement of the theater of the handover events as well as the rhetorical strategies of the media logic, making it appropriate to talk about the handover as a global media spectacle fitted with varying national themes.

International News and Discursive Struggles

Discourse is at the heart of a nation as an "imagined community" (Anderson, 1983). It reproduces the society as a coherent unit of culture, allowing its members to envision a sense of belonging and identity vis-à-vis other units. A discursive community comprises a group of people who feel bound through shared interpretations and representations of their everyday experiences within a common cultural, political, and economic environment (Fish, 1980; Lincoln, 1989; Wuthnow, 1989). The discursive binding of such a community shines particularly at critical moments when certain events of historic proportions inspire a wealth of symbolic resources to solidify cultural values. These events force members of a society to form their self-conceptions through cultural practices and thus renew their shared identity.

The ceding of Hong Kong to a Communist regime in the post-Cold War era represents one of those "hot moments" to different national communities in varying degrees. In this study, as said above, we start with the premise that on the global scale, different national communities will construct different media discourses about an issue of such momentous ideological import. It is true that globalization of modern media has made the symbolic bond of a community often more dependent on mediated representations than on territoriality (Appadurai, 1996), but international news about distant events happening in faraway places must be "brought home" via discursive means. Cultural representations of a "discursive community" are closely related to the activities and artifacts of their producers in concrete social and historical settings. Media discourse, in Wuthnow's words (1989: 16), occurs within "the communities of competing producers, of interpreters and critics, of audiences and consumers, and of patrons and other significant actors who become subjects of discourse itself." This sociological grounding calls for an examination of how different media discourses invoke their cultural symbols on behalf of their national interests, and how they articulate enduring values of the society often in support of the power authority.

Put otherwise, mass media stand at the forefront of institutional venues through which each national community acts out its shared experiences and the underlying cultural premises (Edelman, 1988; Esherick and Wasserstrom, 1994). Events of historic importance absorb the "attention resources" of the public arena (Hilgartner and Bosk, 1988), which "tames" a distant event through selective domestication in tandem with core social values. Global news must be filtered through the domestic system of commonsense knowledge (Berger and Luckman, 1967) or "local knowledge" (Geertz, 1993); media texts are constructed in the multilayered organizational, cultural, economic, and political frameworks. We aim to achieve some understanding about the discursive contestation of national media systems in the international terrain over tensions between cultural particulars and transcendent values. These tensions sharpen the continuities and ruptures between national interests in the world order.

The handover of Hong Kong forms a concentric circle of relevance and vested interests to various national discursive communities and is thus open to divergent media construction. International newsmaking follows the same logic of domestic newsmaking, but under different political conditions. It is widely accepted that the media produce and reproduce the hegemonic definitions of social order. There are four general claims to this overall thesis. First, "news net" of the media (Tuchman, 1978) corresponds to the hierarchical order of political power and the prevailing belief system that defines this order. Occurrences outside the centralized organizations or standard genres would not be recognized as news. Secondly, even in a democratic society, news production must inevitably epitomize the capitalist mode of production and serve the financial-ideological structure and interests of the dominant class, race, and gender (Mosco, 1996; Thompson, 1990). Thirdly, the ideology of journalistic professionalism, as enshrined by the creed of objectivity, is predicated on an unarticulated commitment to the established order (Gitlin, 1980; Said, 1978; Schlesinger, 1978; Tuchman, 1978). News media "index" the spectrum of the elite viewpoints as an essential tool for domestic political operation (Bennett, 1990; Cook, 1998). In a similar vein, Donohue, Tichenor and Olien (1995) maintain that the media perform as a sentry not for the community as a whole, but for groups having sufficient power and influence to create and control their own security systems. Fourthly, when elite consensus collapses or is highly divided, or when there is strong mobilizing pressure from social movements, the media may have to reflect such opinion plurality (Chan and Lee, 1991; Hallin, 1986; Page, 1996). Such plurality does not, however, question the fundamental assumptions of power in society.

The international order being more anarchic, the *state*—rather than specific individuals, classes, or sectors within a country—acts as the repository of "national interest" (Garnett, 1994), as the principal maker of foreign policy, and as a contestant in international news discourse (Snyder and Ballentine, 1997: 65). Operating as "little accomplices" of the state (Zaller and Chiu, 1996), the media rely on political authorities to report foreign policy cum national interest. Moreover, the media, the domestic authorities, and the public tend to perceive the international news reality through shared lenses of ideologies, myths, and cultural repertoire. The media resolve around the head of state, foreign ministry, and embassies to make news because these institutions are assumed to have superior if not monopolistic access to knowledge about what national interest is abroad. Foreign news agendas are even more closely attuned to elite conceptions of the world than domestic news agendas. The U.S. media therefore tend to "rally around the flag" in close alliance with official Washington (Brody, 1991; Cook, 1998), especially when the country is in conflict with foreign powers. By this process of "domesticating" foreign news as a variation on a national theme (Cohen et al., 1996), the media serve to sharpen and legitimize national perspectives embedded in the existing order of power and privilege (chapter 3). Gans (1979) maintains that in the U.S. media, foreign news stories are mostly relevant to Americans or American interests, with the same themes and topics as domestic news; when the topics are distinctive, they are given interpretations that apply to American values. Media domestication is an integral part of the international political economy.

News media participate in a broader discursive process in constructing the domestic elite's images of "the other" and legitimizing the state's effort in safeguarding geopolitical interests abroad (Said, 1981, 1993). They produce a local narrative of the same global event through employment of unique discursive means of rhetoric, frames, metaphors, and logic. In "tangling" with distant contestants in the game of international newsmaking, they impute different causes and effects to reality to advance national interest and promote national legitimacy. During the Persian Gulf War, CNN became a stage for the U.S. and Iraqi governments to verbally attack each other, paving the way for and extending the eventual armed conflict (Kellner, 1992). Unlike the institutional struggle in which central authority allocates tangible material resources (Jabri, 1996: 72), the discursive struggle wins or loses symbolically in terms of expression of preferred values and orders. The latter may be mobilized into an institutional struggle, while the former may derive its legitimacy from a discursive struggle (Edelman, 1971; Gamson, 1988; McAdams, McCarthy, and Zald, 1996). During the Cold War, superpowers contested over intangible public opinion, images, and rhetorical discourse in order, ironically, to prevent the hot wars of guns and missiles (Medhurst, 1990).

The Making of a Media Event

The arrival of the world media turns Hong Kong into a theater of performance. Although the basic script for the event was long written in the Sino-British Joint Declaration in 1984, the actual staging of its performance had been in serious dispute between the two principals (Lee, 1997, 2000a). The handover is thus a long anticipated and carefully scripted event that unfolds with real and potential drama of conflicts. The predictability of its prescheduled nature facilitates "calendar journalism" (Tuchman, 1978). Following the meticulously scripted events may neither require much enterprising journalistic effort (Sigal, 1973) nor satisfy the "entertainment logic" of television age (Altheide and Snow, 1979). Yet, given the logic that bad news is good news and given the rancorous diplomatic skirmishes and war of words between Britain and China until the final moment, the world media had committed considerable resources to covering an event of presumed worst-case scenarios under Communist takeover. But the handover turns out to be smooth and peaceful, not as bad as previously envisaged. Somewhat disappointed, the large presence of international journalists in a crowded island becomes a story—a media spectacle—more important than the event itself. A Canadian journalist compares this "thin massive event" to "a small pellet of fish food being attacked by 8,000 piranhas." *Newsweek*'s bureau chief, when asked, agrees that thousands of competitive egos probably end up talking to the same set of 20 to 50 people in town, but the *Daily Telegraph* reporter defends this practice as an inherent logic of journalism not different from covering South Africa or Bosnia. The logic of making news is hijacked by the logic of staging a media spectacle.

According to Dayan and Katz (1992), a media event may fall into one of three categories: a contest, a conquest, or a coronation. In spite of consuming efforts made by the dismayed international journalists, the handover story did not seem to rise to various qualifications of a *spectacular* media event. As it began, the event seemed to contain all the exciting elements of a conquest or those of a contest. As the event went through a process of transformation during its life cycle, elements of a contest and conquest receded, and the media began to focus on it more as a coronation.

First, a contest "pits evenly matched individuals or teams against each other and bids them to compete according to strict rules" (Dayan and Katz, 1992: 33). Media events of this type should generate much excitement over the process of competition and reduce the uncertainty about its outcome. The Sino-British rows over sovereignty negotiations and Governor Patten's democratic reforms (Dimbleby, 1997) began to fade in significance as Hong Kong inched toward the handover.

Second, a conquest refers to great men and women with charisma who "submit themselves to an ordeal, whose success multiplies their charisma and creates a new following" (Dayan and Katz, 1992: 37). Indeed, all of China's official and media proclamations hail Deng Xiaoping, the paramount leader, as the ingenious author of the "one country, two systems" idea, through which the previously impossible task of reclaiming Hong Kong becomes a reality. Thus, Chinese patriotic heroes roundly beat British imperialist villains. China's official television constantly shows a picture of Margaret Thatcher falling on her steps in front of the Great Hall of the People, almost as a favorite icon that "provides an occasion for journalists and their sources to refigure cultural scripts" (Bennett and Lawrence, 1995). The Prime Minister had just emerged from her first excruciating encounter with Deng, during which he lectured her that China would not take humiliation from foreign powers any more. That showdown forced both sides to embark on painful negotiations leading finally to the handover. This icon was coined in 1982, and by 1997 Thatcher had retired from public life and Deng was already dead, but the image lives on as a soothing symbol of conquest for China's injured national psyche. The People's Republic of China (PRC) media are also fond of flexing military icons to relish the story of national strength in front of the doubting world. To counter this, the world media depict that the small and efficient Hong Kong will play the role of a "Trojan Horse" to subvert the huge and clumsy Communist China from within. This story of conquest is, however, set in the future, and its confirmation requires a time horizon that goes far beyond the drowning ritual ceremonies.

A coronation, a third kind of media event, deals in "the mysteries of rites of passage" which "proceed according to strict rules, dictated by tradition rather than by negotiated agreement" (Dayan and Katz, 1992: 36). Media coverage of a coronation serves to pledge allegiance to the political center and to renew contract with it. Persons of authority are signified and dignified by costumes, symbols, titles, and rituals. Media presentation, which tends to be reverent and priestly, enacts the tradition and authority that are usually hidden from everyday life. A prime icon of Hong Kong's handover coronation is a picture of the brief moment at the midnight of June 30, seemingly frozen in history. The Union Jack is being lowered, and the Chinese flag being raised. All principal actors—including Prince Charles, President Jiang, Governor Patten, and Chief Executive Tung—are solemnly arrayed on the stage to commemorate a change in the authority structure and to usher in formal absorption of Hong Kong into the motherland. In spite of its historical significance this still moment produces no lively journalism.

The media event thus transformed, journalists must do something to save the integrity of their paradigmatic structure. They repair part of the assumptions, cull more supporting data, dismiss contrary evidence, or try to fit their stories into generic narrative structures of media events (Bennett, Gressett, and Haltom, 1985; Chan and Lee, 1991). Above all, they must "hype" up the event in hopes that their domestic audiences may find reasons to participate in the media rites and rituals. Through the display of repetitive, familiar, and exaggerated images often out of the context, hyping creates a mythical ritual that is confirming of the dominant ideological framework (Nimmo and Combs, 1990). The media are not passive reflectors of the media event, but active participants in its making. The media not only provide a stage for an event scripted by authoritative agencies outside of media; they also "coauthor" the event with event organizers and their own domestic authority structure. They rescript the event to fit their respective national narrative and annotate the performance of the principal actors with reverence. They add their own "star performers"—the celebrity anchors and famed correspondents—to share the stage with, if not take over the title role from, the actors of the official script. They hype the elements of the event in resonance with the domestic audiences.

Methodology

This study interweaves (a) indepth interviews with international journalists, (b) a content analysis, and (c) a discourse analysis of elite newspapers and television networks from eight countries or regions. The main body of evidence comes from a discourse analysis of media representations. The result of content analysis provides information about the basic parameter and orientation of media coverage. Interviews with journalists are indispensable to understanding the sociology of news regarding their professional biographies, organizational resources and strategies, news competition and collaboration, and the cultural map on which they draw to cover the handover. These interviews generate important insights for formulating and confirming the "ideological packages" in our constructionist discourse analysis. Published documents, press reports, the proceedings of media fora and symposia, and our field notes fill the background gaps in terms of the motives, actions, and behind-the-scene maneuvers of various key individuals and regimes, thus piercing through the surface of media content. Needless to say, all of them are to be interpreted in light of the insights we have built up over two decades as critical analysts of the media in Hong Kong and elsewhere (Chan and Lee, 1991; Lee, 1997, 2000; So and Chan, 1999). Without doubt, our comparative framework sharpens our interpretation of media accounts.

Countries and Media Outlets

To investigate the national prisms through which the handover of Hong Kong is inflected, we select for examination eight "national" media systems that form a concentric circle of relevance and vested interest: the PRC, Hong Kong, Taiwan, the United States, Britain, Canada, Australia, and Japan. Within the immediate circle of relevance are the primary constituencies of "Cultural China" (Tu, 1991)—namely, the PRC, Taiwan, and Hong Kong—fraught with conflicting identities and historical memories. (Strictly speaking, Hong Kong is not a "nation" but a British colony returning to the PRC's possession, while Taiwan has *de facto* but not *de jure* nationhood, constantly struggling against the PRC over issues of national sovereignty. To avoid repeated references to more accurate yet cumbersome "nations or regions," we shall treat Hong Kong and Taiwan as if they were "nations.") In broader circles of relevance, the PRC seems ideologically at war with the outside world at large, in what appears to be an extended East-West conflict. Not only has the outgoing Britain marshaled possible moral, political, and media resources to fend off assaults on its legitimacy from the PRC. The United States, particularly, has led a western ideological united front in support of Britain against China in this power game of words and images. Incorporated as junior partners in the western camp are Canada, Australia, and to some extent, Japan, which display different national interest within the common western ideology.

We set out to select a sample of 32 newspapers, four news magazines, 14 television channels, and seven news agencies from the eight countries (Table 1.1). The criteria for selection include:

- Influence in terms of circulation and the perceived status.

- The range of ideological variation with a national media system.

- Level of operation: International, national, regional, and local.

- Modes of financial operation: Official organ or private enterprise.

- Type of medium: Newspapers, magazines, television, and news agencies.

- Type of audience: General interest or specialized interest.

Table 1.1
The Sample of Media Outlets[1]

Countries	Print Media	TV	News Agencies
PRC (n = 8)	*People's Daily** *Economic Daily* *People's Liberation Army Daily* *Guangming Daily* *Guangzhou Daily**	CCTV* Guangzhou TV	Xinhua
USA (n = 11)	*New York Times** *Washington Post** *Wall Street Journal** *Chicago Tribune** *Los Angeles Times** *Des Moines Register** *San Jose Mercury News* *Newsweek* (magazine)	CBS* CNN*	AP
Britain (n = 8)	*The Times** *Guardian** *Daily Telegraph** *Independent** *Financial Times*	BBC* ITV*	Reuters
Hong Kong (n = 10)	*Ming Pao Daily News** *South China Morning Post** *Apple Daily** *Oriental Daily News* *Yazhou Zhoukan* (magazine) *Far Eastern Economic Review* (magazine)	TVB* CTV CTN	(GIS)[2]

(continued)

We compile media content of the sampled organizations from two weeks before the handover and one week after it, thus covering the period between June 16 and July 5, 1997. We ask many professional colleagues in various locales to collect the sampled newspaper issues and to tape sampled television programs (including regular evening news, special programs, and live coverage on June 30). It should be noted that we decide not to include the endless stream of wire stories in further analysis, although we do incorporate insights from interview with wire reporters. We are also confident that the "discursive packages" of news agencies do not differ markedly from those of print media and television.

Table 1.1 (*continued*)
The Sample of Media Outlets[1]

Countries	Print Media	TV	News Agencies
Taiwan (n = 7)	*China Times** *United Daily News* *Central Daily News* *Liberty Times* *Mingzhong Daily*	TTV*	Central
Japan (n = 7)	*Asahi Shimbun* *Yomiuri Shimbun* *Sankei Shimbun* *Nihon Keizai Shimbun*	NHK Asahi	Kyodo
Australia (n = 2)	*The Australian**	ATV*	
Canada (n = 5)	*Globe and Mail** *MacLean's* (magazine)	CBC*	Canadian Press Southam News

Notes:
1. All print media and television outlets listed in this table are qualitatively examined in the discourse analysis. Only those with * are also content-coded. We do not examine the news agencies in either study. For further information, see Appendix I–IV.
2. The Government Information Services serves the international journalists by providing press releases, briefings, field trips, and other assistance.

Interviews

Based on this media sample, we interview a total of 76 journalists (Table 1.2), including 37 from the print media, 29 from the broadcasting media, and 10 from news agencies. The country distribution is, except for Australia, fairly balanced. (See Appendix II for a complete list of interviewees.) Most interviews are based on a detailed, semistructured protocol (Appendix III), each lasting 30 to 180 minutes, fully taped and transcribed. A small number of interviews take the form of more casual conversation to validate our inferences from more formal interviews. Many of the interviewees are Hong Kong-based, others on special assignment for the occasion.

We aim to discern patterns of professional journalists at work within various organizational and cultural milieus. We probe journalists on (a) their professional biography; (b) their working conditions in relation to the sources, editors, competitors, and audience; and particularly (c) their discursive activities—namely, invocation of themes, frames, images, and metaphors to narrate the story. This thick description of their professional world later comes to life, enriching our interpretations of the stories they produce. We ask them to name a story they think would

Table 1.2
National Origins of Journalists Interviewed

	Print Media	Broadcasting	News Agencies	Total
PRC	2	4	1	7
USA	7	2	1	10
Britain	5	4	0	9
Hong Kong	7	4	0	11
Taiwan	6	9	2	17
Japan	4	3	4	11
Australia	1	1	0	2
Canada	5	2	2	9
Total	37	29	10	76

capture the essence of Hong Kong. This would lead to a better understanding about how they draw on certain political ideology and cultural repertoire in the process of "translating" foreign reality for their home audiences. We also ask them about their game plan for covering a series of competing events situated in the web of time and geography on the day of the handover. It is important to know how they construct the news net, divide the labor, and cope with intense competitive pressure under the punishing deadline.

At first glance, the interviews seem to suggest the emergence of a "global" culture of professional journalism. Rooted in western origins of market economy and liberal polity, this professional culture seems to have been widely accepted as general if not universal norms of journalistic conduct and judgment (Schudson, 1978; Weaver, 1998). All journalists profess their commitment to the pursuit of fact and "truth," in their capacities as avowed observers, transmitters, and interpreters of reality, and they take offense at being viewed as partisan activists with an ideological ax to grind. Even Communist journalists from the PRC seem no longer to hold their Leninist teachings with deep conviction (He, 2000; Pan, 2000; Zhao, 1998). This general impression is superficial and shallow at best, for what constitutes the fact or truth is culturally relative and ideologically indeterminate. Despite being professional cynics, journalists usually do not defy the assumptions of the power structure in their work (Gans, 1979; Manoff and Schudson, 1986; Schlesinger, 1978; Tuchman, 1978). Media discourses in the international terrain, in particular, tend to possess strong national personalities that sharpen the us-against-them boundaries in reductive and limiting categories (Herman and Chomsky, 1988; Lee and Yang, 1995; Said, 1981). Notwithstanding claims to the contrary, this reliance on national ideology is also true of such global-scale media outlets as the BBC or CNN that speak in perfect English to the elite in the rest of the world.

Content Analysis

Of the sampled media outlets, we perform a content analysis of a subsample of 26 outlets totaling 3,883 stories, across seven media systems except Japan (Table 1.1). The main purpose is to set the basic comparative parameter of media coverage, but content analysis does not yield a deep understanding of the discursive structures. Appendix IV provides a more detailed description of the research procedure.

Three general points deserve initial remarks here. First, all eight media systems have covered the handover extensively (see Appendix IV for statistics). In terms of newspaper space, Hong Kong and the PRC rank highest, followed by Taiwan, Australia, and Canada. The United States ranks lower because the "local" papers devote a smaller space to the handover, but the elite papers produce large amounts of long interpretative stories. The pattern of television coverage differs only slightly: CCTV (China) ranks the first, followed by TVB (Hong Kong) and TTV (Taiwan), and Australian, British, and U.S. networks.

Second, the handover, as a prescheduled calendar event, has a clear life cycle. Media coverage peaks on June 30 and July 1. During the prehandover preparatory period (June 16–29), daily media coverage is only 11% to 33% of the amount produced in the peak period. The posthandover coverage (July 2–5) tapers off to range from 7% to 39% of the amount produced in the peak period.

Thirdly, as will also be clear (Table 3.1), the PRC faces a doubting world. The PRC media see no negative change will take place after the handover; in fact, everything in Hong Kong will look brighter under the loving care of the motherland. But those from the four English-speaking countries—the United States, Britain, Australia, and Canada—predict that profound negative change is likely to occur in political, if not economic, areas. Hong Kong and Taiwan media, concerned with self-survival, are also negative but not as negative as the western media. The content analysis confirms and sharpens the results of our discourse analysis.

Discourse Analysis

For the most important part of our work, we take a constructionist approach to discourse analysis as developed by William Gamson and his associates (Gamson and Modigliani, 1987, 1989; Gamson et al., 1992) in an effort to link media texts and broader ideological underpinnings of national prisms. We first deconstruct stories that comprise each national media account into what Gamson and Lasch (1983) call "signature matrix," a device that lists the key frames and links them to salient signifying devices. We then reconstruct their major theses into genotypical categories—or what Gamson calls "ideological packages" or "discursive packages"—replete with metaphors, exemplars, catch phrases, depictions, visual images, roots, consequences, and appeals to principle. These frames serve as an organizing scheme with which journalists provide coherence to their stories and through which some critical issues can be discussed and understood. Gitlin (1980: 7) writes, "Media frames, largely unspoken and unacknowledged, organize the world both for journalists who report it and, in some important degree, for us who rely on their reports." These frames relate media texts to overall social and ideological contexts.

This analysis involves examining the text along the paradigmatic and syntagmatic dimensions (Fiske, 1982). The former calls for an examination of the choices of textual units and their interrelationships within a news paradigm. We focus on "macro" and "midlevel" units in terms of journalists' choice of story details, quoted statements, metaphors, images and exemplars, as well as their source dependence. The syntagmatic dimension concerns the placement of textual units in a syntactic structure according to certain linguistic rules or the "story grammar" of an event (Pan and Kosicki, 1993; van Dijk, 1988). This dimension entails three levels of abstraction, each forming a template for storytelling:

(1)   At the level of the story, we must first analyze the "macro structure" (van Dijk, 1988) or "story grammar" (Franzosi, 1989) of news items—how signs are put together according to certain rules. A regular news item consists of the headlines, the lead paragraph, and the story (or event)—woven with actors, actions, and consequences.

(2)   We must analyze how official event organizers author a "mega-story" composed of a series of activities and events (with a cast of actors and roles) leading up to the sovereignty transfer. This is an analysis of the "superstructure" or "global structure" (van Dijk, 1988).

(3)   We must analyze how, within this "global structure," journalists bring certain professional norms, journalistic paradigms (Bennett, Gressett, and Haltom, 1985; Chan and Lee, 1991), and organizational routine (Tuchman, 1978) to make sense of the events.

In sum, we examine the narrative structure (headline, lead, main body, and sources), the thematic structure (rules of citing sources and evidence to support a theme), and the rhetorical structure (rules and conventions of using certain symbolic resources to create meanings and cultural resonance) of media discourses (Pan and Kosicki, 1993).

We examine the texts of all sampled media organizations (Table 1.1), with an estimated total of 7,600 print stories, hundreds of hours of television coverage, and supplemental magazine stories. Two of us on the team are responsible for analyzing a country to achieve cross-verification. Frequent—initially, almost daily—communication is conducive to furthering our common understanding about the framework for scrutinizing the discursive packages of each media system. We develop "country reports" based on cross-examining and traversing media texts, interview transcripts, our "other knowledge," and theoretical concepts. We make back-and-forth attempts at proposing alternative and supplemental interpretations to settle some conflicting hypotheses. For example, given our understanding of the general literature, we were initially skeptical about a claim made by a prominent CNN corespondent that his network is an objective international entity not tied to U.S., or any, ideology. We nonetheless treated it as a plausible hypothesis and reminded ourselves to pay special attention in the discourse analysis to determine if there is a significant difference between the ideological structure of CBS and CNN. We found little differences between them and hence rejected his claim (see chapter 3). Painstaking and disciplined cross-fertilization between theoretical concepts and different facets of data has led to the development of thematic outlines as herein presented.

Framework for Analysis

News has to come from somewhere and somebody. It does not reveal itself without human construction. Our framework for analysis, as sketched in Figure 1.1, highlights the following points:

1. International news is a series of complex processes that involves making political, economic, and cultural choices.

2. Each of these news processes is constrained by the political economy of the home country, as well as its role and place in the larger international political economy.

3. Event organizers, often the authorities, produce the first-order script to structure the universe of news activities.

4. Professional journalists, working for and within media organizations, write the second-order script as narratives based on their observations and interpretations—within the constraints mentioned above.

In essence, this volume consists of two major parts: chapters 2–4 deal with the sociological, cultural, and ideological processes and strategies in the making of a global media event, while chapters 5–8 analyze the very stuff of life in discursive contestation.[3] The first part—the sociology of international media— is important in its own right, but it also paves the way for the second part, where national prisms are the central site of ideological wars.

News Staging and News Agendas

   The authorities outside the media set the news stage—ranging from the controlled access, facilities and the infrastructure, to schedules and arranged activities—that have a decisive influence on the news flow (chapter 2). The nature of the event—whether prescheduled, conflict-ridden, or fast-paced—varies. The first injunction of journalists is to stay with the facts; they cannot portray a peaceful march as a bloody crackdown. Next, the configuration of domestic and international forces shapes the parameters of potential news topics within which journalists construct their narratives. Journalists transform occurrences into news agendas according to professional norms, orga-

Figure 1.1
Conceptual Scheme of Comparative International Media Discourses

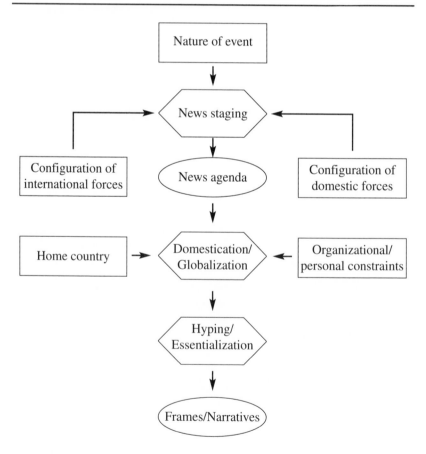

nizational constraints, national values and orientations, and the law of the market. The stronger nations tend to have a stronger media presence. The media enjoy less latitude in setting the agenda if the organizers minutely script the stage. All centralized authorities and dominant nations attempt to control the flow and rhythm of news, even though they cannot completely monopolize it.

Domestication and Globalization

Global news, about events happening in distant places, has to be brought home through the process of "domestication" to make it familiar and intelligible to home audiences (chapter 3). The conversion of a global agenda into a home agenda—that is, treating foreign news as an extension of domestic news—starts out with selective framing of issues or topics through the lens of professional norms, national interest, cultural repertoire, and market dynamics. As the public is generally apathetic to international news, foreign correspondents must go to extra length in imparting relevance or adding entertainment value to the story. This "domestic" perspective tends to be state-articulated "national" perspective, suppressing subnational, local differences. The extent to which the global-scale media outlets (such as CNN and the BBC) can be free from national ideological constraints bears further analysis.

Hyping and Essentialization

Hyping and essentialization are two processes by which news is domesticated and globalized (chapter 4). Hyping is a strategy for the media to reduce the gap between what is expected of a media event and scripted reality, thus bringing to the forefront (and to make up for the lack of) theatrical elements (such as conflict, competition, suspense, and emotion) to electrify the audience. The resultant media product tends to portray a reality that is larger than life. Intensified media competition in the commercial market has made hyping an imperative in today's news business. Essentialization means stripping an event to its core properties as if they were invariant and immutable; the reductive and frozen narratives, often manifested in crude us-against-them cliché, conceal many complex and contradictory contexts of reality. We present a case analysis of essentialized narratives about nationalism and colonialism in chapter 7.

National Prisms: Frames and Narratives

Another core concern is to analyze international newsmaking as a form of ideological contestation (chapters 5–8). As the end product of the news process, these frames and narratives provide journalists with organizing coherence to their stories, through which some critical issues can be discussed and understood. These frames help organize the world of events both for those who report them as journalists and for those who consume such reports as audience. We shall examine four outstanding discursive battles, each with internal skirmishes.

The first discursive battle is fought between the United States and the PRC over grand ideologies and conflicting systems (chapter 5). The PRC finds itself becoming the chief villain of the U.S. media in the post-Tiananmen era and in the post-Cold War order. Seeing Hong Kong through the ugly mirror of the Tiananmen crackdown, they proclaim that the United States, as a "new guardian," will prevent Hong Kong's fragile democracy and existing freedoms from China's abuse. Hong Kong will also play the "Trojan Horse" role to subvert China's authoritarian system. Television networks are particularly blatant.

Britain and the PRC, the two sovereign powers involved in the handover, join the second discursive battle over the interpretations of colonialism and nationalism (chapter 6). China's media *essentialize* British colonialism as inherently evil while touting Chinese nationalism as inherently supreme; this narrative, while partially valid, loses sight of several key complex and paradoxical historical developments. The British media largely ignore their inglorious colonial beginnings. Instead they *de-essentialize* the evilness of colonialism by emphasizing that Hong Kong is Britain's creation as a free, stable, and prosperous enclave against relentless turmoil in the PRC. They personify Governor Patten as democracy's apostle who stands up to Communist bluster. These selective historical depictions, while partially valid, typify what Said (1978, 1981, 1993) portrays as the imperial construction of Orientalism.

The third discursive battle occurs within "Cultural China" over the meaning of Chinese nationalism, China, and Chinese (chapter 7). The state-controlled PRC media approach the handover primarily as a domestic issue with global implications for national glory. Relying exclusively on domestic and friendly sources, they construct China as a unified nation-state centered in Beijing yet supposedly inclusive of global Chinese communities. The handover is a "national ceremony," marking an end to western colonialism and a beginning to national reunification. On the receiving end, Hong Kong media treat the handover as the unfolding of a crucial chapter in local history, praying that global watch will keep the place out of Beijing-inflicted harm's way. A thriving democracy in search of identity, Taiwan media focus on "what's next" for the island nation.

The fourth discursive struggle concerns a supporting cast of the western camp who seems to fight against the PRC and the United States at the same time over the primacy of ideology and national interests (chapter 8). Both Canada and Australia have become Hong Kong's new diaspora, while Japan has enormous economic interests in Hong Kong. Australia and Japan also emphasize their "Asian identity." This means that the "minor three" not only play ideological variations on the western themes of democracy and human rights, but also seek to advance their own economic and security interests that require certain struggle against the U.S. policy.

Finally, we shall conclude this volume in chapter 9 with focused discussions on the implications—the structures, processes, consequences, and limits—of this discursive contestation in relation to media events in the age of globalization.

Chapter 2

News Staging

All the world's a stage, and all the men and women merely players.
—Shakespeare, *As You Like It*

Staging is a transitory world of make-believe.
—Gerald Millerson (1982: 10)

For the foreign press, we won this battle. We were not just a side story on July 1. In the foreign press, we were the focus. That was our intention.
—Lau Sai-leung, Senior Executive Officer,
the Democratic Party of Hong Kong

Help us stop 5 billion people being fed garbage.
—Advertisement by a PR consultant in the *South China Morning Post*, referring to foreign journalists' "rubbishing" Hong Kong

International journalism is performed on a local-cum-world stage. In the literal sense, the handover of Hong Kong's sovereignty takes place at a specific time and place. The date of July 1, 1997 was in a way set in 1842 by the Nanjing Treaty and rectified in 1982 by the Sino-British Joint Declaration. The official site makes Hong Kong a stage for the Chinese and British leaders to perform courteous but strained rituals for the invited political and social dignitaries in front of the mediated world audience. Symbolically, the Hong Kong handover is also a stage for ideological contestation between East and West, and between capitalism and socialism in the post-Cold War context. The media, representing national discursive communities, are the principal reality constructors and ideological contestants.

We borrow from the literary and theatrical traditions the concept of stage and apply it metaphorically to look at the acts of the world media and journalists in the context of regime change. We shall describe and analyze, at different levels, the various news gatherers and makers as well as media scenes as components of a news stage. With news stage as a macroscopic framework to visualize the roles of the media and journalists, we shall also use the literature on media sociology to make sense out of their strategies and activities.

News Stage

In an early handbook on the production of plays, Nelms (1958) spells out the essential theatrical elements as the stage, script, casting and actors, acting, scenery, lighting, make-up, set design, and costumes. More broadly, this "art of presentation" (Beckerman, 1990) encompasses the audience, the place (scene), the performers, the "theatrical hierarchy" (managers and playwright), and media or scholarly critics. The theory of dramatism (Gronbeck, 1980) notes that not only do the actors perform according to the scripts written in languages or symbols; other constituencies would then interpret the scripts via their knowledge of cultural rules and significant symbols. Consequently, social meanings and actions are produced within certain sociocultural contexts of scenes. In the modern setup of a television studio, Millerson (1982: 10) describes controlling the staging as "whenever we deliberately arrange or contrive a scene in front of the camera." He further comments that "staging is a transitory world of make-believe, where the fantastic and the imaginary are given substance, where for a brief while we build an illusion." Staging can be used to provide a background for a subject, to create an atmospheric effect, and to enhance a subject either by stressing its importance or by distracting our attention from it.

Media are essential to staging a major international event like the Olympic Games. The organization of games entails marketing, security, tourism, transport, volunteers, and everything else, but the media are assumed to be "the last judges" of its success (Gratton, 1999: 122). The media televise rituals and symbols (the flame, torch, flag, ceremonies), prominent individuals and athletes, events and performances—most importantly, they also make "numerous judgments about the host country and its society and how well the Games have been organized" (pp. 130–131). That is why the Sydney Olympics in 2000 regard it as a high priority to rectify the shortcomings of the press center in the 1996 Atlanta Olympics.

The best competition to a media event is another media event. At the time of the Hong Kong handover, there are no other major crises brewing nearby or elsewhere, so the world media can focus their attention on this tiny "giant" island-city. In June, it was rumored that Pol Pot, the Khmer Rouge killer, had been captured; the Associated Press for example reassigned half of its handover staff to Cambodia, only to discover that it was a false alarm. Similar rumors spread that hell had broken loose in North Korea, diverting some media attention away from Hong Kong. But none of these events ultimately equals or threatens the prominence of the handover.

First and foremost actors in staging the theatricals of the handover are the Chinese and British governments, complete with their political showmanship. Both sovereign powers' clash of interests had been glaringly played out in the public arenas of media diplomacy until the last end. Any details relating to the handover must be carefully planned to avoid being elevated to a test of national dignity. The flags used in the handover ceremony must be of equal size. Turquoise, politically neutral, is the chosen color of the handover logo. Media representations were judiciously negotiated. All other onlookers to the political spectacle have their own interests at stake: the tourist industry intends to cash in on the mania, after years of promotion, to make real profits; the business community wants the goose to continue to lay golden eggs. For Hong Kong people, after years of patient or impatient waiting, this day of reckoning has come, exposing their fear and hopes to the world media.

The stage cannot be complete without the presence of the world media and journalists as key observers and participants. The two sovereign powers set the stage to aid and filter world media coverage, each competing to establish different agendas. They set the outer boundary conditions of media operation in terms of schedule, activities, and primary content. They write the first-order script (Dayan and Katz, 1992), within which the media build their own news stage and write their own second-order scripts. The media's "news net" captures the essence of the event in ways that not only aim to win journalistic competition but also reveal their deep-seated ideological assumptions. Metaphorically speaking, this news stage is made up of (a) various locations and scenes; (b) journalists and their organizations; (c) their sources and interviewees; and (d) their scripted texts. This news stage allows the journalists to transform occurrences into newsworthy stories for the public consumption.

Journalists do not have unlimited freedom in creating their news agenda. For any event, there is a defined set of potential news topics for the journalists to tap. News staging defines news agendas; the nature of the event and the configuration of domestic and international forces give slanted prominence to selected occurrences. The larger the event, the more difficult it is to block out all competing social forces. The more concentrated is power distribution in society, the less likely the event will allow room for the competing social forces to operate in a given society. Journalists have room for negotiation, but only within given parameters.

Journalists, as professional storytellers, invoke their ideological premises and professional codes to understand the events, ceremonies, people, institutions, and psychology, and finally to produce oral or visual texts accessible to the public. Journalists seldom openly discuss their own work. Their ideological framework is more often implicitly embedded in the larger culture, thus outside the range of critical reflection. A discursive struggle starts with the unmasking of ideological assumptions that inform professional codes. A global-scale media event engenders international discursive contestation over its causes, processes, and consequences. This contestation, however, seems to consist of a series of independent and parallel self-declarations by the media of their national desires, hopes, fear, and agendas without fierce frontal attacks or encounter of direct battles.

The GIS as Controlling Host

As the official host, the Government Information Services (GIS) in Hong Kong is responsible for coordinating the government's communication efforts with local and foreign journalists. The 9,300-square-meter Press and Broadcast Center (PBC), located in the newly expanded Hong Kong Convention and Exhibition Center, is the main journalistic site to gather basic information for their organizations back home. The PBC is officially open on June 15 and closed on July 10, operating twenty-four hours a day. According to the GIS, the PBC provides 150 booths for use by the electronic media, more than 80 booths for the print media, and a free-seating area that accommodates more than 600 journalists. There are also photo-finishing booths and snack counters.

The GIS accredits 8,423 media representatives from 778 organizations. As Table 2.1 shows, Hong Kong contributes 2,816 (or one-third) to this pool; many of them are TV reporters and technicians as well as freelancers. Local media submit as many names as possible "just in case," for accreditation does not incur any cost or effort. The rest are from Japan (1,300 or 15 percent), the United States (1,047 or 12 percent), Britain (688 or 8 percent), China (610 or 7 percent), and Taiwan (528 or 6 percent). Canada and Australia are more modestly represented. According to a Japanese media specialist, Japanese TV stations are notorious for sending a huge number of people to file reports from abroad because they prefer not to work with local stations. There is no precise breakdown of how many actually arrived, but by any measures the total number remains astonishingly large. While the United States is third in number of journalists, following Hong Kong and Japan, it is first in number of media organizations represented. Hong Kong, Japan, and China have many journalists but fewer media organizations; some media outlets dispatch a large army of journalists. China's state-run "Big Three" virtually monopolize the entire team.

The PBC, which carries a price tag of U.S.$11 million and takes two years to plan, is the largest of its kind ever built in Hong Kong. This huge physical stage can be regarded as a symbolic backstage for world journalists to cover the handover. The GIS has an information counter working around the clock during the span of PBC's operation. Journalists located in the PBC can have 18

Table 2.1
Number of Media Organizations and Journalists Registered
with the Handover Ceremony Coordination Office*

Country/Region	Number of Media Organizations		Number of Journalists	
	N	%	N	%
Hong Kong	106	13.6	2,816	33.4
Japan	45	5.8	1,300	15.4
USA	108	13.9	1,047	12.4
Britain	63	8.1	688	8.2
China	16	2.1	610	7.2
Taiwan	42	5.4	528	6.3
Australia/New Zealand	34	4.4	159	1.9
Canada	22	2.8	76	0.9
Other European countries	233	29.9	727	8.6
Other Asian countries	91	11.7	441	5.2
Other regions	18	2.3	31	0.4
Total	778	100.0	8,423	99.9

*Source: Handover Ceremony Coordination Office as of May 8, 1997

feeds from different venue locations around Hong Kong. They can book studios, editing suites, and a video library with record and playback facilities. Some 400 kilometers of video and audio cables are used to link the broadcast booths to the master control center. Over 40 tons of TV equipment is installed in the technical nerve center for broadcasters to get signals and uplink to satellites for global distribution. Inside the PBC are information counters for the Tourist Association and the Trade Development Council. Each accredited journalist receives a packet of souvenirs, information materials, a book promoting Hong Kong's economy, and even a belt pouch with six rolls of film and lens cleansing kits. The GIS facilitates journalistic operation and promotes Hong Kong's tourism and business opportunities.

One notable arrangement inside the PBC is the size and location of official media from China and Britain. Literally, CCTV and Xinhua (New China) News Agency, symbolizing the new sovereign power, take the most prominent locations at the center stage of the PBC's floor plan. CCTV occupies the largest booth (540 square meters), paying a weekly rent of U.S.$13,000 and the total renovation cost of U.S.$39,000. A neighboring area with the same size is originally saved for the BBC, but the BBC decides to make a low-key retreat by renting only two small units inside the PBC. (For comparison, Reuters rents seven units.) This space is ultimately assigned to a group of official Chinese media including Xinhua News Agency, the *People's Daily*, the *PLA Daily* and the English-language *China Daily*. Our informants disclose that even if the BBC or anyone else had offered top money, it would not have got the top spot anyway. The BBC finally chooses the rooftop of the neighboring Academy of Performing Arts as its coverage headquarters. The Hong Kong government could not promise the BBC to have the PBC early enough, and the BBC wants to have a closed and secure site for its huge team, responsible for both its domestic and world radio and TV broadcast services. The official TV representative of Hong Kong, RTHK, is located in a relatively obscure position on the middle left side of the PBC. Many reporters mill around the huge free-seating area, where they gulp massive amounts of GIS handouts and watch a big TV screen to keep abreast of various ongoing activities. A television producer, having overheard its rival station's conversation about "news budget" held in a thinly separated cubicle next door, sighs in relief, "We are doing OK." Reporters from two poorer Taiwan papers had initially fretted about having to rely heavily on organized sources, but the event turns out to be so colorless that they scoff at their richer colleagues for being overzealous.

The GIS arranges a program of 70 package tours for visiting media, including 30 briefings and 40 visits over a three-week period. Some 1,000 journalists attend the briefings, and 1,200 take part in the visits (Knight and Nakano, 1999: 35). Since the news net "identifies some sources and institutions as the appropriate location of facts and dismisses others" (Tuchman, 1978: 13), the GIS is the most prominent source of information exerting decisive influence on the media. Building on routine journalistic practices, the GIS generates a form of manipulated journalism "for its instrumental value in the service of particular interests" (Fishman, 1980: 15). The GIS facilitates foreign journalists in various ways: interviewing senior officials, visiting government departments and new constructions, and touring local industry and commerce as well as "fun spots." The most popular site to visit is the border that divides Hong Kong and the mainland, where the People's Liberation Army was to cross to make its entry. The GIS has a team of 26 photographers going to all major events in the last five days, who provide digitized photographs to all journalists on the Internet free of charge (*Ming Pao Daily News*, June 6). The GIS is, in effect, providing subsidized visual scripts to media "clients."

As the major propaganda arm, the GIS is extraordinarily skilled in controlling the flow of government information and in "marshaling" the media. The GIS establishes a website to facilitate information delivery but restricts the number of journalists to various ceremonies. Media accreditation has a deadline on April 7; latecomers can partially use the PBC facilities but cannot apply for attending the major ceremonies. Major officials convey their speeches to the media via the GIS. The GIS releases a time schedule of daily events and the arrival time of major dignitaries from China and the United Kingdom. (The list of VIP guests for the handover ceremony totals over 4,000 from more than 40 countries, since the Chinese side is eager for celebrating the international "coronation," while the British side hopes for a grand finale to mark a retreat in glory.) One journalist complains that the operational details are too tightly but unnecessarily controlled (Knight and Nakano, 1999: 40). Journalists schedule their work around the official itinerary, as for example on the June 30 countdown day:

4:15 pm: Governor Patten and his family leave the Government House

6:15 pm: The Sunset Ceremony for the British administration

8:15 pm: Firework Display

9:00 pm: Reception Banquet

10:00 pm: Variety Show

12:00 pm: Handover ceremony

1:00 am: Royal Yacht Britannia departs

1:30 am: The Provisional Legislature swears in

5:00 am: The People's Liberation Army (PLA) moves in

The only "nuisance" that received most eager media attention is the staged protest by the Democratic Party in the immediate wake of the handover ceremony and before the swearing-in of the Provisional Legislature (see below).

Journalists remonstrate about Beijing's "closed door" policy, but praise the GIS for trying to wear them down by helping to secure five to six interviews a day. Kristi Khockshorn of the *San Jose Mercury News* observes: "You call people here nine at night and they are at their desks working . . . Everybody from the PR section calls me back at midnight." AP's Marcus Eliason echoes, "They are on the board. They give you accurate information, quick, the transcripts of the speeches; the trips they organize are very useful." However, Yau Shing-mu of the *Hong Kong Economic Times* opines that the GIS provides good daily routine help (such as looking for phone numbers) but is not forthcoming with in-depth information. Even the invited guest list to the handover ceremony was not released until after it was over.

Competing for Media Attention

Besides the GIS, numerous social organizations and political groups vie for media attention to promote their causes. In the days leading up to the handover, the media-savvy Democratic Party holds different types of street shows, concerts, talks, and exhibitions. Other activist groups of different ideological stripes take advantage of the presence of foreign journalists by staging protests near the handover ceremony site. The police have to block off several streets next to the Convention Center and designate a small site for the demonstrators 200 yards away so that they would not see or be seen by the invited guests. Nearby newsstands are suspended.

Led by the most eloquent English-speaking lawyer Martin Lee, the Democratic Party stages a protest on the balcony of the Legislative Council Building right after the handover ceremony and before the swearing-in ceremony of the Provisional Legislature on the midnight of July 1. The event is carefully timed to occur in the brief span when television camera is momentarily not captivated by official proceedings. The site, a stately and photogenic building perfect for visual attraction, is chosen to tell the world that the democrats have been driven out from the PRC-installed body that displaces the elected legislature. A senior party official admits that they orchestrated this event with the foreign media in mind (Knight and Nakano, 1999: 43). Moreover, Lee delivers his speech in Cantonese and in English, with somewhat different emphasis and tone, to satisfy different needs of the local and foreign media. The Democratic Party has two slogans; the foreign media harp on "Fight for Democracy," whereas the local press finds "Support the Return of Sovereignty" also palatable. The Party considers it a coup for Lee to be quoted by English-language newspapers—invariably praised as a "democracy hero"—more often than Prince Charles and the incoming Chief Executive Tung Chee-hwa on July 1. But the headline on the cover of an earlier edition of the *South China Morning Post* magazine reads: "Martyr Lee."

The Foreign Correspondents' Club (FCC), headed by the *Washington Post*'s local bureau chief Keith Richburg, also sets itself up as a miniature news stage; it creates and legitimates news agendas by sponsoring seminars and press conferences with a parade of local and foreign personalities. Parachute journalists, new to Hong Kong and lacking linguistic competence, find such staged news of particular benefit (chapter 3). Resident correspondents, many of whom claim to be independent loners rather than members of the news pack, nonetheless tend to clarify and reinforce their shared definition of news through press conferences and informal social contacts (Bennett, 1996). We find journalists well aware of the range and quality of their colleagues' work. Even Edward Gargan of the *New York Times*, a self-proclaimed loner, admits that he occasionally shares observations and insights with other colleagues. The British *Guardian* correspondent credits the *New York Times* and the *Washington Post* for doing more thorough coverage thanks to their abundance of resources. These leaders in the pecking order are treated so reverentially that their accounts helped to set the basic tone of news agendas for the U.S. if not world media. The FCC may play a dual function akin to Crouse's (1973) description of U.S. journalists on the campaign trail who compete, compare notes, and swap tales with one another. News is a mutually confirming process; the agenda is intersubjectively constituted by members of the journalistic community (Zelizer, 1993). Consequently, certain events receive more prominence, while others fall into obscurity.

In one of the FCC's guest-studded seminars, the speaker is a local banker who takes a pro-China stand. We find that about 30 journalists are present, mostly from the English-language media, one from Kyodo News Agency, and one crew from Hong Kong's ATV. While many journalists ask the banker about the property market and economic situation in Hong Kong, an unidentified journalist (probably just parachuted from abroad) asks him if he is a member of the Communist Party. The banker announces that he is a citizen of the United States. His agenda was to release a packet of survey findings conducted by the Asia Society (of which he is chair) depicting Hong Kong people as increasingly optimistic about their future. He also tries to blame Governor Chris Patten and the Democratic Party chief Martin Lee for presenting a bad image of Hong Kong overseas. We doubt any news organization would pay him much respect; at best, veteran journalists would treat his remarks as background statements to be inserted into a larger story as a show of balance and depth. Those from pro-Beijing papers, if they had been present, might have been more than happy to use him to denigrate Patten and Lee. We check the *South China Morning Post* (June 20), which carries a short story about the talk, with a markedly skeptical title: "Tycoon on the Offensive."

In a relatively open environment of diverse interests and perspectives, the media can subvert the intentions of various major organized groups so far as these fora and symposia are concerned. While the GIS coordinates numerous field trips to impress journalists from abroad, some local social workers want to expose social problems by taking them to slum areas to see the poor live in a "cage." To mold a more favorable opinion environment for the handover, the pro-Beijing Foundation for a Better Hong Kong Tomorrow had been inviting journalists from midsized cities in the heartland of the United States to take paid visits to the territory since 1996. Now this foundation is also sponsoring seminars and symposia for journalists but, for credibility's sake, finds itself having to invite its ideological opponents to share the limelight, even sharing the same speakers with the FCC. On these occasions, the media habitually shower attention on democracy activists to the neglect of pro-China sources whom the sponsors mean to spotlight. Parachute journalists, brought in for the occasion, are, however, more vulnerable to the manipulation of activist groups (see chapter 3).

Apart from the FCC, the Freedom Forum also sponsors a number of talks and seminars for the media right before the handover date. For example, CNN's Mike Chinoy gives a speech organized by the Freedom Forum on May 6. Earlier in March, the Freedom Forum had a luncheon talk featuring the editor of the *Far Eastern Economic Review*. Other stage-setters include the Hongkong Telecom that provides more than 1,500 phone lines, 275 fax lines, more than 200 telex lines, 300 video lines, private exclusive lines, mobile phone and pager rental services. In addition, it has three satellites for worldwide broadcast, and two-thirds of the world's population can directly pick up their signals.[1] Physically adjacent to the PBC is the Academy of Performing Arts that rents out its rooftop, equipped with satellite dishes, to more than 50 media organizations, including the BBC. DHL Worldwide Express begins to pick up brisk business in early June, for reporters have to send photos and materials back home.

The Broadcast Feed: A Stage of Mini Struggle

The broadcast arrangements for the handover ceremonies were an act of political wresting in the Sino-British Liaison Committee. The BBC and CCTV, designated representatives of the two sovereign states, were to be official co-producers of live footage of the major events and handover ceremonies for free satellite transmission to the rest of the world. Our informants reveal that the BBC, acutely aware of the fact that even when it takes charge on June 30 it will have no significant role to play after the next day, has been inclined from the start to let the local television take the lead. The PRC was reluctant to concede the primacy to Hong Kong on grounds of national sovereignty; not until the last moment did CCTV relinquish that control, realizing that local people can do a better job. So a local television consortium, led by RTHK with the three local broadcasters (TVB, ATV, and cable) as members, takes over the responsibility to produce the core feed. The BBC remains in the consortium as an associate member but CCTV refuses to be part of it and wants to make productions of its own. In the end, the BBC agrees to take up the Sunset Ceremony at Tamar and the leaving of the royal yacht Britannia, while CCTV covers the official establishment of the SAR and the PLA's incoming. Nevertheless, the whole episode gives a glimpse into Hong Kong's awkward roles between the hegemonic PRC and the sunset British.

The BBC focuses on the Flag Lowering Ceremony and the Sunset Ceremony as a dignified retreat. They report the demonstration by the democrats while ignoring the swearing-in of the Provisional Legislature. The moving in of the PLA troops is done live but negatively covered. The core feed supplied by the Hong Kong TV consortium also shows a memorable farewell with friends and well-wishers of Chris Patten, with his daughters' tearful eyes. For Fiona Andersen, the bureau chief, the top story is the departure of the British entourage, Prince Charles's speech, and the ceremony itself. The second story turns immediately to the new regime and the problems it will face, airing the speech by Martin Lee in the Legislative Council balcony. In contrast, CCTV pays little attention to the lowering of the Union Jack and other British ceremonial rituals. It covers the swearing-in ceremony, praises the PLA, ignores the protests, and highlights the celebration activities in Beijing and other parts of the world.

In the end, the television consortium delivers 96 hours of live broadcast from June 29 midnight until July 2 midnight, involving ten crews, 76 video cameras, and more than 300 people. It also has 48 hours of nonstop broadcast over the Internet. From June 23 to early July, over nine million people have visited the consortium's Internet site, and a quarter million have watched or listened to the live broadcast. (During the 48 hours on June 30 and July 1, more than six million people visited the consortium's website.) Among the audience, 20% are from Hong Kong, 31% from the United States, 16% from Canada, 14% from Australia, 11% from Malaysia, 4% from China, and 2% from Britain (Leung, 1997). The handover is truly a staged international media event, and the distribution of audience reveals not only the Internet strength of individual countries but also their psychological affinity toward this spectacle.

The Media as Stages

While the GIS and other organizations set the stages for the handover, the media as participants construct different stages for the political actors to perform. We can differentiate the print media from the broadcast media (basically TV) as two stage environments, and also the local media as a stage to assist the foreign media acquainted with the Hong Kong scene.

Television

The biggest challenge for television is a technical one. Local TV does not have to remind its viewers of the political and historical significance of the handover; instead it prefers to let them "see everything for and by themselves." Live coverage and technical excellence overwhelm substance. To fill up its airtime, CNN tries to showcase a troop of key players on all sides of the political fence, hiring a full-time person to book interviews. Its comprehensive coverage is an important point of reference for parachute journalists. To Mike Chinoy, its Hong Kong bureau chief, the handover is "a bit of a logistical nightmare." Bringing in 70,000 pounds of equipment from the United States, CNN has to make sure that cameras will catch the events as they are happening; the sheer mechanics of getting the right technical stuff, the right camera, the right people at the right place and the right time is a formidable challenge. Chinoy says that he spends a lot of time fighting with the handover committee for the right to do a stand-up commentary before camera in addition to getting a picture of the ceremony from the pool. Since there is not much chance to flaunt its breaking-news specialty, CNN ends up doing a lot of profiles, analyses, and features. A producer flies in from Congo to team up with its senior European correspondent in the filming of a local bartender with a king cobra tattooed on his arm in a tattoo parlor. Another CNN team spends half a day trying to find a restaurant willing to be filmed for serving snake and lizard on the menu.

The BBC's team of 180 people is, as a senior management describes it, "one of the most ambitious projects we have ever attempted in every respect." The BBC builds a studio in Britain, ships it to Hong Kong, and spends four months to install it on the rooftop of the Academy of Performing Arts, guarding it against possible typhoons. The European Broadcasting Union (EBU) provides technical infrastructures for 66 European member stations in 54 countries, but editorial coverage is the responsibility of individual members. EBU has a master broadcast control room for its members to share. It ensures proper functioning of satellites, phone lines and fax machines, and tries to meet different requests from member stations.

CCTV's 300-strong staff, including reporters and technicians, began to arrive in 1996. A building was bought for use as their dormitory. Beijing dispatches its own people to handle CCTV's local transportation and travel to mainland cities, to protect the security of their booth at the PBC—and to cook daily meals for 300 people. CCTV erects in its booth a 1.5-meter-high photo, along with a huge model, of Hong Kong as a background for live broadcast, so the presenters can point out places such as the arrival of the PLA. Everyone speaks from a completely written and preapproved script, but the anchor tries to read it as if it were "live."

Hong Kong's TVB had intended to hire helicopters to cover the entry of the PLA in the early morning of July 1, but darkness, cloud interference, and insufficient microwave links made it infeasible. TVB's "war plan" looks like a huge spiderweb of high-cost communication lines and points connecting its headquarters, the PBC, and different venues. The setup, with the help of additional optical fibers and mobile crews, is more complex than anything TVB has ever attempted, as its news manager Carmen Luk stresses: "The most important thing is to ensure the infrastructure is well built."

The resource-poor television stations must try to impose stringent order on the news schedule by producing canned programs well in advance. The Hong Kong-based CTN, having not enough equipment and cameras, makes 100 fillers of 30-second MTV-style films, statistics, Q & A, and sound bites from the audience for use between scheduled events. Taiwan's TTV prelists 35 story ideas for June 23 to 27, each with assigned reporters, a story outline, and a target date for completion and airing. The local cable television organizes professional and public fora to fit its "transition in people's heart" theme. RTHK prerecords its regular programs early on to free up resources.

The Print Media

The newspaper is more analytical and contextual than television. TV stories can whet some audience's appetite so they will look for more information in the newspaper. On the other hand, television can also create what Lazarsfeld and Merton (1948) call "narcotizing dysfunction," so the public mistakes superficial knowledge for action. Jan Wong of the *Globe and Mail* considers what she does is "sociology in the daily news." Graham Hutchings of the *Daily Telegraph*, as a historian, finds the Hong Kong story very "absorbing, interesting, and fantastic" to cover, as his job is not only to report what happened yesterday but to explain it in context. Most western media try to explain Hong Kong in the China context.

Chris Wood of *Maclean's* puts it nicely, "The actual story is before, after, and around." Before: Go back to 156 years ago when Hong Kong was ceded. After: What will happen? Around: What is going on in Guangzhou, Shanghai, Beijing, and Taipei? With the transition seemingly smooth and peaceful, many western journalists—such as those from the Associated Press, the *San Jose Mercury News*, and Canada's Southam News—set their eyesight on the future: What will happen a year from now? Can Tung handle it? Will Hong Kong remain upbeat? Will China suppress the Democratic Party? The *New York Times* has been working on a series of "Waiting for China" projects. International (*Newsweek* and *Time*) and regional (*Far Eastern Economic Review* and *Yazhou Zhoukan*) newsmagazines publish a number of cover stories or special issues, as the date of the handover is drawing near. *Asahi Shimbun* vividly compares Japan's orderliness with Hong Kong's order-within-chaos and China's complete chaos.

Local Media as "Clues"

Many journalists take cues from the English-language *South China Morning Post*, the *Asian Wall Street Journal*, and to a lesser extent the *Hong Kong Standard*. Those who read Chinese get information, rumors, and story leads from major local Chinese-language newspapers. Major local media inform foreign correspondents of the basic community concerns, foreign coverage feeds back into the local circuit, and news spawns news in the global-local nexus. Kristi Khockshorn of the *San Jose Mercury News* admits that she only knows about the illegal immigrants as a big issue in Hong Kong after reading the *South China Morning Post*, as the wires do not write much on it. TV Asahi gets news ideas from the local media, and they do follow-up stories. ITN admits to receiving helpful advice and source materials from the local media, while the BBC also hires many local journalists whose families and friends the network can film. Most sophisticated journalists read such political journals as the *Nineties Monthly*, *Zheng Ming* (Contending), and *Kaifang* (Open) for indepth and critical analysis. Many foreign journalists get the daily GIS news summary of the local Chinese-language media. They also read the local China-controlled *Ta Kung Pao* and *Wen Wei Po* to decipher Beijing's rhetoric and motives.

The *Apple Daily* and Radio Television Hong Kong (RTHK) deserve special mention. As a vulgarly populist paper thriving on commodifying anti-Beijing sentiments, the *Apple Daily* is seen as a test case of press freedom; many foreign journalists rush to its premises to take pictures and ask its reporters whether they are "afraid" of China's takeover. Its publisher, Jimmy Lai, whom Beijing detests, is a darling of the western media; even CNN does a live interview with this paper's political editor. RTHK, a government arm, has established itself as a source of high credibility (top-ranked in public opinion polls) in the last two decades by modeling after the BBC's professionalism, but for this very reason it has been assaulted by the Beijing authorities and pro-Beijing figures in Hong Kong. ITN films the making of RTHK's controversial current affairs program "Headliner," which is often satirical of the Hong Kong government and the PRC. Whether RTHK will be allowed to continue as usual is a burning question for the western media. Given its former pro-British background and now being suspected of self-censorship, the *South China Morning Post* also courts journalistic attention as an indicator of the political wind. Edward Gargan of the *New York Times* (April 18) and Joseph Kahn of the *Wall Street Journal* (April 22) develop lengthy and widely discussed reports on the softened voices of the *SCMP* and *Ming Pao Daily News*.

Media Sociology

Many local journalists prepare for the worst but hope for the best, so far as Hong Kong's future is concerned. The best-case scenario, as outlined by Anson Chan in a speech delivered in Manila two months before the handover, is this newspaper headline: "Hong Kong goes back to China; Nothing happens." A local TV news editor puts it: "You get up early in the morning (on July 1), Nathan Road did not turn into Liberation Road." But for the foreign journalists "nothing happens" would be a disastrous anticlimax. They had scripted all sorts of scenarios beforehand, knowing what to look for, who to talk to, and what kind of events to cover. BBC's James Miles observes that journalists' diaries are well written out because the handover itself, with saturated coverage, "scripted all the way down to the second in the grand hall." The western media expected Martin Lee to get arrested and the People's Liberation Army to provoke a major confrontation, but in the end, the better wish of local journalists comes true; the transition is smooth.

Competition

Competition is the engine of news business. The wire services pride themselves on beating their rivals by minutes or seconds. The local bureau of the Associated Press assigns junior reporters the task of monitoring Reuters and AFP. The BBC television competes with ITN at home; the BBC World Service considers CNN (television) and the Voice of America (radio) as its chief competitors. The BBC headquarters takes satisfaction in airing, before ITN does, an interview with Tung Chee-hwa. After the BBC does a piece on Lantau Island, its reporters bump into an ITN reporter interviewing the same person, so the BBC arranges to run the piece one day ahead of ITN. A satellite television news team from Taiwan decides to do 37 hours of live coverage from June 30 to July 1, just to beat its competitor, CTN, by one hour (*Yazhou Zhoukan*, May 19).

On the other hand, journalists have to bow to the pressure of standardization (Bennett, 1996; Zelizer, 1993). There may be some kind of "herd journalism" in which several thousands of journalists interview a few dozen people. It is not uncommon for them to seek mutual aid in updating and providing incidental information, giving referrals and "global leads," as well as exchanging gossip (Crouse, 1973; Fishman, 1980). Mutual back-scratching and pooled resources are all the more pronounced when covering in a foreign land an event too huge for anyone to do it all. Reporters sometimes compare notes. Kristi Khockshorn of the *San Jose Mercury News* admits, "You share with your community, but you do not share with outside your community. You steal the sources, see other people's stories, and see who sounds intelligent. You definitely steal. I see CNN, and I write down the name of the people they interview for different subjects." Before arriving in Hong Kong, many Canadian journalists—from noncompeting organizations—got together to exchange information and to enlarge personal contacts, vowing to be in touch while there. The *Liberty Times* from Taiwan teams up with the western media—to compensate for its weaker resources—through the friendship its deputy chief editor had made with leading western colleagues while translating their books into Chinese. In return, his western partners profit from his expert knowledge of Chinese economy. Cable TV in Hong Kong has a partnership deal with CNN to exchange news and feature programs about the handover. The *Wall Street Journal* is assisted by its subsidiary, the Hong Kong-based *Asian Wall Street Journal*; so is Taiwan's TVBS backed by its parent company TVB in Hong Kong. But Edward Gargan of the *New York Times* claims that he is happiest when he is alone and out in the jungle.

The Hong Kong stories are too routine to get a scoop or to be scooped. Andrew Higgins of the *Guardian* thinks of them as "bordering on the impossible of finding anything new to write about," but journalists still closely watch their competitors' moves. Rarely do print journalists regard television reporters as their direct competitors and vice versa. The competition is likely to be most fierce between rival oligopolies, such as the *Apple Daily* and the *Oriental Daily News* in Hong Kong, ITN and the BBC in Britain, and the *China Times* and the *United Daily News* in Taiwan. They bring forward rather homogeneous stories, though with a certain degree of product differentiation. An ITN reporter considers his organization as more light footed and fresher, while BBC as more worthy and stodgy in approach. The *China Times* is perceived to report more about the mainland and Hong Kong, while the *United Daily News* is more interested in the Taiwan-Hong Kong relationship. In Hong Kong, Cable TV does not regard the terrestrial ATV and TVB as a threat.

Competition can be won by getting exclusive stories, coming up with original feature-story ideas, or making small scoops on details (Gans, 1979). Since Beijing controls the "first-order script" (Dayan and Katz, 1992) of the event and did not finalize the arrangements until the last moment, the media are left to construct their own "second-order script." With little chance of getting a big scoop, journalists are not terribly keen on documenting the mundane details. In search of colorful stories tailored for domesticated consumption, journalists also become spectators to the tightly controlled extravaganza of official ceremonies. Without substantive competition, it is customary for the Taiwanese press to overwhelm their rivals with more space, which the editors take as a sign of victory.

Reporting Strategies

Major western media have sent in additional reporters to join forces with those already stationed regularly in Hong Kong. Many outlets have hired a mixed lot of local assistants. Some media have worked out detailed plans in advance, others simply follow their intuitive "noses for news." These differences notwithstanding, they invariably follow the principle of domestication (chapter 3) and build their "news net" around seven principles:

- Get big names. Favorite names include Governor Patten, Chief Executive Tung, and democracy advocates (Martin Lee and Emily Lau). Martin Lee has to attend two to three hour-long press conferences every day in order to satisfy "thousands" of requests from journalists. The leader of a pro-Beijing party, Tsang Yok-shing, has been meeting the press frequently since March and sometimes has to grant five interviews per day. The news net is set up to catch the big fish—not the small fish, let alone shrimps—but the less prestigious media cannot have access to these media celebrities who are either too busy or very selective in granting interviews. Many foreign journalists are left empty-handed.

- Interview "relevant" people, especially one's own official representatives and expatriate communities. Canadian journalists would hunt for the Canadian commissioner in Hong Kong, and Japanese reporters would look for Japanese expatriates there. U.S. Secretary of State Madeleine Albright, as the de facto spokesperson of the western world, is a prized source for the American and other western media. The PRC media only seek out the pro-China people, while Taiwanese reporters would find people inclined to air a pessimistic view of the handover.

- Talk to other journalists when "real" sources are unavailable. The *Liberty Times* of Taiwan, for example, interviews the BBC's bureau chief in Beijing and ABC's diplomatic correspondent. Many foreign journalists seem to take cues from the English-language *South China Morning Post*. Resident correspondents may read local political journals. Jan Wong of the *Globe and Mail* is interviewed by ABC News, the U.S. network, for her feature stories on "cheungsam" (Chinese gown); the *South China Morning Post* interviews her for her recent book on China.

- Cover the media phenomenon if there is no real news. Editors in New York or London are bombarded with so many pictures and stories as to think of them as something interesting. Andrew Higgins of the *Guardian* said stories he filed normally would be cut in half, but the handover stories get printed twice as large as the "usual" size. The active international media presence heightens the level of the event's perceived significance more than what it really is.

- Interview the street people to put a human face on the story. The supply of these "sources" is virtually unlimited, but western journalists tend to pursue English-speaking people. Linguistic barriers may prove formidable for low-budget media organizations that cannot afford an interpreter's help to interview "ordinary" street people.

- Make use of stereotypes to typify events and people (chapter 4). It is reported that an Australian network hopes to find "a pro-mainland spokesman who would appear belligerent," and a Norwegian broadcaster is seeking "an elderly colonial Brit with an intelligence background who is upset about what's going on" (*Far Eastern Economic*

Review, July 10). *South China Morning Post* (May 2) takes an informal count of stories in selected western newspapers. Out of 237 headlines about Hong Kong from 10 prominent newspapers from the U.S., Britain, and Canada between March 1 and April 29, 89 are negative, 32 positive, and the other 116 neutral. A local reporter notes that western colleagues "always report the pessimistic side" and "discard the not-too-bad opinions when they ask people how they feel about the future of Hong Kong" (*Yazhou Zhoukan*, July 7). These stereotypes are consonant with core values and not likely to be challenged by the public (Nimmo and Combs, 1990; Said, 1981).

- "Peg" the news to special dates and "hype" the event. News peg is the use of a recent event or a public official's statement as a "handle" to "hang" stories (Gans, 1979: 168). In the handover saga, certain dates are given special significance. For example, the *Independent* focuses on the last 100 days and begins to print stories about the Hong Kong handover; TVBS starts the "100 days countdown"; the *Ming Pao Daily News* officially kicks off the coverage on the same day. Typical of many television stations, the BBC did special reports on days marking one year, six months, and a week before the handover. Kyodo News pegs its articles to three years before the handover, then two years, one year, six months, one hundred days, three months, two months, and one month. TV Asahi plans to do a special "one month after the handover in Hong Kong."

Given the media logic, the set of people (mostly from the elite plus a few "ordinary" persons) to be interviewed by the journalists is small. The pool of news sources are rather homogeneous among western media, but the PRC media's heavy reliance on domestic and pro-China sources indicates little overlap with the sources of western media. The news rhythm of the scripted event is decidedly slow, while the spot news is boring. Deprived of any real scoop and tired of the rituals and government planned tours, many journalists are keen to develop nonscheduled soft stories—the British "color" stories or the American "mood" pieces. Being "there" to see and feel it, journalists provide a personal touch to hook up with the audience. They are keen to describe the thunderstorm falling when ordinary people line up outside the Government House to bid farewell to Patten. Perhaps hoping to invoke his audience's familiar image of the Demilitarized Zone dividing the two Koreas, a TV reporter from South Korea points his camera and places his palm against one of the concrete pillars of the barbed-wire fence built to halt illegal immigrants at the Hong Kong-China border. He then explains: "This is the border between capitalism and communism" (*Far Eastern Economic Review*, July 10). Jan Wong of the *Globe and Mail* writes about the gay bars, the souvenir craze on stamps, the subway passes, and the elevator closing seconds earlier than elsewhere as a sign of quick life tempo. She also recounts her having a last afternoon tea in the Peninsula Hotel in the old colonial tradition. The "side stuff" is not necessarily less ideologically loaded.

Conclusion

Power is reflected in the sociology of news organization, which also affects the media content. There are event-centered, journalist-centered, and organization-centered theories to explain how occurrences are transformed into news (Gans, 1979: 78-79). But all these factors have to operate within larger contextual factors—including technology, economy, politics, and culture—that lie outside the boundary of the news organization. This chapter has dealt with the play of power between journalists and their sources: journalists cultivate sources to gain information, whereas the sources seek to publicize certain events or influence news agendas. The GIS as the official organizer and centralized news source is not shy about taking advantage of its privileged status and from profiting from its interaction with the media. Other nongovernmental organizations also enter the fray to have their say. The local media serve their audience and play host to the foreign media. Journalists are constantly battling for scoop and speed, but sometimes may help each other out in small ways. They have developed reporting strategies to deal with different situations, even for a much scripted and predictable event like the handover.

The availability of resources determines the size of reporting teams, ranging widely in numbers from hundreds (such as China's state-run television) to tens, to several, to a lone stringer. Many resource-poor journalists collaborate with colleagues from a different type of medium who are not direct competitors, or those from other countries—and better yet, with the local media. Major outlets call upon their Beijing correspondents, in addition to those from the home headquarters, to reinforce the effort of the Hong Kong bureau. Many media outlets use CNN cuts or wire stories, which approach the global status. On the other extreme is Epicentrum, a news organization from Czechoslovakia, which rents a small office (also used as living quarters for the four reporters) in a village house in the outlying island of Cheung Chau. It can only afford to use a computer, a secondhand TV, a Beta VCR, and two digital cameras, to produce feature stories and analyses (but no live coverage) for its domestic media clients. The four reporters came in November 1996 and hope to stay until the end of 1997 (*Apple Daily*, June 30).

In the sociology of journalism, a striking feature is predominant interest in people, especially when the event itself proves to be inadequately attractive. TV stories need to have faces and images, and people are the best vehicle to convey meanings and emotions of remote foreign events in personal terms. "Everything must be about people, about human beings, then everyone will be interested," notes Steve Vines of the *Independent*. People orientation is useful for lesser organizations such as the *Baltimore Sun* to produce dramatic human-interest stories, leaving formal and stately ceremonies to the wire services. If there is a central theme, the Southam News correspondent says, it is "what Hong Kong people feel about this." The *South China Morning Post*'s Chris Yeung echoes: "For the media as a whole, the handover was about how 6 million people felt about the changes." The *Ming Pao Daily News* also wants to capture the feelings of the general public. Unlike the historians who have the luxury of sitting in a nice office to read what the journalists write about, the journalists often write about what is happening under great pressure. The first drafts of history that journalists are writing always start with people and events.

Chapter 3

Domestication of Global News

One of our great problems is to make some people in Pakistan, in Hong Kong, in Iowa, the head of the CIA, the Russian Foreign Ministry, all understand the (handover) stories and learn something from them.

—Mike Chinoy, Hong Kong Bureau Chief, CNN

I am sure that on the night of the handover I would be looking for someone from San Jose.

—Kristi Khockshorn, Correspondent, *San Jose Mercury News*

For Britons and Americans, the Hong Kong storyline is simple: The place is going down the tube after 1 July.

—Jonathan Fenby, Editor, *South China Morning Post*

Newsweek produces a cover story on Hong Kong, as the handover approaches. The international issue is a "souvenir issue" whose cover portrays Hong Kong as a "Land of Survivors" against the backdrop of its towering skyscrapers, but the U.S. edition features the face of a female model blindfolded with a red ribbon, asking "China Takes Over Hong Kong—Can it Survive?" People wonder why *Newsweek* has two different covers for the same story. Is it not a blatant example of western attempts at "demonizing" China?

Rarely can a foreign topic make the domestic cover story of *Newsweek*. A foreign topic, with the notable exception of Princess Diana, has invariably hurt the magazine's newsstand sales in the United States. Maynard Parker, the editor-in-chief of *Newsweek*, admits that China is the international news that causes the least decrease in circulation, and the handover of Hong Kong is seen primarily as a China story. But then even the grim irony of Hong Kong coming into China's possession, against the world trend of collapse of Communist regimes since 1989, is judged not enough to "grab" the attention of the American audience, so Parker decides that throwing in a question mark may "energize" the cover story. Apparently, the uncertainty this question mark implies is controversial and yet quite in tune with the prevailing political culture of the United States that tends to cast doubt over the future of a capitalist jewel snatched by the Communists. This story typifies how a global media event is "domesticated."

Bases and Processes

Globalization, a useful yet elusive concept, has its fair share of supporters and skeptics. World economy, politics, and culture are becoming more interdependent, but also with sharpened disparity between center and periphery on the globalized stage. It is widely accepted that globalization brings about "the time-space compression of the world" (Tomlinson, 1999) and the "intensification of consciousness of the world as a whole" (Robertson, 1992). To Giddens (1991: 63) globalization is the consequence of modernity marked by the increased level of "time-space distanciation" and "the intensification of social relations which link distant localities in such a way that local happenings are shaped by events occurring many miles away and vice versa." Waters (1995: 3) defines globalization as "a social process in which the constraints of geography on social and cultural arrangements recede and in which people become increasingly aware that they are receding."

Globalization and localization are a pair of conceptual opposites that at the same time imply each other (Chan, 2002; Chan and Ma, 2002). Globalization represents the universalization of the particular, whereas localization is the particularization of the universal; one cannot be divorced from the other. Local happenings may move in an obverse direction from the very distanciated relations that shape them, and local transformation is as much a part of globalization. While time and space have been compressed in this globalized world, they have not been eliminated (Wang et al., 2000). The perspective of globalization tends to exaggerate the extent of deterritorialization, with references to "the end of geography" and "the end of sovereignty" (Scholte, 1996: 51). The very existence of time and space is an important basis for locality to assert its influence in the midst of globalization, because locality anchors cultural meanings of a discursive community through shared language, experience, and knowledge. Robertson (1992) and Featherstone (1995) therefore use "glocalization" to capture the mutually constituting and dialectical nature of the global and the local.

One of the most vexing questions in this formulation is: How "local" is "local"? The global system of international relations consists of a network of nation-states (Giddens, 1985). In the international discursive terrain, the "local" is most likely to be the "national" that is tied to domestic political authority and interests at the expense of subnational differences (Sreberny-Mohammadi, 1991). Globalization may have weakened national feelings to some extent, but nation-states remain very relevant in contemporary politics. Nationalism has seen a rapid revival in Eastern and Central Europe after the collapse of Communism, while instability of a nation-state in Yugoslavia has triggered intense and often destructive subnational "identity" struggles, leading to ethnic cleansing and religious strife. Instead of viewing globalization as "a process that uniformly subverts the national," the nation-states are thus regarded as "powerful players in the process of constructing the global" (Sreberny-Mohammadi et al., 1997: xi).

Given the inexactness of "the local," we posit the concept of "domestication" to refer to the way that journalists try to transform global events, through adaptation, into the relevance structure of a national home audience in accordance with the primary definitions of the nation-state. In this context, the metaphor of "domestication" in the taming of wild (thus alien, uncertain, unknown, unpredictable) animals into being part of the home environment is an apt one. Journalists use domestic frames to turn "nonrecognizable happenings or amphorous talk into a discernable event" (Tuchman, 1978: 192); otherwise, without domestication, foreign news may remain as nonrecognizable happenings. Domestication of global news can be viewed as a major procedure of "reality-maintenance to safeguard a measure of symmetry between objective and subjective reality" (Berger and Luckmann, 1967: 167)—in other words, to avoid cognitive discontinuity and inconsistency. In order to render distant happenings salient, familiar, intelligible—or, less wild—to a home audience preoccupied by the "here and now" issues, journalists must therefore construct foreign news stories in connection with their own political, cultural, and historical systems of meaning (Cohen et al., 1996). The process of news domestication enables journalists to convert foreign agendas into home agendas and to tailor international news for domestic consumption, with the implications of reproducing the prevailing ideology and renewing national self-identity. Said (1981) demonstrates that Orientalist media discourses are clearly constructed through the eyes of imperialist nations in grossly self-serving and reductive terms, thus obfuscating and distorting the complex reality of the Orient itself. Gans (1979) observes that international news in the U.S. media is often presented from a purely national perspective, hewing closely to the State Department line. Hallin and Gitlin (1994) show that the U.S. media try to emphasize the "home dimension" and local relevance of the Gulf War. Lee and Yang (1995) attribute the different causes of the Tiananmen incident as imputed by the U.S. and Japanese media to their different foreign policies that are crystallized expressions of respective national interests.

Various national media systems routinely apply the three criteria of "authority, credibility and availability" differently in choosing their sources (van Ginneken, 1998); this may create a particular slant to the constitution of their news net. The application of these criteria is situated within the sphere of elite consensus and the field of acceptable discourses (Hallin, 1986; Bennett, 1990), thereby privileging official sources and marginalizing other voices. Hearing other sides and checking information are done only within this overall framework, not outside it. Journalists, like other people, live in a "common-sense world in which the meaning of things, of facts and relations, is taken for granted and self-evident" (van Ginneken, 1998). Their socialization into the larger culture, professional subculture, and organizational milieu (in that order) further reifies this taken-for-grantedness of reality (Tuchman, 1978; Schlesinger, 1978). No wonder journalists may "depart (for a foreign country) with a repertory of stereotypes, tend to interpret an ambiguous confrontation with strange cultures in these terms, and tend to return with their preconceptions reconfirmed" (van Ginneken, 1998: 70).

International relations are at the core of international news, but international relations are ridden with contending national interests. The powerful countries tend to impose their worldviews by setting the parameters for discourse on international affairs, but they can count on few laws to govern the behavior of different countries. The discourse on international affairs leaves open the space for national struggles within the world order. From the cognitive perspective, the less well defined the stimulus, the greater the contribution of the perceiver (Fensterheim and Tresselt, 1953). Hall (1974) observes that the media exert their maximum effect on labeling an unfamiliar or ambiguous situation. The ambiguity and indeterminacy embedded in the multifaceted nature of international reality necessitates journalists to provide accounts that suit their preconceived conceptions. Even the sophisticated readers of the *New York Times* and the *Guardian*, their correspondents confess, would find "other people's politics boring." To enliven the boring and familiarize the unfamiliar, "framing" (Goffman, 1973) through typification of unknown phenomena into known categories is an inevitable yet potentially distorting bridge for understanding. These conceptions are, however, not random but have national and cultural embeddings. We agree with van Ginneken (1998) in regarding the nation-state as the primary definer and the media as only the secondary definer of international reality. This ambiguity also enhances the interpretative role of government officials and other sources endowed with institutional authority. In this sense, media accounts reflect the nation's perspectives and outlooks on world affairs. Journalists do not necessarily toe the line of the foreign office, but they rarely question the premises of foreign policy.

Domestication is also necessitated by the needs of audience and media organizations. Cohen (2002) argues that television viewers may not possess certain cognitive abilities to make sense of news if it is not put in a domestic context, because some formal features of news pose problems for comprehension. Newscasts consist of a rapid succession of brief items with no pauses between them, often with no relationship between them or with little or no context or background given. Thus both proactive and retroactive interferences occur, unless foreign affairs are cast in a culturally familiar framework. Organizationally, the media outlets have to justify why they have to send correspondents overseas, particularly in this age of high cost and easy access to wire news. Providing a customized and domesticated perspective gives the media outlet an edge over its competitors. The need for domestication is thus built into the organizational and economic logic of any competitive news medium.

Strategies

Journalists tend to "hype up" the boring news to inflate its appeal or significance (chapter 4). Hyping is a general process that can apply to domestication of foreign news and reportage of domestic news as well. Domestication is first mediated by the professional routines—such as norms and conventions of source attribution and reliance on the powerful to make news—that media organizations develop to achieve efficiency and to safeguard themselves from external pressure (Tuchman, 1978; Gans, 1979). To begin with, given the considerable latitude in making source selection, journalists often take pains to tell a foreign story through the words of celebrities and familiar faces. Journalists have absorbed organizational and cultural definitions of foreign reality as their own "second nature," which lets them accomplish their news task without having to be conscious of the professional rules and values. In covering critical events where greater interests are at stake, the home editorial office plays a more active role and flies in star anchors, well-known commentators and experts from half a world away to "tell as news is happening" in a foreign locale. U.S. television network anchors, despite their lack of expertise in Asian affairs, are prominent television personalities who extend their news battlefield to Hong Kong. The Asahi Broadcasting Corporation boosts its ratings by inviting Agnes Chan, a local pop singer turned Japanese through career and marriage, to report from Hong Kong. A Taiwan TV personality admits to his lack of expert knowledge about Hong Kong but is put in the anchor's chair because of his popularity.

Moreover, the media put the news spotlight on high-ranking officials from their home countries. Gans (1979) notes that the majority of foreign news in the U.S. media concerns "Americans abroad" or "foreigners at home"; of them, many are no doubt high-ranking officials. Officials are highly visible and in a position to express certain views as a representative of political institutions, thus establishing relevance of foreign reality to the home base. Authority figures of international stature, whose reputation and influence reach beyond national boundaries—such as Tony Blair, Margaret Thatcher, Madeleine Albright, and Chris Patten—are keenly sought after by various national media systems. Taiwan's media for days speculated on the seating arrangement for its representative to the handover ceremony and its implications for renewing the talks with the mainland, which had been stalled by Beijing's missile threats in 1995 and 1996.

In addition to officials, the media may give voice to the "ordinary people," especially those from or related to home, to incorporate foreign reality as an extension of local interest. Kristi Khockshorn of the *San Jose Mercury News* specifically looks for visitors from her hometown or the San Francisco Bay area to construct a "typical" narrative. When previously reporting from Somalia, she stood in front of a line of tanks with a "San Jose" sign and shouted once every few minutes for someone from "home" who could probably help to throw some light on what's going on. The growing influence and profile of Chinese-Canadians prompt the media to rely on both ordinary and other not-so-ordinary Canadian citizens of Hong Kong origin as key news sources. To mimic western methods of professional objectivity, a local Guangdong television station interviews a parade of clearly arranged "passersby" against the breathtaking Victoria Harbor, as if each were wholeheartedly joining the chorus of national patriotism in unison. One of them, allegedly retired from the Taiwan army, chokes with tears, "I have been waiting for this day all my life." The old animosity seems to have magically dissolved all of a sudden, but poor editing reveals artificiality of the atmosphere. The *Australian* notes something as trivial as the glass-and-chromium interior of the handover hall that was made by a Melbourne company.

Distant events may stand out more visibly if cast in larger political or historical contexts. Most of the *New York Times* pieces are highly interpretative rather than straightforwardly factual, focusing on how life will be in Hong Kong under Chinese rule. Mike Chinoy of CNN in an interview with us argues that one has "to keep coming back to the big issues and themes" and "to try to put the local thing into a broader perspective." His point is to make people understand the handover not just as boring local politics but as an important issue related to China and the U.S.-China relationship. The story line should not be too detailed to be incomprehensible, but it is important to "to realize that you are talking to people who do not necessarily understand Hong Kong." Chinoy illustrates with this example:

> I am working on a story on housing. Although it is interesting, it is not an international story. It will be if people start rioting and burning down apartments. Anyway, it is a significant social issue here. But how Tung Chee-hua, the Chief Executive of Hong Kong, deals with it is a test of his leadership and (of his claim) that Hong Kong people are more concerned about standard of living issues than freedom issues. . . . I put it in that kind of context, so that somebody seeing it in Argentina, who did not care about housing in Hong Kong, will watch it.

In reporting foreign stories, correspondents naturally turn to their personal frame of reference based on their upbringing and their understanding of comparable events, historical antecedents, and equivalent concepts in their home culture. They make direct or indirect comparisons, draw analogies, and use metaphors or similar historical allegories to illuminate the ramifications of the foreign event on their home country (Cohen, 2002). In the summer of 1997, the majority of media outlets take the high stock market and real estate values in Hong Kong as an assurance of continued economic vibrancy despite political trepidation. Only Japanese journalists read the same "data" as a precursor to the bursting of a "bubble economy"; they are to be substantiated by the Asian financial crisis in less than a year. Japanese journalists' insight or "foresight" bears the conspicuous imprint of their own recent painful economic meltdown. A journalist from a former Communist country in Europe, still beset by the memories of past political brutality and repression, makes the bleakest forecast about the plight of Hong Kong. American visions of Hong Kong are filtered through the lingering images of the Tiananmen crackdown and the long-term memory of the Cold War, thus linking the handover to the capture of a beautiful lady by an ugly beast. Moreover, journalists generally develop preconceived notions, likely scenarios, and journalistic hypotheses that would inform them where to look for what kind of facts, even before the events occur. Many western media assume that the PRC would lose little time in teaching the outspoken *Apple Daily* the first lesson through forced closure. Chris Yeung, political editor of the *South China Morning Post*, describes this journalistic instinct as a "perspective" rather than "purposive spinning."

Journalists produce "color" stories—a genre that uses a lot of anecdotes as supports for the main theme of the story—to reduce the audience's resistance to distant or general ideas and happenings. To Kristi Khockshorn of the *San Jose Mercury News*, a "color story" means "something that gives you a sense of place, that has real people talking, not the officials," and people will feel "more attached" to a story that has "real people" in it. Chris Wood of Canada's *Maclean's* magazine thinks that his readers look for a mix of "color" and "texture" that gives the "sight, sound, smell, and voices of a story." On June 19, Edward Gargan of the *New York Times* wrote a front-page story recounting the life experiences of a teacher, a waiter, a fishmonger, and a tycoon—families across the socioeconomic ladder—"to show what makes up Hong Kong." To catch the mood of the first day after the handover, Seith Faison of the *New York Times* talks to diners at a small noodle shop. The *Chicago Tribune* interviews colonialists, born and bred in Hong Kong, who were saddened by the end of their era. The *Washington Post* (July 5) publishes a feature contrasting a former mainland refugee who now owns a stylish Italian restaurant—once burned by the Communists, she is afraid of going near the fire again—with her aunt who has led a nightmarish life in Shanghai.

We ask the journalists what story in their minds would epitomize the essence of Hong Kong. Invariably their answers point to the ability of the story to elicit the attention and emotion of the home audience. Fiona Anderson, the BBC Hong Kong Bureau Chief, says:

> My colleague made a story that had me in tears. It was a story about a father of a family who came here from over the [Hong Kong] border in the 1950s and 1960s, the most difficult years. They filmed with him, talking about his memories about his days in Hong Kong. And his family is doing really well. His daughter is a senior executive officer in the Hong Kong Bank, his son as well. The father had not given up any chance; he created something for his children and they built on it. And they are now doing well, so they are looking after the father. And they were filming him eating with his grandson on Sunday. To me this is what Hong Kong people are like: Start with nothing and made something out of nothing. And that's what I like about here. That's a beautiful story because it tells the Hong Kong story.

This is a specific story endowed with generalized human values that readers can share with empathy. It also involves a considerable degree of simplification, by way of personification, that enhances its accessibility. The reductive quality of labeling the complex political setup as "the Beijing-appointed Provisional Legislature" makes freedom and democracy black-and-white issues that the unsophisticated audience at home can comprehend on ideological cues.

Secondary Factors of Domestication

Given the relative stability of nationalist interest and its important location as a basis for domestication, national differences in international newsmaking tend to overshadow the internal differences within a nation. Other secondary factors may influence the process of domestication: medium type, nature of target audience, organizational constraints, journalists' biographies, and the local news perspectives.

Medium Type

Television thrives on exciting action-packed pictures. Seeing is believing. Network television news lives with the contradiction between the prestige of elite journalism and the mass appeal of television. As a "cool medium" (McLuhan, 1967) it thrives on live images rather than traditional print-media linear flow of logical reasoning. This visual logic abhors pictorial stillness and dullness, as compelling images often overwhelm the words uttered. Acknowledging television as not a good medium to "convey subtle ideas," Mike Chinoy of CNN says that journalists must work around technological constraints by "looking for visual images and talking to people." War over television ratings further intensifies oversimplification of foreign news lest the viewers who lack requisite background knowledge would not put up with details. Jane Hutcheon, an Australian television reporter, concurs that television is most effective when it presents a few simple ideas with an ensemble of contrasting images in almost black-and-white terms. While television caters to the taste of undifferentiated mass audiences, elite newspapers have to be more thoughtful in offering cause-and-effect interpretations to their more sophisticated readers.

Inasmuch as CNN has a global presence with a need to satisfy the needs of multinational and multicultural audiences, Mike Chinoy claims that its news represents a global view—not from the U.S. perspective but "from nobody's perspective." As a parallel, Epstein (1973) recounts in his study that many U.S. network news people disavow any personal biases and argue that they produce news from nobody's point of view but faithfully reflect the reality. Epstein proceeds to debunk this myth of neutral objectivity by analyzing the immensely powerful political, regulatory, and economic influences on network news. He shows network news to be primarily shaped by organizational considerations: the budgetary requisite, the demand for the news division to maintain the ratings, the high value placed on action or motion footage, and the government's requirement for network news to conform to standards of fairness. Our analysis finds little differences in the ideological structures between CNN and CBS, or between the BBC and ITN. If whoever pays the piper calls the tune, then CNN and other western media organizations active on a global scale will clearly cater to the values of "the global class" in the First World. Even the editors for CNN's World Report admit, "To say that we do not have a point of view is dishonest" (Flournoy, 1992: 23). Poor clients from the Second and Third Worlds are obviously of marginal concern, particularly if their sensibilities clash head-on with those of clients from the First World (van Ginneken, 1998: 44). Even the primary audience members in the subsidiary markets are English-speaking elites. Wire services, supposedly more factual than interpretative, are not free from "national" prisms either (Lee and Yang, 1995). In addition, "local" television stations largely regurgitate national narratives, with little new perspectives to add.

Correspondents vs. Home Editors

Domestication works smoothly when the theme of the news reports agrees with the preconceptions of the home editors and audience; in that case, journalists need not justify their stories. Experienced journalists, especially those whom Tunstall (1971) calls "specialist correspondents" with expert knowledge, should have the trust of their editors and enjoy considerable autonomy—after

all, they share the same professional ideology and organizational culture
(Breed, 1955). Edward Gargan of the *New York Times*, who had previously stationed in Beijing and New Delhi, claims with pride that all his five colleagues
have a reservoir of knowledge to "get below the superficial stories" rather than
"do cliché stories." Gargan and others, like Graham Hutchings of the *Daily
Telegraph*, all emphasize that they take charge of the news agendas with a minimum of interference from their editors. Jonathan Mirsky of the *Times* of London is quick to correct us: "Look, I don't get assignment. I work on stories. I
decide on the topics." Joseph Kahn of the *Wall Street Journal* seems to suggest
that the editor may intervene more often in how the story is presented rather
than what it is about:

> As long as you can present substance in an interesting, proactive and well-
> written way, they are quite enthusiastic. But if you take absolutely accurate,
> very well reported information and present it to them in a dry, just-the-facts
> kind of manner—even if it is completely right—they would say 'ah, not in-
> terested in that.' Quite boring, you know. That is the influence the editors
> exert. They want you to be kind of provocative and intelligent, and forceful as
> a writer.

Veteran editors, of course, command greater authority. Chris Wood, the world
editor of *Maclean's* magazine who had worked for a newsmagazine in Hong
Kong for ten years, insists that he only "discusses" with his reporters about
what should be covered, but to avoid confrontation he does not "dictate" his
agenda to them.

Parachute vs. Resident Correspondents

The summer of 1997 sees a swarm of parachute journalists pulled off from
their regular posting—mostly from Beijing or from their home headquarters—
and flown into Hong Kong either as lone crisis managers or as reinforcement to
the existing organizational strength. Their lack of proficiency in language or
culture makes their task of covering a flood of competing activities at the same
time difficult if not impossible. They have to rely quickly on local media to get
their bearing. They establish alliances and exchange stories with various colleagues who are not their direct competitors, preferably from a different country or from a different type of medium, to "scratch one another's back."
Parachute reporters, lacking resources, must then turn to institutionally organized tours, seminars, and symposia for strategic assistance; many have indeed
reported about their tour trips arranged by the GIS. A most striking example is
the lavish international media attention given to the "cage men," people who
live in crowded space, courtesy of the arrangement by some local social service
organizations.

We observe a parachute reporter, representing a reputed midwestern newspaper from the United States, at work. Upon arriving from Beijing, she rushes to attend a symposium of invited speakers in a crowded room at the Foreign Correspondents' Club (FCC). Midway through the question and answer session, she manages to put in a rather cursory question about land prices to a speaker who is a pro-Beijing banker. Having furiously scribbled down his zealous but uninspiring answer on her notebook, she immediately stands up and leaves the room—presumably to file her story or to scramble for other stories—without bothering to listen to other parts of more substantive conversation. Sitting beside her, we follow her to the door and ask for an interview with her. She nervously replies that she would be too busy to do it before the handover, inviting us instead for an interview about the conditions of press freedom in Hong Kong. (She had promised to call us back after the handover to honor our request, but the call never came. When we called her again, she apologized for having forgot it. Was she available now? "No, I am leaving for vacation before heading back to Beijing.") We later check on her FCC story in her paper—decidedly shallow, clichéd, and probably not one of her proudest moments.

Generally but not invariably, resident journalists command better grips of the local conditions with a wider network of contacts to consult as sources. A self-described supporter of democracy in Hong Kong, Marcus Eliason of the Associated Press says that he is convinced that China will not make Hong Kong Communist, but instead will carry out "one country, two systems," though not necessarily in all its details. Instead of solely blaming China for disbanding the elected legislature, he opines that journalists should explain why Chris Patten insulted the Chinese by changing the rules without consulting them in the first place. On the other hand, veteran China correspondents may also have their own liabilities; their knowledge of China and its leaders have made them excessively cynical. The most cynical journalists before the handover are those who have worked in Beijing, especially those who saw the Chinese system at its worst in the spring of 1989.

In 1989, awed by the student protesters in the Tiananmen Square, Dan Rather of CBS announced to the world, "China will never be the same again." But it should be noted that CBS News has not maintained a bureau in Hong Kong for two decades and has paid scant attention to China in the 1990s when the country underwent the most profound change. Suddenly, in 1997, the first time in eight years, Rather takes his team back to Tiananmen to set the motif for Hong Kong, constantly mixing the handover with the bloodshed to create the scenario of "Tiananmen II" (see chapter 5). (Several of our American colleagues teaching in Hong Kong received phone calls from their relatives and friends who, having seen the network reports on the PLA, urged them to "get the first plane out of Hong Kong tomorrow morning.") CNN's old China hand in Hong Kong, Mike Chinoy comments:

> One of the things that I am proud of is that, unlike some of our competitors, CNN took a much measured approach, not Hong Kong is to be raped by the butchers of Beijing. We are pretty level-headed even in the issues like the arrival of the PLA. This is where my experience in China pays off. It is pretty obvious to me that a lot of the fussing about the dispute between the British and the Chinese over the PLA had to do with the issues of face and sovereignty, and rectifying historical injustices. While some of the other presses think that the PLA coming in are the storm troopers into Hong Kong. . . . My gut feelings in those last few days is that the Chinese wanted to make the point that as soon as Hong Kong was theirs, they had the right to station troops here. It is a matter of sovereignty. I think my experience in China makes me understand how emotional an issue this was to China.

Chinoy of CNN and Joseph Kahn of the *Wall Street Journal* are among those who have regularly visited China since 1989 to see a more "positive" and more "upbeat" country.

Lastly, the drawback of parachute journalists should not be overstated. If they are good journalists, they can see with clarity what is sometimes invisible to resident colleagues. A resident journalist looking for nuances and subtleties may also lose the broader picture. Journalists, as Graham Hutchings of the *Daily Telegraph* maintains, "should, up to a point, jump the hurdles of language and culture" (Knight and Nakano, 1999: 130).

The Situs News Perspective

All journalists, whether resident or parachute, must read the situs press either by themselves or through translators to identify important concerns to the community. But this is only the beginning, not the end of their job. They get tips to follow up on. News is a mutually confirming definition of reality, and the journalists proceed to frame local (situs) issues in national and global contexts. The situs press is a necessary point of reference, but as Steve Vines of the *Independent* argues, the best stories invariably are obtained from the contacts, friends, or people journalists know, rather than from reading the situs press.

There are 13 Chinese newspapers and two English dailies to span the entire ideological spectrum. Most foreign journalists interviewed name the *South China Morning Post*, the *Asian Wall Street Journal*, and online newspapers as major sources of information. Fiona Anderson, BBC Bureau Chief, discloses that they carefully watch the local media, especially the pro-Chines press, for "good tips." The daily digest of the Chinese press published by the GIS is also accessible and useful. Other journalists proficient in Chinese also expand their reading range to include major Chinese newspapers and critical political journals. In fact, many Beijing-based correspondents follow these political journals also. NHK buys local television programs, which are translated and edited for Japanese consumption. The fact that foreign journalists in Hong Kong rely on the local media for information and news clues is similar to those in Washington, D.C., who must rely on the *Washington Post*, the *New York Times*, and the Foreign Broadcast Information Service to shape their news (Cohen, 1963). What looms large in the Hong Kong media tends to capture their attention, and they may continue to use local reportage as a major source of information, though the story will eventually be cast in domestic terms and logic.

Consequences

We expect that domestication would lead to systematic differences among various national media systems in terms of the origins of news sources, the tone of coverage, and the political orientation of news sources. This is borne out by the results of our content analysis (for more information, see Appendix IV).

Table 3.1 summarizes media references to the prospect and direction of changes thought likely to occur after the handover of Hong Kong. Each story may (a) mention that changes will occur, (b) mention that changes will not occur; or (c) not mention this prospect at all. If the story mentions possible changes, it may indicate (a) changes for the better; (b) some changes for the better and some changes for the worse; (c) changes for the worse; or (d) changes hard to determine. What we have measured is, in essence, a conservative estimate of the media's explicit references; given its implicit and embedded nature, the ideological overtone in the text should be much stronger.

One distinct pattern is, as expected, that China differs significantly from the rest of the world. Its media report virtually no change in Hong Kong in any of the aspects; whenever they do, the change tends to be positive. They avoid any substantive issues related to Hong Kong's reality in order to present the festivity of a national celebration. The media from all the other societies, however, predict changes to occur. The four English-speaking media systems—the United States, Britain, Australia, and Canada—make more references to changes than do the Hong Kong and Taiwan media, partly because western media are more interpretative and hew more closely to western values of democracy and human rights vis-à-vis Communist authoritarianism. Hong Kong and Taiwan seem more realistically concerned about preserving their own autonomous status than about waging an impossible fight against the Communist regime in Beijing. Most notable changes are expected in these specific areas:

- Democracy: Australia (36.5%), the United States (34.8%), Canada (28.6%), Britain (23.4%).

Table 3.1
References to the Prospect of Changes after the Handover[1]

	Autonomy	Democracy	Press Freedom	Rule of Law	Economy	Daily Life	N
% of asserting change[2]							
PRC	0.0	0.8	0.0	0.1	3.6	1.4	739
USA	15.2	34.8	14.0	10.4	7.6	13.7	328
Britain	6.6	23.4	7.7	1.4	2.6	3.1	351
Hong Kong	5.8	11.2	3.1	4.7	3.9	4.2	1351
Taiwan	3.6	6.6	2.2	1.2	3.2	3.0	500
Australia	6.6	36.5	10.2	10.9	4.4	8.0	137
Canada	9.5	28.6	2.4	7.1	13.1	16.7	84
Of the changes mentioned, % of claiming that they will be for the worse[3]							
PRC	—	0.0	—	0.0	0.0	0.0	44
USA	27.5	73.7	54.3	50.0	0.0	57.8	314
Britain	34.8	61.0	51.9	40.0	11.1	54.5	157
Hong Kong	38.0	41.7	36.6	34.4	9.4	15.8	444
Taiwan	33.3	45.5	45.5	66.7	6.3	25.0	99
Australia	44.4	62.0	42.9	53.3	16.7	8.3	105
Canada	0.0	58.3	50.0	50.0	18.2	21.4	77

1. Categories: (a) Autonomy of HK SAR: Refers to the relationship between HK SAR government and Beijing, HK's ability to handle its own affairs without Beijing's interference, and the workability of the "One Country, Two Systems" policy; (b) Democratization, Civil Liberties: Refers to the promises and activities related to democratizing HK SAR political institutions (e.g., setting up the timetable and procedures for Legislative Council election and potentially for electing the Chief Executive) and individuals' rights to association and speech; (c) Press Freedom: Refers to change in media policies, media structure, journalists' self censorship, and professionalism, as well as any influences or attempted influences of political forces (including the PRC forces) on Hong Kong's media; (d) Rule of Law: Refers to HK's legal independence, continued functioning and independence of the ICAC, changes in or maintenance of the Common Law system and its relations with the Basic Law and Chinese legal system; (e) Economy: Refers to the activities, performance, and structure of the consumer and financial markets, the manufacturing, real estate, and service sectors. Examples include relocation of manufacturing factories, rise or plunge of the real estate market, injection of mainland capital; (f) Political/Social Realignment: Refers to changing political orientation, allegiance and posture of various associative and political organizations, influential individuals, and commercial firms (e.g., Jardines repositioning itself to mend the fence with Beijing); (g) Daily Life in Hong Kong: Refers to the livelihood of people not directly systemic in nature or scope (if it is, it will be in one of the above six categories).

2. 1 = Hong Kong will change after the handover, 2 = Hong Kong will not change after the handover, and 3 = no changes mentioned.

3. 1 = Changes will be for the better, 2 = Some changes will be for the better and some will be for the worse, 3 = Changes will be for the worse, and 4 = Cannot be determined

- Press freedom: the United States (14%), Australia (10.2%).

- The rule of law: Australia (10.9%), the United States (10.4%).

- Autonomy of Hong Kong: the United States (15.2%), Canada (9.5%).

- Daily life: Canada (16.7%), the United States (13.7%).

In this context, changes in Hong Kong's democracy and civil liberties clearly are the most salient areas of concern. Six or seven in ten stories in the English-speaking media systems (compared with four in ten stories in Hong Kong and Taiwan media) predict democracy will deteriorate in Hong Kong. The U.S. media seem to be most pessimistic, followed by Australia and Canada. Insofar as Britain touts its good legacy and is a cohost of the handover, its media may be somewhat self-congratulatory and somewhat defensive, and do not go overboard to be extremely cynical. The western media also hold a gloomy view about the preservation of press freedom and local autonomy, but they are rather optimistic about continued economic prosperity in Hong Kong. These points will be sharpened by the discourse analysis (chapters 5–9).

Table 3.2 shows the tones of the media's references to the PRC. The categories include (1) positive; (2) positive in some aspects but negative in others; (3) negative; and (4) no indication of any direction in coverage. The pattern appears to confirm that displayed in Table 3.1. While the PRC media are supportive of their government, most others tend to cast a negative shadow on Beijing to a varying extent. The U.S. (42.3%), Canadian (39.3%), and Australian (34.3%) media are more negative than the British (20.9%), Taiwan (22%), and Hong Kong (10.9%) media.

The domestication hypothesis expects the media from a given nation to seek information from sources from the same origin. If the sources of that origin are not appropriate for a particular issue, the media will go for the sources that best approximate their own. Table 3.3 tabulates the news sources by their origins. The PRC media derive the highest proportion from domestic sources (44.7%). Sources from Hong Kong are otherwise the most popular, which account for the majority of sources in Canadian (62.8%), Hong Kong (62.5%), British (49.7%), U.S. (48%), Australian (42.2%), and Taiwan (34.9%) media. The PRC media have more mainland sources (44.7%) than Hong Kong sources (33.8%), reflecting the power gap between Hong Kong and the central government. Domestic sources also stand out in Taiwan (28.9%), British (23%), and U.S. (13.9%) media, though by no means as dominant as in the PRC media (44.7%).

Table 3.2
Tones on the PRC Government (in %)[1]

	Positive	Positive/ Negative	Negative	None	N
PRC	53.9	0.0	0.0	46.0	714
USA	6.2	15.7	42.3	35.8	324
Britain	0.6	9.4	20.9	69.1	1352
Hong Kong	3.8	1.8	10.9	83.6	1352
Taiwan	8.6	5.4	22.0	63.9	499
Australia	2.2	3.6	34.3	59.8	137
Canada	1.2	2.4	39.3	57.1	84

1. The figures across each row do not add up to 100 due to rounding error.

Table 3.3
News Sources from Different Countries

	PRC media (N = 767)	Britain (N = 880)	Hong Kong (N = 1795)	Taiwan (N = 470)
PRC sources	44.7%	12.3%	14.8%	15.1%
UK sources	3.5%	23.0%	8.8%	8.9%
HK sources	33.8%	49.7%	62.5%	34.9%
Taiwan sources	0.5%	3.8%	3.9%	28.9%
U.S. sources	2.0%	3.9%	4.5%	7.0%
Sources from other Asian countries	6.8%	1.3%	1.6%	2.8%
Sources from other non-Asian countries	8.7%	6.3%	4.0%	2.3%

	U.S. media (N = 757)	Canada (N = 196)	Australia (N = 344)	World (N = 5719)
PRC sources	15.9%	7.7%	11.1%	18.0%
UK sources	14.0%	9.7%	13.1%	11.5%
HK sources	48.0%	62.8%	42.2%	50.6%
Taiwan sources	4.6%	1.0%	8.7%	6.0%
U.S. sources	13.9%	1.5%	4.7%	5.5%
Sources from other Asian countries	1.1%	1.0%	3.8%	2.57%
Sources from other non-Asian countries	2.6%	16.3%	16.6%	5.9%

Table 3.4 shows that the media rely heavily on official sources from their own country and from countries of cultural and political proximity. More than half (53.6%) of the official sources in the PRC are from within, and 24.7% more from Hong Kong. Official sources also figure prominently in Taiwan (40.2%), British (39.4%) and U.S. (18.4%) media that are concerned with the implications of the handover to their own national interest. Media in the two more marginal members of the western camp—Canada and Australia—also use high proportions of British official sources.

Table 3.5 sums up the ten most frequently cited sources by country, further confirming heavy media reliance on domestic officials. Six of China's top ten sources are from its own leaders (President Jiang, Prime Minister Li, Vice-Premier Qian, Qiao, Chui) and the official Xinhua News Agency; others (Tung, Fan, Fok) are pro-China figures in Hong Kong. Governor Patten heads Britain's list, followed by Foreign Secretary Cook, Prime Minister Blair, Prince Charles, and the Foreign Office. Taiwan focuses on its representative in Hong Kong (Cheng), the vice president (Lian) who was interviewed by foreign media, and other officials (Gu, Li, and Zhang). The American media include Secretary of State Albright and President Clinton. Canadian media include Foreign Minister Axworthy and a diplomat in the list, as Australian media feature Foreign Minister Downer. Besides domestic officials, top Chinese (Jiang), Hong Kong

Table 3.4
Official Sources from Different Countries

	China sources (N = 263)	Britain (N = 388)	Hong Kong (N = 706)	Taiwan (N = 214)
China media	53.6%	16.2%	18.4%	18.7%
UK media	5.7%	39.4%	17.4%	11.7%
HK media	24.7%	28.1%	44.2%	17.3%
Taiwan media	0.4%	5.2%	6.9%	40.2%
U.S. media	1.9%	4.1%	6.2%	7.9%
Others	13.7%	7.0%	6.8%	4.2%

	U.S. sources (N = 207)	Canada (N = 47)	Australia (N = 164)	World (N = 1990)
China media	20.3%	8.5%	12.8%	22.2%
UK media	29.0%	29.8%	20.1%	21.3%
HK media	21.3%	40.4%	25.0%	31.5%
Taiwan media	6.8%	4.3%	14.0%	9.8%
U.S. media	18.4%	4.3%	4.9%	6.6%
Others	4.4%	12.8%	23.2	8.7%

Table 3.5

Top Ten Most Frequently Cited Sources by Country

Ranking	China (N = 739)	Britain (N = 881)	Hong Kong (N = 1795)	Taiwan (N = 470)
1	Jiang Zemin (China's president) (N = 28)	Chris Patten (HK governor) (N = 47)	Chris Patten (HK governor) (N = 34)	Cheng An-kuo (Taiwan's representative in HK) (N = 11)
2	Tung Chee-hwa (HK chief executive) (N = 24)	Tung Chee-hwa (HK chief executive) (N = 39)	Tung Chee-hwa (HK chief executive) (N = 31)	Lian Zhan (Taiwan's vice-president) (N = 9)
3	Xinhua News Agency (N = 23)	Martin Lee (HK democrat) (N = 26)	Martin Lee (HK democrat) (N = 22)	Chris Patten (HK governor) (N = 9)
4	Li Peng (China's prime minster) (N = 14)	Robin Cook (British foreign secretary) (N = 25)	Robin Cook (British foreign secretary) (N = 21)	Xinhua News Agency (PRC's official voice) (N = 8)
5	Qian Qichen (China's vice-premier) (N = 13)	Jiang Zemin (China's president) (N = 25)	Rita Fan (Head of HK's new legislature) (N = 20)	Tung Chee-hwa (HK chief executive) (N = 8)
6	Rita Fan (Head of HK's new legislature) (N = 7)	Emily Lau (HK democrat) (N = 9)	Jiang Zemin (China's president) (N = 17)	Gu Zhenfu (Taiwan official) (N = 7)
7	Prince Charles (N = 7)	Tony Blair (British prime minister) (N = 9)	Elsie Leung (HK official) (N = 15)	Li Dawai (Taiwan official) (N = 7)
8	Qiao She (Head of China's legislature) (N = 5)	Prince Charles (N = 8)	Emily Lau (HK democrat) (N = 15)	Robin Cook (British foreign secretary) (N = 6)
9	Henry Fok (pro-Beijing tycoon in HK) (N = 4)	Britain's Foreign Office (N = 8)	Madeleine Albright (U.S. secretary of state) (N = 14)	Zhang Jingyu (Taiwan official) (N = 6)
10	Chui Tiankai (China's foreign ministry spokesman) (N57)	Michael DeGolyer (HK academic pollster) (N = 13)	Szeto Wah (HK democrat) (N = 5)	Martin Lee (HK democrat) (N = 4)
% of total no. of quotations	17.5% (N = 129)	23.0% (N = 203)	11.3% (N = 202)	16.2% (N = 76)

(continued)

Table 3.5 *(continued)*
Top Ten Most Frequently Cited Sources by Country

Ranking	U.S. (N = 759)	Canada (N = 222)	Australia (N = 344)
1	Tung Chee-hwa (HK chief executive) (N = 36)	Tung Chee-hwa (HK chief executive) (N = 12)	Tung Chee-hwa (HK chief executive) (N = 19)
2	Chris Patten (HK governor) (N = 34)	Chris Patten (HK governor) (N = 7)	Martin Lee (HK democrat) (N = 15)
3	Jiang Zemin (China's president) (N = 24)	Martin Lee (HK democrat) (N = 7)	Jiang Zemin (China's president) (N = 11)
4	Martin Lee (HK democrat) (N = 22)	Emily Lau (HK democrat) (N = 5)	Chris Patten (HK governor) (N = 11)
5	Madeleine Albright (U.S. secretary of state) (N = 15)	Jiang Zemin (China's president) (N = 4)	Alexander Downer (Australian foreign minister) (N = 8)
6	Emily Lau (HK democrat) (N = 13)	Andrew Wong (head of HK's legislature) (N = 3)	Zhang Jingyu (Taiwan official) (N = 7)
7	Prince Charles (N = 9)	Lloyd Axworthy (Canada's foreign minister) (N = 3)	Li Denghui (Taiwan president) (N = 6)
8	Bill Clinton (U.S. president) (N = 9)	Lee Cheuk-yan (HK democrat) (N = 3)	Tony Blair (British prime minister) (N = 5)
9	Xinhua News Agency (PRC's official voice) (N = 7)	Lee Yee (HK commentator) (N = 3)	Emily Lau (HK democrat) (N = 5)
10	Tsang Yok-sing (leader of a pro-Beijing party) (N = 7)	Garrett Lambert (Canadian Commission in HK) (N = 3)	Robin Cook (British foreign secretary) (N = 4)
% of total no. of quotations	23.2% (N = 176)	22.5% (N = 50)	26.5% (N = 91)

(Tung, Patten), and British leaders—plus leading democrats (Lee, Lau) in Hong Kong—are favored sources for almost all media. Australian media surprisingly give Taiwan sources a rather high profile.

Conclusion

The notion of "glocalization" (Robertson, 1995; Featherstone, 1995) captures the global media production of the local and the local media production of the global. In this nexus, the nation-state serves as the primary definer of global news. Domestication takes place because the home audience ultimately consumes international news. The relevance of global news is defined from a domestic perspective in relation to the international political economy, the prevailing ideological framework and cultural symbols, as well as the authority structure. The domesticated news tends to represent a national perspective, with a narrower and more unified scope of ideological field than domestic news. Partisan differences over domestic issues often are transformed into bipartisan support of a national policy on international issues. Officials are privileged. Stories are simplified, personified, and put in a national context. Television is more patently ideological than elite newspapers. Explicitly or implicitly, various domesticated national perspectives join battles in the international discursive terrain.

Domestic media outlets compete within national boundaries; the *San Jose Mercury News*, for example, regards the *San Francisco Chronicle* as its chief rival. The global-scale media have to compete within and across national borders; CNN battles not only with the three U.S. networks (and increasingly with such cable operators as Fox and MSNBC) but also with the BBC, which has the largest international reach. Chinoy admits that the BBC "keeps us on our toes." The global-scale media must first of all serve their primary markets in the United States and Britain, even if they have also to allow for an assortment of other national perspectives from the "secondary" markets. Even the viewers in the secondary markets are likely to be English-speaking elites who have affinity for western values. Volkmer (1999: 156) notes that CNN journalists are dedicated to "fact journalism," trying to stay away from ideological overtones—"value-laden terms" and "words that could potentially have some values injected into them"—as far as possible. But the question is that facts do not speak for themselves without political or historical contexts. As van Ginneken (1998: 42) puts it: "Naïve empiricism thus often becomes a way of recycling ideologies into 'hard facts.'"

We find little ideological differences either between CNN and CBS or between BBC and ITN. These global-scale media probably do not deliberately trumpet the prevailing ideology of their turf, but they undoubtedly see the "global perspective" through the prisms of generalized western values—and, doing so in the name of objectivity. Mike Chinoy does not consider CNN a U.S. network; if CNN sometimes carries an American angle, it is because that angle is meaningful beyond the United States. Canadian and Australian journalists are, however, quite vocal in our interviews in chastising American journalists' self-presumed monopolistic interpretations of democracy and human rights. Chinoy stakes his claim of objectivity partly on his long residence in—and cultural understanding of—China and Hong Kong.

Many national media are subscribers of the global-scale media, including CNN, the Associate Press, and Reuters. They often adapt (even twist) imported materials to suit domestic angles (Boyd-Barrett, 1980). News agencies and elite media have been known to exert agenda-setting influences on the media at large in the Untied States. When the wire services interpret a series of protests against Japan's occupation of the disputed Diaoyu Islands as a sign of rising Chinese nationalism, Kristi Khockshorn frames it more as anti-Japanese sentiment than as the rise of Chinese nationalism. Her editor at the *San Jose Mercury News* asks for an explanation; she defends herself by citing the empirical evidence gathered by local scholars in Hong Kong.

To conclude, all news is selective through inclusion and exclusion of information and through the use of particular logic and frames. Domestication is an inherent logic of international journalism. International reporters are trained "to find the story in unfamiliar, often chaotic, situations, to give their reports an attention-getting angle based on a judgement about what their desk editors will and will not like and will go over with their home audience" (Flournoy, 1992: 23). International news represents the global production of the local and local production of the global. The mediating mechanism of the global-local linkage is domestication.

Chapter 4

Hyping and Repairing News Paradigms

The Global Media War breaks out in Hong Kong.
—Headline, the *Oriental Daily News*, June 24, 1997

It is nothing like the Tiananmen in 1989, the coup in Moscow in 1991.
The whole thing (in Hong Kong) is choreographed.
—Andrew Higgins, East Asia Correspondent, the *Guardian*

In societies where modern conditions of production prevail, all of life
presents itself as an immense accumulation of spectacles. Everything
that was directly lived has moved away into a representation.
—Guy Debord (1987: 2)

We live in the age of live television and a world of "hyped" media reality.
Our cognitive and emotional experiences have been shaped and changed by
media spectacles: popular uprisings against the Communist regimes, televised
wars, "live" TV handshakes between enemy leaders, moon landings, and so on
(Dayan and Katz, 1992). The change of regime in Hong Kong is a global
media spectacle of pageantry, personalities, emotions, and contrived dramas.
This is so even though (perhaps because) many journalists concede that the
event, contrary to their hypotheses, has little news other than a series of carefully scripted ceremonies.

In presenting a media spectacle, the media have increasingly infused the
logic and format of entertainment into newsmaking, thus challenging the established codes of media representations and also blurring the boundaries between fiction and news, or between myth and reality. When drama or ritual
"becomes" a fact and when news objectivity gives way to aesthetic authentic-
ity, how would journalism as "the strongest remaining bastion of logical posi-
tivism" (Gans, 1979: 184) be eroded? Are journalists simply "storytellers"—or,

63

are they performers, annotators, and mythmakers of scripted events? This chapter, by analyzing the world media coverage of the Hong Kong handover, addresses these questions.

News Paradigm and Media Events

News is not a "mere occurrence." It is a "cognized happening" that takes shape in the context of complex institutionalized relationships among purposive actors (Molotch and Lester, 1974). Journalists, working in a paradigm-based field (Kuhn, 1962), apply a set of broadly shared understanding about what constitutes news and how to "frame" the reality through the selective gathering and packaging of facts. Such understanding, codified as professional norms and canons, is embedded in the established social order (Bennett, Gressett, and Haltom, 1985; Gitlin, 1980; Reese, 1989; Tuchman, 1978). The news paradigm enables media organizations to "reduce environmental uncertainty by routinizing their recurring task activities, enforcing organizational norms and values, and exercising social control in the newsroom" (Chan and Lee, 1991: 24). Journalists rely on the authoritative sources and standard narrative codes (including positivistic methods of determining the facts as well as the storytelling conventions) to reproduce standard themes (Bennett et al., 1985; Bird and Dardenne, 1988). Gans (1979) argues that these journalistic codes and themes constitute and are constituted by the "enduring values" in the larger U.S. society: ethnocentrism, altruistic democracy, responsible capitalism, small-town pastoralism, individualism, and moderation. Therefore, a news paradigm operates within the larger framework of ideological hegemony; different national systems breed and follow different national news paradigms, albeit with minor internal variations.

A news paradigm is as stable as its underpinning foundation of "enduring values" and social consensus, inherently conservative, and hence resistant to change. The dominant assumptions are internalized, thus unrecognized by journalists and media organizations. These assumptions are stable unless and until challenged by such irreconcilably "anomalous" situations as economic meltdown, a political crisis, social protests, collapse of elite consensus, or regime change. Even then, the first instinct of the media would still be to "repair" the existing paradigm (Bennett et al., 1985) to the extent that modifying parts of the assumptions can help to preserve the paradigmatic whole. To this end, they may cull more facts to confirm their assumptions; twist new facts to the old conceptual framework; fit the emerging reality into the established news genre; or concede such ruptures as exceptions to (rather than a refutation of) historical continuities. In addition, the interpretive community of journalists reflexively reinterprets exemplary cases in history to rearticulate the professional principles and the accepted practices (Zelizer, 1993).

Sometimes repairing work is good enough to prolong the life of a news paradigm, but other times it may require an overhaul. Bennett (1990) argues that media discourses "index the range and dynamics" of elite discourses. Media discourses are most wide-ranging and diverse when different forces—none of which hold a monopolistic, even privileged, access to media representations—hotly contest the power. But suppression of insurgency or resolution of power conflicts would necessitate the media to reorient their perspectives and "news net" toward the new authority structure. Therefore, change in the news paradigm stems more often than not from change within the power establishment—and only occasionally from social movements—which does not necessarily lead to a change of the system itself. For example, the U.S. media had cheered for President Johnson's war against Vietnam for years before the alliance between antiwar national leaders and antiwar movements began to take hold and alter the contour of national discourses. At that point, what had been safely assumed as a terrain of "consensus" and "deviance" became problematic. The news paradigm underwent major shifts to admit a wider scope of official and dissenting voices with regard to a national issue of "legitimate controversy" (Hallin, 1987).

Challenges to the news paradigm may also arise from changes in the practices of news production (Zelizer, 1992). Technological change, such as CNN's continuous live broadcasting of the Gulf War, may have altered the gatekeeping process, but it has left the core of the news paradigm unaffected. The rise and prevalence of "media events" may present a greater challenge in that they have been modifying the traditional concept of news—in terms of taste, judgment, and news definitions—among media professionals and the audience. Jacobs (1996) shows that in the midst of the unfolding drama of a media event, broadcasting journalists had to change their news routines accordingly. The event generates a huge buzz of excitement, expectations, and emotional hysteria in society and the newsroom. Journalists are then drawn into the swirl of the event to catch the latest development and to satisfy the escalating audience expectations. Thus, there is a powerful dynamic of "ritual separation" (Jacobs, 1996: 389) that distinguishes the practices of producing media events from those of routine news.

Media events are constructed to fit the media appetite for drama and spectacle (Becker, 1995), whose "excitement" factor satisfies the "pleasure" of the consuming-public-cum-passive-spectators. As media events unfold "live" around the clock, television becomes a "kind of control center for decisions about news" (Sharkey, 1994). The "aesthetics of television" (Dayan and Katz, 1992: 18), responsive to the audience's incessant expectation for a "good show," has in part displaced the traditional canon of professional objectivity.

The elevation of Princess Diana's unexpected tragic death into a world-media spectacular (Cleghorn, 1997) illustrates how a media event turns into media hype. Not long before the incident, the BBC news team had rehearsed its operation in the unlikely event of "the death of a leading royal in a car crash in a foreign country" (Bridgman, 1999). This rehearsal was more than installing an "emergency routine" to cope with nonroutine news (Berkowitz, 1992). It enabled the BBC to retrieve from the archive photogenic footages of the Princess's life and to script a ritual of mass mourning. The resulting spectacle mixed news reports with archived footages over a soundtrack of *Candle in the Wind* and created a tale of modern-day Cinderella turning into a saint (Bridgman, 1999). In contrast, the story of Mother Teresa, who died around the same time, was all but buried under an avalanche of media attention for Diana (Martin, 1999).

The Media Logic and Hyping

In media events, the entertainment-based "media logic"—the rules and formats of drama, emotional display, personalities, primacy of visuals, and the rhythm and tempo mimicking the real life with varying intervals (Altheide and Snow, 1979)—is infused into news production. This media logic is driven by business and ratings; it not only shapes the media organizational dynamics but also incorporates "the perspectives and activities of audience members," making its organizing features taken-for-granted reality (Altheide and Snow, 1991: 53–54).

As the media occupy the center stage of contemporary politics, political actors interact according to the rules of "popular reality" that the media help to perpetuate (Edelman, 1988; Hartley, 1992). The media do not simply report news; they stage a social performance in which "the knowns"—individuals and agencies of power and authority—become "star performers" (Becker, 1995; Gans, 1979). Media events whet the public's voracious appetite for more excitement; the public then naturalizes them as a reality. Public sphere is turned into a media arena for spectacles, in which audiences play as supporting members of the cast or as spectators (Becker, 1995; MacAloon 1984). A major news story becomes an occasion, a "creative moment," for the power structure to be enacted in what has been variously called "press rites" (Becker, 1995; Ettema, 1990; Real, 1989), "press performance" (Elliot, 1982), "media drama" or "media spectacle" (Manning, 1996; Tomlinson, 1996).

Hyping conforms to this media logic to generate "an artificially engendered atmosphere of hysteria" (Aronson, 1983: 23) to the point that a news story is larger than life. Hyping is a set of rhetorical strategies that helps the journalist to fit a story into the genre of media event, thus turning up the voltage of the report to garner a wider appeal. It uplifts entertainment to reality and enlarges the voltage to enthrall a large audience. With its attendant hysteria, a media event may interrupt the routines of newswork and draw journalists into the whirlpool of intense competition. Live broadcasting of a big media event, such as assassination of kings and presidents, can also interrupt the flow of the public's daily life (Dayan and Katz, 1992).

Media events are not necessarily hyped to disrupt the status quo; indeed, many of these ritualistic performances promote social cohesion, consolidate communal experiences, and reaffirm shared beliefs that are steeped in tradition (Alexander and Jacobs, 1998; Hallin and Gitlin, 1994). Often, media events are hyped as "hot moments" for a society to overcome tensions in the established system; hyping relies upon the existing power and serves to strengthen it. Through its well-publicized performances in the mourning spectacle of Princess Diana, the British royal family ridded its image of aloof and dysfunctional patriarchy.

In this chapter, we identify four major methods of hyping, based on our inductive categorization of media texts and interview protocols coupled with the literature. They are certification, visualization, amalgamation, and mystification. *Certification* refers to the way in which the media inflate the significance of an event by resorting to authoritative "news personalities," celebrity politicians and star journalists. The media deploy journalists at various locations to "lift" a media event from routine to extraordinary. The star performers, placed as the central cast, express social power and imbue media narratives with energy from the authority in the real world. Media events thus "anthropomorphize" politics and legitimize power in society (Sigal, 1986: 30).

Visualization involves selecting and collating images of certain activities that typify the key elements of an event and objectify the flow of the event in a "real" temporal sequence. It creates an "event reality" through the application of the rules of "sampling" and "ordering/sequencing" (Manning, 1996). By presenting a bundle of images in "real time," the event draws audiences to "witness the history"—a participatory experience that is objectively illusive but subjectively real. Using the tempo and rhythm of reality entertainment, media presentations also authenticate an event as a "social drama" (Turner, 1982).

Mystification takes place at two levels: first, it involves the uses of mythical images and symbols of a culture to create a majestic aura of authoritative figures and cultural icons. These mythical images and symbols reify "essential qualities" of the power relationships in society. Secondly, it involves narrating a media event in the myths of a culture and its bearers, and authenticating it in the meaning system of the culture (Bird and Dardenne, 1988).

Amalgamation refers to juxtaposing images and activities from diverse locales and moments to build a narrative flow and thematic unity. It extends the core plot of a media event and draws out a historical causal sequence embedded in the event. In this process, tidbits are signifiers disguised as "facts," becoming meaningful as part of a particular grand historical narrative. As a result, in narrating a media event, "opinion is metamorphosed into reality" (Said, 1981: 108) and even certified as historical in a particular ideology.

The Hong Kong Handover

The Hong Kong handover is typical of "prescheduled" news events culminating in a series of carefully choreographed ceremonies. Much is predictable about the outcome of this scripted event. If the outcome of a race in the Olympic Games is already known, it must be anticlimatic to report about the process of winning and losing. No wonder Chris Wood, a Canadian reporter, complains about its being a "nonevent." Jonathan Mirsky of the *Times* of London thinks it "ridiculous" to send an army of reporters to Hong Kong, whereas Edward Gargan of the *New York Times* believes that the ceremony is "only good for television." Why does this event receive such overwhelming attention from the global media in the post-Cold War order and in the post-Tiananmen milieu? Each nation seems to have some sort of vested interest at stake in Hong Kong.

The large number of journalists becomes the cover story of *Asiaweek* (May 19), entitled "The Media War at the End of the Century." It also prompts the *People's Daily* to proclaim that Hong Kong is the center of world media attention. There are more journalists covering the event than there are members of the People's Liberation Army (PLA) sent in to symbolize Hong Kong as part of China. The handover does not turn out as traumatic as most of the visiting world journalists had envisaged—which, as CNN's Mike Chinoy said, "probably is good for Hong Kong, but not good for the media because it does not lend itself to easy coverage." Having expected civil disturbances and police arrests, *Newsweek*'s Dorinda Elliot quipped, on June 30, "Nothing happened; just a bunch of nice ceremonies." *Guardian*'s Andrew Higgins complains that there is no drama in the handover "like in the Tiananmen event, the Russian coup, or the war in Africa." *Daily Telegraph*'s historian-cum-China watcher, Graham Hutchings, observes, "If I were a journalist who wants to jet around the world, going to big journalistic stories, I would have found the Hong Kong thing very boring." Many Taiwan journalists are surprised, upon arriving in Hong Kong, at its apparent calm. Summing up his professional frustration, a *Los Angeles Times* reporter wryly notes, "Thousands of competitive egos who were thrown into one land-starved city woke up every morning feeling the pressure from home to justify the $450 per night hotel room and $5 cups of coffee."

Before arriving in Hong Kong many foreign journalists had concocted various worst-case scenarios of political disorder. Facing the contrary evidence, they hang on to their presumptions. Instead of admitting to their own epistemological biases, they advance ad hoc hypotheses to explain away what they see as a "momentary calm" before a big storm hits. To make up for the lack of suspense, drama, and excitement in these staged ceremonies, they choose to "hype up" the stories, especially when they are all hunting for the same object. Otherwise, why did 1,000 journalists turn up to cover Governor Patten's farewell ceremony, which was only attended by less than 10,000 people (Knight and Nakano, 1999: 27)? And why did foreign journalists often out-number protesters at the scene (Xu, 1997)? Hyping the handover story becomes a necessity to repair unconfirmed assumptions of the news paradigms and to justify enormous commitment of media resources.

Certification

In a warlike atmosphere fraught with professional tension and intrigue, top-notch journalists arrive in the ideological battlefield of Hong Kong. The sight of densely concentrated journalists, along with the conspicuous camera crews carrying their equipment roaming about the crowded streets, only heightens the frenzy and hysteria in the air. Andrew Higgins, the East Asian correspondent for the *Guardian*, speaks of the "combustion" factor in the journalistic herd:

> The story that would have cut to 500 words now gets printed twice as big be-cause the momentum makes it seem more important. It's like 8,000 journalists suddenly show up in New York and they write about McDonald's. News events acquire certain momentum—a weird combustion occurs once you have certain cameramen, journalists, radio people cover the same thing. Even if the focus is on the ashtray, when editors in New York or in London are bom-barded with pictures of the ashtray, the story gets built up; they begin to think that the ashtray is interesting and something they don't want to miss . . . There is a lot of herd mentality to the story.

For Taiwan, however, Higgins may have missed the point. News value or not, Taiwan will be China's next target now that Hong Kong is back to the fold. *The Liberty Times*, favoring Taiwan's secession from China and usually pay-ing little attention to China, this time sends in a team of ten reporters led by a deputy editor-in-chief to cover the handover stories. The *Central Daily News*, the organ of the KMT that has been rapidly marginalized by political democ-ratization on the island, finds itself in a particularly awkward position because Hong Kong is after all returned to the Communists, not to the Nationalists. The paper, having a much smaller presence, is an "also-ran." The competition be-tween the two press conglomerates, the *China Times* and the *United Daily News*, is rancorous. Through the aid of a noted pro-KMT journalist who had re-cently been befriended by Beijing, the *China Times* holds an exclusive inter-view with Zhou Nan, the head of China's command post in Hong Kong. Zhou does not say anything new, but his sensitive status is enough for the *China Times* to outsmart its chief rival.

Competition in an imaged ideological war cries out for the attention of the world's top TV anchors and reporters. CBS flies Dan Rather in from half a world away; with him are Washington Chief Correspondent Bob Scheiffer and two veteran foreign correspondents, Bob Simon and Tom Fenton. CNN's familiar faces include Bernard Shaw at the anchor desk, Richard Blystone and Tom Mintier from home, and the specialist correspondents Mike Chinoy in Hong Kong and Andrea Koppel in Beijing. All four U.S. network anchors (Tom Brokaw, Dan Rather, Peter Jennings, and Bernard Shaw) are on the scene to "move the show" and to inflate the significance of the event. Undeterred by the criticism, Brokaw insists, "I do think that I bring in here a pretty general good understanding of what the situation is, and when I don't know something, I have quick and easy access to the correct answers before I put on the air" (Buerk, 1997). Ignorance necessitates their further reliance on ready-made cliché and stereotypes. Dan Rather claims that "the quality and depth of our coverage, particularly inside China, sets us apart" when, in fact, CBS's reportage is most ideologically laden (chapter 5).

A celebrity anchor performs as a chief narrative organizer. Usually a middle-aged man looking dignified, assuring, and authoritative, he occupies the center of a TV broadcast, directing the narrative flow with a macrointerpretive framework. Using the "language of transportation" (Dayan and Katz, 1992: 11), he connects the studio live with field reporters. His familiar "star" quality brings remote realities from afar closer to the audience at home and authenticates the event as a "real" occurrence. He is a condensed icon of the taken-for-granted authoritative structure in news.

Media and their celebrity journalists, no matter where they are, certify—even amplify—news values of a story. China's national channel, CCTV, rents the largest booth in the Press and Broadcast Center as a show of national pride. Its coverage team consists of 289 people in Hong Kong and 22 crews in various cities at home and abroad. A popular prime-time public affairs program anchor, Shui Junyi, hosts the program from Hong Kong. He teams up with four regular evening anchors in Beijing headquarters, rotating to host the 72-hour "non-stop live broadcast." CCTV heavily promotes the millions of dollars it had invested into equipment and its grand-scale live show. At 7 am, June 30, as the live broadcasting is about to begin, chatting with the anchors in Beijing, Shui assures the home audiences that he and his colleagues have "well rehearsed the live coverage."

Media feed on one another's frenzy, not only to heighten the intensity of a story but also to prolong its life cycle. When the journalistic herd competes for the same drama, it creates pressure on the political actors to perform certain tasks for the media. This logic was vividly displayed in 1989 by the interaction between the escalation of student uprisings in Beijing and the world media that happened to gather there to cover the Soviet leader Gorbachev's visit (Lee, 1990; Esherick and Wasserstrom, 1994). This time, in Hong Kong, it comes alive again. As the handover is to take place under the watchful eye of the world media, British and Chinese negotiators struggle to hammer out minute details of the ceremony; such tense negotiations in turn provoke the media to speculate if Hong Kong is going to survive. Under similar pressure, the G-8 leaders, holding an economic summit in Denver, Colorado, pledge support to Hong Kong's continued freedom; such remarks in turn make the headlines of such papers as the *New York Times* and the *Times* of London. Similarly, in Hong Kong, the democrats' staged protest is geared primarily toward the foreign media. To dramatize the expectation of encountering difficulties with the authorities, Martin Lee, its leader, vows that if necessary, he would "climb a ladder" to reach the second-floor balcony to deliver his speech. His remark ignites the imagination of western journalists, who had come to Hong Kong to see how Beijing would oppress civil liberty (Knight and Nakano, 1999: 42–61). *Newsweek*'s Dorinda Elliot muses afterwards, "We were all waiting to see Martin Lee getting arrested." Lee is not arrested. The protest proceeds without an incident. However, all but the PRC media outlets are present to await the anticipated drama. Lee's speech is covered "live" on CNN, and the protest is given two segments of "live" coverage on the BBC.

Visualization

Pictures speak louder than words. Given the awesome power of television, a story gets hyped up through visual authentication of events; it creates a sense of intimacy and produces a good "reality show." A Taiwan TV reporter says, "Camera is the story!" He is elated over a compliment he had received from his home editor, not for the substance of his story, but for the careful use of lighting. Good pictures are good stories, especially when the stories lack substantive significance. The official script of the handover is heavily loaded with emphasis on generating good visuals—pageantry, rituals, fireworks—for television cameras. Using inflated terms to describe the event, journalists intensify the visual spectaculars. At one point on the night of June 30 in Beijing, Andrea Kopple of CNN gasps that the Tiananmen Square is now a "sea of joy." CCTV uses even stronger terms to elicit emotive responses throughout the evening.

Visual images crystallize the overall theme of each country's coverage. Although we do not do a quantitative count, some visual images appeared in newspapers and TV so frequently as to catch our attention (Table 4.1). Some of these images might even have achieved the status of an icon—a vivid and memorable image that crystallizes an ongoing news story, evokes larger cultural themes, and

Table 4.1

Key Visual Devices from the Media Coverage

China	Hong Kong	Taiwan
1. Count-down clock	1. Horse racing and dance continues	1. Taiwan's democracy
2. Chinese national flag raising in Tiananmen	2. The PLA soldiers and armored personnel carrier	2. One country, one better system
3. Deng Xiaoping	3. The Royal emblem and insignia	3. "Say no to China"
4. Fireworks, dances, and music	4. Chris Patten	4. The Nanjing Treaty original
5. Hong Kong and mainland having the "affection as close as bones and flesh"	5. Lu Ping, Deng Xiaoping	5. Seating arrangement for Taiwan emissary, Gu Zhenfu
6. Mother and lost child	6. Anson Chan, the Chief Secretary before and after the handover	
7. The Yellow River, the Great Wall	7. Hong Kong people run Hong Kong	
8. The tomb of the Yellow Emperor	8. Union Jack and the Chinese national flag	
9. The Forbidden City	9. Broken-legged caldron	
10. Bell of National Awakening in Nanjing	10. Bauhinia	
	11. Torrential rain	

U.S.

1. PLA soldiers in battle-ready posture in Tiananmen
2. Lone man facing a tank column in Tiananmen
3. The PLA armored personnel carrier
4. "Hand-picked" "shipping tycoon" as the Chief Executive
5. "Freely elected" legislature dismantled
6. Martin Lee, the leading Hong Kong democrat
7. Capitalist jewel, jewel of the Orient
8. The Trojan Horse

Australia

1. Tiananmen Square Massacre
2. PLA soldiers
3. Horse racing
4. Skyscrapers and Central District of Hong Kong
5. Demonstrations by democrats
6. British and colonial emblems
7. Chris Patten
8. Martin Lee
9. Emily Lau

Canada

1. Canadian soldiers' graveyard in Honk Kong
2. Tiananmen Square massacre
3. Stock market and Hang Seng Index
4. Handover souvenirs
5. Hong Kong immigrants to Canada and return migrants
6. Junk
7. Star Ferry
8. Rickshaw
9. Sampan
10. Fortune-teller
11. Temple

Britain

1. Chris Patten
2. The Royal Yacht Britannia
3. The Union Jack
4. Bagpipes
5. Buglers playing *Sunset*
6. Patten bowing to the Union Jack
7. PLA soldiers in battle-ready posture in Tiananmen
8. Lone man facing a tank column in Tiananmen
9. Skyscrapers of Hong Kong
10. Torrential rain

symbolizes values (Bennett and Lawrence, 1995). It is obvious that both the British and Chinese media make effective uses of visual images as dramatic displays of emotive condensation. In Beijing the countdown clock at the Tiananmen Square is the media icon, where the feelings of patriotism and national pride are elevated. On the British side, Governor Chris Patten, hailed as a "guardian" of democracy in Hong Kong—and to a lesser extent, the "beautiful and graceful" Royal Yacht Britannia—personifies the dignity and popularity of Britain. In contrast, other media systems, notably those from the United States, Canada, Australia, and Taiwan, constantly peg the handover to the Tiananmen crackdown with footages from 1989 showing roaming tanks and soldiers in battle positions. Hong Kong media have many scattered visual images—horseracing, the Royal emblem, the bauhinia, the PLA, the broken-legged caldron, and so on—and yet none of them stands out, reflecting its prevailing ambivalence toward the handover. In pursuit of good visuals despite the heavy torrential rain, the media deploy cameras at various points of the territory, including the border crossing, where the PLA troops roll into Hong Kong in the early morning of July 1.

Even the print media increasingly follow the visual logic to spice up their stories. The *People's Daily* publishes special photo sections featuring the former supreme leader Deng Xiaoping and jubilant mass celebrations in cities across the country. On July 1, all the major newspapers in China publish special photo sections to capture key moments of the handover activities. On the same day, the English-language *South China Morning Post* carries on its front page President Jiang Zemin's address at the ceremony, alongside a frontal close-up shot of him looking grim and solemn. Looking up from the bottom of the page is, notably, an array of photos of world leaders, each accompanied by a brief well-wishing message, as if to create the impression that "the whole world is watching." Habitually using outlandish and eye-catching photos, the leading market-driven mass paper, the *Apple Daily*, carries a full front-page photo of the hoisted Chinese national flag and Hong Kong SAR flag, with a huge-size caption at the top of the page that reads, "Hong Kong *Ought to* Have a Tomorrow" (emphasis added). This photo and caption express the mixed feelings of hope, anxiety, and desperation.

Spatializing the Stage

Visuals help to map out the geography of an event. Manipulation of space in the symbolic terrain is a significant feature of what Foucault (1986: 22) calls "the epoch of simultaneity," meaning that the historical depth is compressed by emphasis on the spatial configuration. Popular wisdom in the media age presumes that the geographical reach of an event, especially if reported "live," connotes its profundity. TV anchors serve the narrative function of weaving different sites into a single stage for a media event. Through the extended geographical coverage, the ideologically intoned script for a media event is given added dramatic excitement. For CBS, the world is the stage. Dan Rather deliberately takes his handover coverage beyond the city of Hong Kong when he frames it as part of the larger "China story." His revisit in Beijing, his train ride from Beijing to Hong Kong, and the computer-generated graphs of his travel route are all broadcast to "appropriate" the visual space for the spectacle.

The home-base orientation of news parallels the spatial arrangement of anchors. The PRC media shape the event as an unprecedented celebration for all-inclusive ethnic Chinese, but by using the countdown clock to synchronize all celebratory activities, they are visually and ideologically oriented toward Beijing as the center of the family-nation. All reports, including those from the outpost of Hong Kong, must be sent back to Beijing before they were relayed to the whole nation. Reflecting this center-periphery relationship, CCTV's Beijing anchors serve as the control center for reports from home and abroad, whereas the Hong Kong anchor is but a coordinator of local activities. Similarly, for BBC and ITV, London is the main anchor with the Hong Kong studio as an outpost. Traffic control of Taiwan's TTV originates from Taipei and reaches out to Hong Kong and China. As an exception to this pattern, the center of gravity for U.S. television networks moves with the anchors, who direct their evening news shows from Hong Kong and pass the microphone back and forth between the anchors and reporters in Beijing, London, and other cities in the United States. The language of transportation ("We now take you to . . .") is invoked to create pseudorealism in light of the "eyewitness news" tradition.

Other production techniques—split screens, quick cuts, field reporter's stand-ups, and so on—are employed to connect various sites into a single stage of performance. On the night of the handover, CNN uses split screens repeatedly to show the activities taking place at different locations. Around midnight on June 30, the lower-left screen shows Bernard Shaw talking to guest analysts in the Hong Kong studio, while the other screen shows the ceremony about to commence, the buzz and background music from the Convention Hall laying over the conversation between Shaw and his guests. A few minutes later, a split screen appears again to show simultaneously the scenes of the ceremony in the Convention Hall and those of the ticking countdown clock in Tiananmen Square. CCTV uses quick cuts in MTV style to flash a string of euphoric celebratory scenes: an ocean of national flags, cheering crowds, fireworks, from one city to the next.

Even newspapers "spatialize the stage" of the handover spectacle through both their layout and their selective reporting from various sites. For days, the *People's Daily* fills its "International News" page with reports of celebration around the world and official statements by leaders of other nations. On July 2, five feature articles of equal length, arranged from the left to the right in a rectangular box, take up half of the page, featuring celebrations in five Chinese embassies or Chinese communities in London, Washington, Tokyo, Melbourne, and Johannesburg (each city representing a continent). The selection of these capital cities is ostensibly to convey a sense of global significance of the event.

Simulating the Tempo and Rhythms of "Reality Entertainment"

Compressing space is simultaneously compressing time. As official organizers script the handover activities for the media, the media rescript them for their presentation. Spatializing the stage conveys a realistic flow of activities, making media coverage conform to the internal tempo and rhythm of TV entertainment. Using split screens by CNN and CCTV to show the countdown clock continuously ticking gives suspense and anticipation to what is clearly a flat and boring ceremony of raising and lowering flags. At the precise moment of midnight on June 30, as the Chinese national anthem is played, CNN cuts its camera to Tiananmen Square, and then interlaces scenes in the Convention Center with the thunderous applause and fireworks in Tiananmen Square, juxtaposing the soundtracks from both sites. As President Jiang speaks solemnly, the screen is periodically cut to the giant TV screen in Tiananmen Square, the nightly tranquility of the Victoria Harbor, only to be interrupted later by scenes of protest staged by democrats in the Legislative Council under heavy rain. Correspondent Mintier covers Martin Lee's speech in full. Lee concludes, "We ask ourselves this question: Why is it that our Chinese leaders will not give us more democracy, that they will take away the modest democracy that we fought so hard to win from the British government?" As Lee utters his last word, the camera changes to the Royal Yacht Britannia—carrying Prince Charles and by-now former Governor Patten—sailing away. Then comes Bernard Shaw's voice, "That (the protest) comes as the *protector* of the fragile democracy in Hong Kong is sailing into the dark" (emphasis added).

CCTV manufactures theatrical elements of its handover coverage by mixing the live coverage of key moments, prerecorded interviews, historical images, and MTV videos. The chief official organs—CCTV, the *People's Daily*, and Xinhua News Agency—all participate in the orchestrating of the "live spectacle"; mixing news with the entertainment logic, ideologically they follow in the footsteps of the commandist mode of propaganda campaigns (Lee, 1990; Liu, 1971). CCTV's marathon coverage starts with highly charged anchors introducing the network's "game plan," followed by reporters in Hong Kong, other cities in China and abroad, who introduce their "local" activities. CCTV also announces that it would wrap its "live coverage" with a selection of MTV videos from a nationwide competition to show patriotic passion and festival elation.

Lacking the advantages and constraints of TV live coverage, print journalists have to use their descriptive power of language to convey a vivid sense of reality. For example, on July 1, Edward Gargan of the *New York Times* reports the sovereignty transfer night under the title "Time of Uncertainty Begins: Will Beijing Honor Vows?" In the seventh of this 41-paragraph-long feature article, he uses short, action-packed sentences to convey quick pace of change. The precise midnight moment is a device for him to "hang" a stream of events together to a narrative:

Changes came quickly as the territory's new rulers assumed control. At the stroke of midnight, Hong Kong's elected legislature was abolished, and a Beijing appointed body of lawmakers took its place. A range of Hong Kong's civil liberties were rolled back as new constraints were placed on the right to protest and association, and any form of speech promoting the independence of Taiwan and Tibet was banned.

Different national media systems appear to share the similar visual grammar: they "sample" the same pool of leads, themes, and visual images in the same spectacle; they all use anchors as star performers; and they employ action-oriented production techniques. Visual images play a central role in media hyping, as the contemporary public life is increasingly mediated through "pictorial representation" (Hartley, 1992). However, this grammar is harnessed to amplify the ideological framework of each media outlet's home country, rendering a country-specific "preferred reading" to the handover event.

Mystification

Hyping transforms an "occurrence" into a media performance by drawing the scripts from cultural rituals (Becker, 1995) and traditionally prescribed format (Esherick and Wasserstrom, 1994). The performance inscribes "star performers" to the established authority structure (Elliot, 1982), enacts familiar symbols and images of a culture, adds majestic aura and mythical qualities to the media event, and normalizes public displays of cultural drama. In the process, journalists may suspend their professional suspicion of the authority and the staged nature of the event to annotate and interpret the officially scripted symbols and rituals with ceremonial reverence. Meanwhile, journalists' annotation completes what Barthes (1982) calls the "second-order signification." Through such "mythological narrative" (Bird and Dardenne, 1988), the "star performers" are further distanced from the viewers in ordinary life routines. They become majestically associated with—even part of—mystified cultural icons. Such mythological narratives are not referenced to the "facts" but to certain culturally acceptable meanings.

In annotating a series of Patten's last-minute ceremonial activities, BBC personifies Patten as representing the best of British legacy in Hong Kong. The media frame bolsters the official British "script"—British successes, honorable and dignified withdrawal, and continued moral support for Hong Kong. After Patten makes a speech at the Sunset Ceremony, he is shown fighting back tears in several close-up shots, with the buglers playing the tune of *Sunset*, as the Union Jack and British Hong Kong flags are being lowered. Then, a lone piper plays the *Immortal Memories*. BBC correspondent Hanrahan reverently comments on this "defining moment" as "the lament for those who gave their lives for us." From the dock of East Tamar, before Patten boards the departing Royal Yacht Britannia, correspondent Eric Robson describes him as "a great man of the people." "Patten says, we put up a scaffolding," he remarks emotionally, "My goodness, what we did with that scaffolding!" Robson describes the yacht in the tone of a romantic lover (chapter 6). At one point, he was so taken as to simply exclaim, "Marvelous!"

Likewise, on June 26, the *Times* of London runs a full-page feature story on Lavender Patten, "I am here to hold his hand." Here is the tale of an affectionate wife committed to her hero husband who had battled against the powerful evil forces of a Communist regime and received consolation from her. On July 1, under the headline, "Final Farewell to Hong Kong," the *Times* reports that when "tears mingle with rain as retreat is beaten," Chris Patten "was cheered to the skies for his role in introducing democracy to Hong Kong and for standing up to Chinese pressure."

Such annotation involves journalists as "aesthetic designers" for media spectacles. They do not only select scenes and camera angles, or adjust lighting to create eye-pleasing shots; they also prepare footages, some specially made for the occasion. Following Patten's final address at the Sunset Ceremony, while the orchestra plays Elgar's *Nimrod*, BBC shows a series of beautifully shot and smoothly edited scenes of Hong Kong at dusk. The ceremony, held under a heavy rain, is accompanied by the live symphonic performance and the beautiful scenes of the Victoria Harbor, the green mountains, and fishing boats scattered on the serene sea under a dusk light.

The official CCTV annotates the handover events with similar techniques in accordance with the official master frame, while tapping into a reservoir of Chinese cultural symbols. In the evening of June 30, CCTV gives live coverage to a drum performance by workers and police forces in Beijing, all in the splendor of traditional costumes, while fireworks shoot vividly into the sky. In one of the specially prepared MTV videos, 100 top pop singers join in to sing the chorus of "1997, the Eternal Love." With the camera roving from one singer after another to the choir, they sing,

> With my heart,
> Rings the 5,000-year-old bell;
> With your love,
> Awaken from the 100-year sleep.
> 1997, I love you.

In another video, the chorus takes place against the backdrop images of the Great Wall, the Yellow River, the Forbidden City, the rising rocket, the Bank of China skyscraper in Hong Kong, all flashed by in rapid succession:

The descendents of the dragon,
Leaning on the Yellow River and Yangtze River;
After a hundred years of suffering,
China is prospering, Hong Kong is returning home.

In addition, the official Chinese media mystify Deng's ingenuity and his tie to Hong Kong. The *People's Daily*, in a typical article (June 23), portrays Deng Xiaoping as "a great man of this century" with "extraordinary courage," whose "one country, two system" conception is "an ingenious innovation." In addition, China's economic reform under his guidance is said to have brought strength to the country and made it possible to "wash away the 150 years of national humiliation." The media keep bringing Deng, by now dead, back to life. In covering President Jiang's arrival in Hong Kong and his delivery of a speech, CCTV keeps turning close-up shots to Deng's widow, who is so frail as to need support from her daughter but is said to be there to fulfill Deng's long-cherished wish of setting foot on Hong Kong as part of Chinese soil. On June 30, CCTV carries a "live report" from Shenzhen, a city adjoining Hong Kong, with a group of students gathered in front of a huge poster of Deng. Under the poster, one student is shown thanking Deng "from the bottom of our heart" for "bringing Hong Kong back to the embrace of the motherland." In CCTV's heavily promoted 12-part documentary series, "Deng Xiaoping," he comes to iconize the reclamation of Hong Kong. It further mystifies Deng with repeated showing of his handwritten note: "I am a son of the Chinese people. I am deeply in love with my country and my people."

The media's ritual performance, as Carey (1989: 18–19) argues, does not improve "intelligent information" to be transmitted or the efficiency of information transmission, but it contributes to the "construction and maintenance of an ordered, meaningful cultural world which can serve as control and container for human action." This performance thus tends to follow the aesthetic criteria of entertainment, rather than the empirical criteria of news, in ways that mystify the political authority and blunt the public's critical faculty. Further, by drawing resources from the mythology of a culture, such performance transforms private feelings into public expressions, ordinary persons into extraordinary heroes, secular objects into sacred symbols, and socially constructed features into culturally essentialized qualities (Becker, 1995; Turner, 1969).

Amalgamation

The script of cultural rituals serves to build a narrative flow and achieve thematic unity by functioning as a template for journalists to amalgamate "microbits" of an event. Amalgamation expands the historical and spatial scope of an event. By so doing, news invariably evokes the past, the present, and the future to suggest causes and consequences of the event (van Ginneken, 1998: 110). In this sense, a ritual performance also explains an event in a grand historical narrative.

The *People's Daily*, in its editorial on June 30, forges a connection between the first day of China resuming sovereignty over Hong Kong and the official "birthday" of the Chinese Communist Party:

> Tomorrow, July 1, is the 76th anniversary of the Chinese Communist Party, also the happy day of Hong Kong's reunification with the motherland that washes away 100 years of national humiliation. Having two celebrations in one day is a rare moment . . . All Party comrades, people of different ethnic groups…warmly celebrate the reunification of Hong Kong and praise our great Party!

Thus, reclamation of Hong Kong was the heights of national salvation and revitalization under the strong leadership of the Communist Party; the handover was congealed into a historical narrative of Communist state building.

Amalgamation is thus an ideological process, rhetorically connecting what otherwise seem disjointed realities and imparting significance to them. Vertically, the narrative ties personal experiences to high political drama; horizontally, it links different life experiences to create some kind of "mood" or "color." National "master frame" endows the media with their interpretive coherence and unity.

In one of its programs, CCTV features a diplomat who had participated in negotiations with Britain over the future of Hong Kong and had once lived with his family in Macau and Hong Kong during his youth. The camera focuses on his dying father, a historian, in a hospital bed. Then comes the diplomat's voice: "The return of Hong Kong has been my father's lifelong wish. Now that people of my generation have won back Hong Kong, we can face history, our ancestors, and offspring." In another program, CCTV shows villagers on the Hong Kong side crossing the border to congratulate a family on the mainland side who moved into a new house. Explaining his family tree, the 70-year-old owner of the new house tells his grandchildren "never to forget that you are Chinese." This implies that with Hong Kong's returning to China, the blood ties should dissolve the artificial border. This story loses sight of many complex historical interpretations, including the fact that that the PRC has continued to control the border after 1997.

Contrived contrasts within a specific ideological framework serve to amalgamate the homologous bits and pieces of reality into a historical narrative; thus, the differences between Hong Kong and the PRC are told through personal life experiences. Steven Mufson of the *Washington Post* files a story on

July 5 contrasting the life of the owner of a stylish Italian restaurant in Hong Kong with that of her aunt, who had been left behind and suffered a lot in Shanghai after the Communist takeover. Gargan of the *New York Times* plans a series on the lives of four families across the socioeconomic ladder: a fishmonger, a waiter, a teacher, and a tycoon. Showing how their lives might have been under Chinese rule fits the grand narrative of freedom-versus-authoritarianism. Dan Rather of CBS refers to Hong Kong and China as "two worlds in one country" and "tales of two cities," while linking the festival mood in Tiananmen Square to the military crackdown of eight years ago. To counter Beijing's "one country, two systems," Taiwan's media drum the official slogan of "one country, one system—the better system." The PRC media contrast past images of poor, weak, and humiliated Chinese people against present scenes of smiles, dances, and songs.

Amalgamation also involves rendering the same signifier to alternative or even opposing ideological decoding. The heavy rain falling on the night of June 30 and July 1 is read by the Chinese media as an act of the Heaven to "wash away 150 years of humiliation"; to the British media, however, God is "mingling rain with tears" over the loss of empire. The *Los Angeles Times* (July 3) calls Hong Kong's new emblems a "sterile hybrid" (bauhinia) and a "nearly extinct" animal (pink dolphin); yet CCTV describes the pink dolphin as "very active, energetic, obedient, lovely" and possessing "a strong sense of kinship." The PLA crossing the border into Hong Kong is a monument to national sovereignty, as CCTV's reporter exclaims in a live report from the border crossing point: "The PLA vehicle is moving! It's getting close . . . It has now crossed the border! The mighty and civilized PLA has now entered Hong Kong!" This reading could not have been more different from CBS's, as Bob Simon declares, "For folks here the PLA means the Tiananmen Square." CNN, BBC, and ITV adopt the same narrative, frequently showing the picture of a lone man facing a tank formation in Tiananmen Square in 1989.

The genre of "color" stories attempting to catch the general "mood" helps to extend the main plot of the handover as a media event. These stories subtly but powerfully hype up the event by adding humor, irony, and human emotions to the core element of news, thus enhancing the values of realism, intimacy, and entertainment. They humanize the stern face of a seemingly hard and cold event. "Reporter's Notebook" on the *New York Times* allows reporters to write more freewheelingly and more subjectively when they bring diverse tidbits into the handover narrative. Most western media relish on writing about rags-to-riches refugees in capitalist Hong Kong, the popularity of fortune-telling in times of anxiety, the exotic Orient that might no longer be as exotic under Communist rule, and the tough time ahead for gay and lesbian communities because of the Communist regime's supposed intolerance of them. The *People's Daily* writes about families happily wrapping dumplings, late-night phone calls to congratulate one another on the return of Hong Kong, patriotic poems and letters. Taiwan's media report a psychiatrist who advises people on how to maintain mental health amid hysteria, about entrepreneurs who sell bottled "colonial air," and about the soaring price of the shark fin (a Chinese delicacy). The Hong Kong media interpreted as a "bad omen" that the tripod gift from the central government in Beijing to Hong Kong had broken a leg.

Through amalgamation, each national narrative is coagulated into a discursive conglomerate, filled with not only the main plot and star performers, but also personal stories of ordinary folks and tidbits of seemingly marginal relevance. While adding historical and cultural texture to the media narratives, these "microbits of reality" (Manning, 1996) serve other rhetorical, narrative, and ideological functions. Rhetorically, they bring the handover event, as remote as it is, closer to a home audience. At the narrative level, such microbits tell the handover story from the vantage point of the people who experienced it with accounts that resonate with common sense. Finally, the power of amalgamation is that the process is so transparent for those sharing the dominant ideological framework that the constructed narrative is authenticated as historical reality.

Conclusion

The Hong Kong handover shows that production of a media spectacle involves the entertainment-based media logic and much repairing work done on the news paradigm. Such repairing work elevates the handover event into a media spectacle, makes it larger than life, and lifts it up to being historic and theatrical. This hyping process involves first certifying the significance of the event, which in turn justifies the commitment of a massive army of journalists. Then the media set up a visual stage for persons in power to perform, while narrating such performance in historically and causally coherent narratives. As Max Frankel of the *New York Times* (June 29) writes, the "media mob" parachuted to Hong Kong "will not teach us as much as the handful of Chinese-speaking reporters who have been tracking the gradual commercial and political accommodation between Hong Kong and Beijing."

The handover ends up consisting of "a bunch of ceremonies," mostly boring and tedious, against the anticipation of, in the case of the western media, a supposed clash between systems and ideologies, and in the case of the PRC media, a watershed event that would electrify the population. Something should have happened, but did not. Hyping becomes important to bridge the gaps between news and reality, and between anticipation and outcome, especially in the rising climate of "reality entertainment" or infotainment. In the process, reporters act as performers, annotators, and narrators of the media event. Hyping "repairs" the news paradigm by infusing the logic of media event into news.

The logic of hyping belongs to "general structure" (Douglas, 1975) found in all media narratives regardless of political systems, ideological contexts, and national interests. But as Thompson (1995: 173) reminds us of the relationship between "globalized diffusion" and "localized appropriation," the hermeneutic process of news production calls for applying the "particular structure" of the dominant ideology in each nation (Douglas, 1975). These particular structures give rise to different national media narratives. The images, symbols, authoritative structure, and historical narratives used are all culturally specific, and they play specific ideological functions in the cultural and political contexts.

There are significant implications when a major news story is turned into a spectacle of theatrical performance. First, a media event, like that of the handover—complete with symbols, enacted through rites according to a script—is bracketed from the flow of everyday life. It is a staged performance with presumed realism. The central cast—authorities that symbolize national sovereignty—are presented with reverence. The narrative of media events thus softens the critical edge of conventional news narrative. Second, while the media set up a stage for the political authorities to perform, the audiences, as spectators, are only allowed to "watch what happens next" but will "never act" (Debord, 1990: 22). Thus, media spectacle reinforces the existing power relationships by drawing clear boundaries of actors and spectators and by imputing passivity and inaction to audiences (Abercrombie and Longhurst, 1998; MacAloon, 1984). The performance of media spectacle thus mars the liberal democratic premise of news as a means of informing the public and encouraging political participation. Third, staged media performance confers identities on the audiences. In some media spectacles, participants possess "double identities" (MacAloon, 1984): for example, athletes in the Olympic Games are both individuals in their own right (with medals awarded to individuals) and "sons and daughters" of the nation they represent (with national flags raised and national anthems played at award ceremonies). In the spectacle of the Hong Kong handover, individuality is largely suppressed; media spectators—euphemistically called "the audience"—are simply members of the national family to reify political, ideological, and cultural differences. In sum, with media hyping, the story of Hong Kong's handover acquires the features of a mythical ritual, celebrating and renewing the symbols of authority, nationhood, and political systems.

Major Chinese and British representatives attend the Hong Kong handover ceremony on the night of June 30, 1997.

Outgoing Governor Chris Patten receives the folded British flag from an officer at the Government House, symbolizing the retreat of the British from Hong Kong.

An armored carrier of the People's Liberation Army arrives in Hong Kong in the early morning of July 1, as onlookers witness the historic moment.

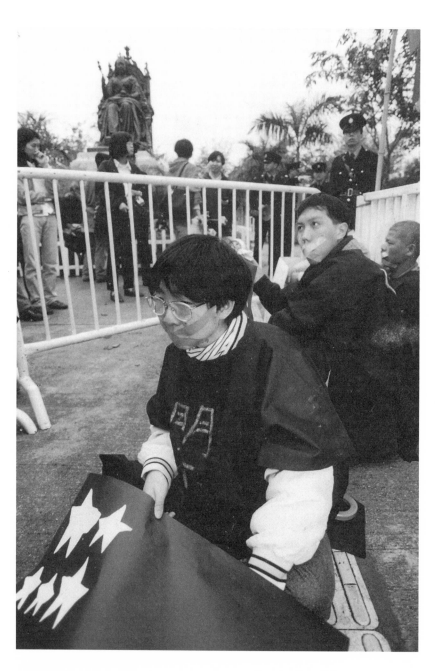

Protesters stage a sit-in with a self-made Chinese flag in black color, with the Queen's statue in the background.

The handover story fills the front pages of major newspapers in Hong Kong on July 1, 1997.

Legislators from the democratic camp protest on the balcony of the Legislative Council building right after the handover ceremony.

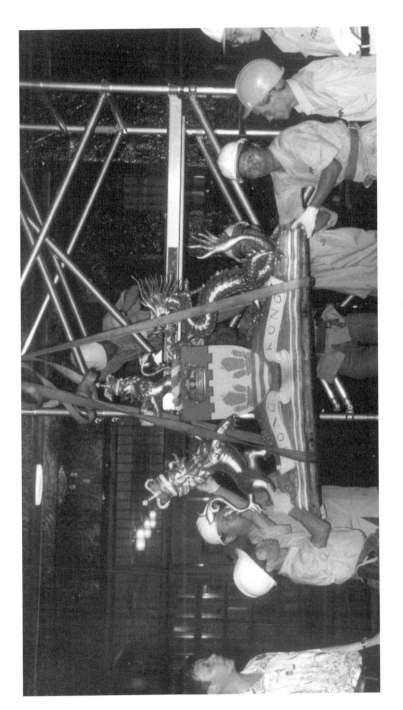

Workers lower the British insignia in front of the Hong Kong government headquarters.

The handover site at the Hong Kong Convention and Exhibition Center, with hundreds of selected media representatives to witness the moment.

Hong Kong citizens learn about the handover details from the newspapers in a surreal atmosphere.

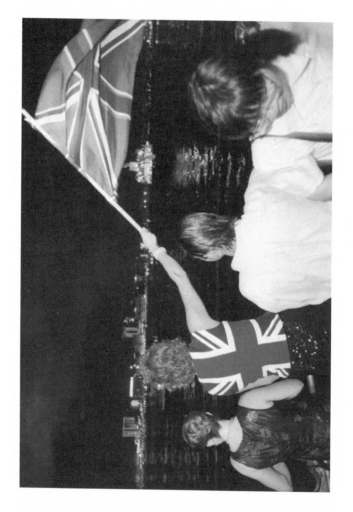

Nostalgic British citizens wave the British flag and say goodbye to the Royal yacht, *Britannia*.

Chapter 5

Banging the Democracy Drum: From the Superpower

There is a sadness in seeing this jewel of Asia transfer to the hands of a dictatorial regime, only 10 years after the fall of the Berlin Wall.
—*Chicago Tribune*, editorial, July 1, 1997

In the American view of the past, the United States was not a classical imperial power, but a righter of wrongs around the world, in pursuit of tyranny, in defense of freedom no matter the place or cost.
—Edward W. Said (1993: 5)

They can walk *freely* now, how long will that last?
—CNN shows pairs of walking shoes in Hong Kong.

They played it up. I had friends in the States who called up and thought there was martial law in Hong Kong.
—Mike Chinoy, CNN Hong Kong bureau chief,
referring to CBS's treatment of the menacing sight
of the People's Liberation Army crossing the border
(Knight and Nakano, 1999: 68)

In the era of "high modernism," Hallin (1994) argues, American journalism domestically followed the New Deal liberal policies and defined foreign policy in terms of bipartisan consensus on Cold War containment. Has the era of "high modernism" indeed passed as he claims? As far as the transfer of Hong Kong from British to Chinese sovereignty in 1997—at a time when the West had supposedly won the Cold War—is concerned, the U.S. media's political reason, agendas, and narratives remain defined primarily by the mighty icon of Americanism. The end of the Cold War, according to Fukuyama's (1992) controversial thesis, represents the total exclusion of viable systemic alternatives to western liberalism. The collapse of the Soviet Union has made the United States the only superpower and the People's Republic of China (PRC) a major hurdle to reconstructing a U.S.-dominated liberal international order (Burchill, 1996), not to mention that China's growing nationalism is a source of regional, if not world concern. Against this backdrop, the handover of Hong Kong becomes a theater, a site and a moment for various national media communities to engage in a discursive struggle.

The transfer of Hong Kong sovereignty reportedly attracts a contingent of 1,047 U.S. journalists from 108 news organizations. They cover Hong Kong but aim at China. American exceptionalism is the motif for this ideological confrontation. Where a Communist power is concerned, the United States— along with its media—always sees itself as "a righter of wrongs around the world, in pursuit of tyranny, in defense of freedom no matter the place or cost" (Said, 1993: 5). Chang (1993) documents that the elite U.S. press has closely followed the foreign policy toward China throughout various administrations. The handover of Hong Kong is but a new chapter in the oscillating history of U.S. media coverage of China between cycles of romanticism and those of cynicism (Lee, 1990), this time perceived through vivid lenses and lingering memories of the brutal Tiananmen crackdown in 1989. During that uprising, the U.S. media strongly and perhaps justifiably endorsed the students' ideological causes, in contrast to the Japanese media, whose primary concern was the impact on Japan's economic interests in China (Lee and Yang, 1995). Dramatized by the televised bloodshed, the U.S. media made what Herman and Chomsky (1988) call "worthy victims" out of Communist China's wanton killings because they "proved" the superiority of capitalist democracy.[1] Since 1989 the U.S. media have continued to portray the PRC as an invariant dictatorship, in fact the last Communist giant to be struggled against, whose promises regarding Hong Kong are not to be trusted. For its part, having issued an unrestrained torrent of threats, China is suspicious of the West's motive to make Hong Kong a base of subversion against the motherland.

Notwithstanding its historical significance, the handover is a "set-piece journalism," a staged spectacle, and a rather bland "media event" with its script written in 1984. Journalists had concocted likely scenarios of riots and disturbances that did not come to pass. Short of surprises and unexpected ruptures, they could only do "theater criticism," a review of some sort of performance not keeping pace with a moving story (Knight and Nakano, 1999: 129). However, even the presumably detached theater criticism flaunts strong ideological underpinnings. The fact that the U.S. media drum up the democracy theme in Hong Kong "recall(s) and celebrate(s) events and persons that are part of their jointly acknowledged generational and cultural identity and common understanding" and "silence(s) the contrary interpretations of the past" (Middleton and Edwards, 1990: 8).

The Sociology of News

Six "prestige papers" (Pool, 1952) are selected: the *New York Times*, the *Washington Post*, the *Los Angeles Times*, the *Wall Street Journal*, the *Chicago Tribune*, and the *Des Moines Register*. (The *Des Moines Register*, relying heavily on the wire services, is included in the content analysis but not in the discourse analysis.) In the absence of a national press tradition in the United States (Bagdikian, 1971) they are highly influential, both reflective of and catering to elite constituencies. The unity or division of elite opinion can influence the effect of mass media on public opinion (Zaller, 1992). These "newspapers of information," vis-à-vis "newspapers of story," provide rational and contextualized analysis that appeals to "the more respectable faculties of abstraction" rather than "the less respectable feelings" (Schudson, 1978: 119). Even the *New York Times* finds it difficult to do "micro stories" on Hong Kong. Edward Gargan, its local bureau chief, tells us that everything has to be placed in a wider context with "some sweeping quality," "with history in it," and "with as much descriptive power in it as you can." But many of its "soft" stories seem to appease "the less respectable feelings" also.

The content analysis of 335 stories (news, features, commentaries, and editorials) is distributed as follows: the *New York Times*, 54 stories (16%); the *Washington Post*, 47 stories (14%); the *Wall Street Journal*, 32 stories (9.6%); the *Los Angeles Times*, 54 stories (16%); the *Chicago Tribune*, 36 stories (10.7%); the *Des Moines Register*, 22 stories (6.6%); CBS News, 35 stories (10.4%), and CNN, 55 stories (16.4%). Table 3.1 shows that the United States is most doubtful among all western nations about the future of Hong Kong's democracy and press freedom. Changes in democracy and civil liberties clearly top the list of U.S. media concerns (34.8%); of these references, seven in ten (73.7%) suggest that these changes would head for the worse. Other major explicit concerns include press freedom (14%), the daily life (13.7%), and the rule of law (10.4%)—more than 50% of these references claim that Hong Kong will deteriorate in these areas. Some 15.2% of media references mention possible, but not necessarily disastrous, changes to Hong Kong's autonomy. The U.S. media seem confident about Hong Kong's continued economic prosperity after the handover.

The size of the news team and the amount of resources vary. The *New York Times* team consists of five experienced China hands, all with a reservoir of knowledge about China and Hong Kong.[2] Gargan explains that since his paper "covers the world" with 44 correspondents, Hong Kong's handover is prominent but not overwhelming. Most of the writing is lengthy and highly interpretative rather than straightforwardly factual. The *Washington Post* also has an equally formidable team headed by its bureau chief, Keith Richburg, and follows similar news routines. (When asked to name the most influential media leaders, a senior British journalist credits these two papers.) The *Wall Street Journal*, besides its own staff, is augmented for local advantages by the *Asian Wall Street Journal*, which it owns. The *Los Angeles Times* has a somewhat more modest presence. The *Chicago Tribune* only parachutes in a reporter from Beijing, whose reports are more event-oriented, shorter, and sprinkled with quotes from a lot of different sources. It also relies on wire services and excerpted foreign press opinions to fill up the missing holes in the news net. Other regional or local papers have different considerations of audience taste. The *San Jose Mercury News* caters to a significant Asian-American community that it serves in California. A reporter from the *Baltimore Sun* admits that a "small fish" like him is disadvantaged to compete with the *New York Times* or the *Washington Post*, so he tries to do something others don't do, but the question is what topics are left uncovered.

The *New York Times* seems to typify the "news net" (Tuchman, 1978) of U.S. coverage. First, topical emphasis is placed on reports of formal and structured aspects of the handover activities. Secondly, in a "Waiting for China" series, journalists take turns to do more informal, interesting, and colorful writing to capture the "mood," allowing their personal values to seep in. Thirdly, corollary reports come from other parts of the world, covering China's nationalistic rallies in Tiananmen Square as well as reactions from Taiwan and other Chinese communities in North America and England. In other words, this news net is centered on the "here and now" of Hong Kong in a web of temporal and spatial significance that is tied to the United States, the PRC, Britain, and Taiwan. All papers in this study publish editorials and commentaries by staff columnists or contributors.

The two networks selected for analysis are CBS News and CNN. CBS Evening News was being broadcast daily in Hong Kong via satellite transmission during the study period. Despite a steady decline in network ratings, television news still has a wider audience reach than the elite press by virtue of its ability to cut across different social strata (Wilensky, 1964). CNN is a quasiglobal network watched in many major cities around the world (Volkmer, 1999); its signals are often received and edited by various national television systems for particular ideological emphasis. The active role of both networks, especially their anchors, during the 1989 Tiananmen uprising was noteworthy (Chinoy, 1999; Salisbury, 1990). The presence of CNN in the Gulf War was a special, albeit controversial, chapter in the history of live broadcasting (Zelizer, 1992). Even though China has been undergoing dramatic transformation, it has almost disappeared from the news maps of ABC, CBS, and NBC since the Tiananmen crackdown, while CNN has narrowly focused on China's dissidents, human rights, and Sino-American diplomatic conflicts (Chinoy, 1999: 413–414).

This study confirms Hallin's (1986) finding that, due to its greater need for simplified thematic unity, television is a much more ideological medium than the elite press. If the elite press provides "knowledge about," television offers "acquaintance with" at best (Park, 1940). Television news knits bits and pieces of images into a plot line, appealing not to understanding but to imagination (Nimmo and Combs, 1990: 49). The anchors perform television's thematizing function by furnishing leading and concluding remarks in the newscast as well as by moderating, interspersing, and posing questions between various reporters. Television narratives also move back and forth between "straight" reporting and commentary; their language is "peppered with phrases strongly charged with moral and ideological significance" (Hallin, 1986: 120).

The four globe-trotting television anchors (Dan Rather of CBS, Peter Jennings of ABC, Tom Brokaw of NBC, and Bernard Shaw of CNN) are flown in to pull off a technological feat. Their celebrity status—projected as more glamorous, wiser, and larger than life, a fame that is beyond the reach of any print journalists—is a creation of modern mass mediation. Despite their well-publicized journeys, *South China Morning Post* gives these anchors a simple test on name recognition and finds them "decidedly hazy on some general knowledge of Hong Kong" (Buerk, 1997). Ignorance does not seem to hamper them but, instead, necessitates their greater reliance on a stock of stereotypes. Nor are their culturally embedded clichés likely to meet with critical challenge from a home audience generally ignorant about world affairs.

CBS News starts broadcasting live from Hong Kong on June 25, six days before the handover.[3] Under the heading of "Red Flag Rising," the network frames the handover "in the context of the ongoing story of China trying to be a world superpower" (Buerk, 1997). Rather claims that echoes from the huge and increasingly more powerful China "reverberate in every American country and town" (Buerk, 1997), but he does not acknowledge that CBS has for years had no presence in Hong Kong. The CBS team consists almost exclusively of its own star correspondents (including Bob Simon, Tom Fenton, and Bob Scheiffer), but these prominent "tourists of history" suffer from a lack of substantive knowledge about China. The anchor, contrary to illusion, is transfixed by the glare of lights and remains in a fixed location. CBS casts a narrow news net with a predictable slate of interviewees: top leaders, English-speaking democrats, a few Britons, a pro-Beijing Hong Kong legislator of British origin, and a controversial radio talk show host. Despite Hong Kong being a foremost center of China studies, curiously, the only person invited to proffer insight in a shallow special live coverage is Sidney Rottenberg, an American sympathizer of Mao's revolution who lived in China until the Tiananmen crackdown in 1989. Having introduced his guest as "a man whose expertise in and of modern China, as an American, is unmatched, from Mao to the market economy, from prison time to information age," Rather asks him: "With your experiences, what do you think?" Live coverage is a most ahistorical and least reflective news genre, one that Katz (1992) has taken to task as the "end of journalism." A noted U.S. journalist describes CBS's overall performance to us as "disgraceful."

CNN has a bigger slab of airtime to fill, in both its regular Worldview program (one hour on weekdays and 30 minutes on weekends) and the special coverage. Bernard Shaw brings in a crew of 59 people, adding to the strength of 16 members in the local bureau led by Mike Chinoy, and reinforced by the Beijing bureau headed by Andrea Koppel. Shaw starts reporting from Hong Kong on June 23, two days ahead of Dan Rather, and anchors a nonstop live coverage of the handover ceremony from 11:30 p.m. on June 30.[4] Shaw claims that CNN tries to cover the handover "as thoroughly as possible" for people "around the world" (Buerk, 1997). It casts a somewhat wider news net than CBS News, albeit primarily with prowestern sources and no official Chinese voices. There are two studio panel discussions, each made up of a local academic and another American professor of Chinese descent (all with American degrees). CNN also depicts the light side of Hong Kong with segments of what could be called an "alien and exotic Orient" theme to close off—and to provide texture for—its Worldview program. These lighter pieces include horse racing (2:48 minutes), the life of the boat people (5:25 minutes), rickshaw (1:46 minutes), shoes and the "frenetic pace" and fortune telling in Hong Kong (1:53 minutes), a ferry ride (2:06 minutes), the fishermen's life (1:53 minutes), and the handover souvenir on sale (1:19 minutes). Many of them seem to match with the sites of tours and visits arranged by the Government Information Services. These seemingly neutral stories contain strong ideological messages. Describing the fast pace of local life, CNN shows a shot of walking shoes: "They can walk *freely* now, how long will that last?"

Media Framing

We identify four "ideological packages" in the U.S. media narratives that are causally related and internally consistent (Table 5.1). First, the United States is now the "new guardian" to protect Hong Kong from China's abuse. Such claims of responsibility are ideologically based on the second package: as the leader of the Free World, the United States has the right and duty to lead in an emerging Cold War. These two abstract packages are concretized by two other packages. The third package concerns how Communist dictatorship will wreck Hong Kong's democracy and freedom, whereas the fourth package posits that the capitalist Hong Kong will eventually spread democracy and freedom over to change Communist China. These two seemingly opposite packages, in fact, postulate the same heroes and villains.

In the arena of international newsmaking, national similarities in media narratives tend to dwarf their internal differences. Television networks and the elite press, despite their fierce competition, play different variations on the same ideological themes. They operate within the same institutional relationship to the power structures and share the broadly similar ideological and cultural prisms. They embrace and reproduce—rather than challenge, weaken, or subvert—elite consensus. The handover of Hong Kong as a political issue never enters into the sphere of "legitimated controversy" in the United States (Hallin, 1986), so the media need not "index" divided opinions, if any, among the elites (Bennett, 1990). It is appropriate to speak of a *nationally* defined media narrative.

New Guardian

The United States is said to have taken over Britain's "guardian responsibility" to protect the treasured capitalist enclave from Communist atrocity. This guardianship is not based on sovereignty or territorial claims but justified on ideological grounds. It should be remembered that as a political candidate Bill Clinton had chided President Bush for "coddling Beijing butchers," and that during the first two years of his administration President Clinton sought to link trade with China to its human rights record. Clinton found his linking policy ineffective and decided to pursue a policy of "positive engagement" instead. Now gingerly announcing that he would make the preservation of Hong Kong's freedoms as part of America's China policy, he also claims that he wants to "draw China in" rather than to "shut China out" (*Washington Post*, June 14). Hence, Secretary of State Albright reiterates that no single issue, not even Hong Kong's transition process, can control the "multifaceted relationship" the United States has developed with China. Columnist David Broder (*Washington Post*, June 24) quotes former U.S. ambassador to China, James Lilly, as arguing that the United States should renew "most favored nation" trade status to China but engage China at every point.

This "engagement" policy is criticized by a hard-hitting *Washington Post* editorial (June 24) for failing to spell out what might be at stake for China if it should trample on Hong Kong's freedoms. Citing China's treatment of the leading dissident Wei Jingsheng and Hong Kong's "puppet legislature," it claims that "sometimes it seems as if the administration wants to champion human rights without risking goodwill in the relationship with China." The editorial urges Clinton to ensure that "China does not feel emboldened to mistreat Hong Kong's 6 million citizens with the same impunity." Similarly, columnist Jim Hoagland scolds Clinton for "sniff(ing) up a version of the old 'quiet diplomacy' excuse" for doing nothing about China's human rights (June 29). He concludes that Hong Kong's reversion "provides an opportunity, and an obligation, for Washington to

Table 5.1
Ideological Packages of the U.S. Media Coverage

	New Guardian	New Cold War	Erosion of Democracy and Freedom	Trojan Horse
Frame	U.S. takes over guardian responsibility toward Hong Kong.	China is a threat to the liberal world order after the fall of Berlin Wall.	China's takeover leads to the erosion of democracy and freedom in Hong Kong.	Hong Kong's capitalism and democracy will spread to China.
Metaphors	The whole world is watching.	ATM machine as the most "efficient diplomatic tool"; the Berlin Wall.	China "will put its virus in Hong Kong's software"; a puppet handler awaits his cue; "nearly extinct" pink dolphin, "sterile hybrid" bauhinia.	"The tail that wags the dragon"; "colossal Trojan Horse."
Exemplars	Clinton wants to "draw China in"; hold China accountable in Hong Kong.	Losing a "capitalist jewel" to the Communists after the fall of Berlin Wall; "Tiananmen bloodbath."	Tiananmen crackdown; democratic Taiwan; authoritarian Singapore.	Soaring Hang Seng Index and Red Chips Index.
Catchphrases	"Exit Britain, enter America."	"Hard-line and old-line communism"; "Red flag rising."	"One country, no system."	Red star over Hong Kong is the end of Maoism.

Depictions	Albright "snubbing an undemocratic body appointed by China's leaders."	Chinese troops "rolling in"; China "trying to be a world superpower."	China's "handpicked legislators"; "democratic legislature dismantled"; Hong Kong as the only decolonized place with less freedom and democracy; Hong Kong media "bend even before the wind starts to blow."	Hong Kong as "a base of subversion"; "Hong Kong capital is reshaping China's landscape"; Hong Kong fever will spread across China; China is big, old, and heavy, while Hong Kong is young, light, and mature.
Visual images	A "jewel of Asia" falling into a dictatorial regime; Patten sailing into the dark.	Tanks, armored personnel carriers.	Tales of two cities; Tung as a "shipping tycoon"; two worlds in one country.	Hong Kong as "crystal ball"; "a flagship of what Chinese people can do"; bullish Hang Seng Index.
Principles	Positive engagement.	Liberal democracy in the post-Cold War era.	Press freedom and free election.	Capitalist democracy.

think and speak more clearly about the future, of China and of U.S. expectations in China."

The conservative Republican chairman of the Senate Foreign Relations Committee, Jessie Helms, writes a tough op-ed page commentary titled "Exit Britain, Enter America" (*Wall Street Journal*, June 25). He asserts that the transfer of sovereignty of Hong Kong to China "signals the handover of responsibility for Hong Kong's fate to the United States." Helms laments about America's "undeniable mistake" not to seek to influence Sino-British negotiations in the 1980s. No matter whether Britain is able to pursue its agenda at the international court, Helms holds that the United States should "employ tactics well beyond legal challenges," until China lives up to its commitments. With Britain gone, he concludes that only the United States "has the will and the way to stand up for Hong Kong." Another critic of China, the *New York Times*'s columnist A. M. Rothenthal, accuses the "China trade lobby" of trying to persuade Clinton to kill human rights as a part of U.S. policy (July 4). The title of his column is: "Laughing in Beijing."

New Cold War

Although almost all western media display antipathy toward China, only the U.S. media frame the handover from the global superpower's vantage point. Because of or notwithstanding its human rights record, China has stepped in as America's convenient enemy in place of the Soviet Union. The *Chicago Tribune* says in its editorial (July 1), "There is a sadness in seeing this jewel of Asia transfer to the hands of a dictatorial regime, only less than 10 years after the fall of the Berlin Wall." The *New York Times*'s editorial on the same day strikes a similar tone. Both invoke the Berlin Wall metaphor to suggest that Hong Kong—Milton Friedman's "wonderful experiment in free-market capitalism"—is in jeopardy.

It is graphically illustrating that Dan Rather embarks on his journey by revisiting, reminiscing about, and reporting from the Tiananmen Square, thus linking the absorption of Hong Kong to that crystallized symbol of Chinese repression. On June 20, Rather reports from Beijing "a rare (housing) protest against the Communist authority on the eve of Hong Kong's transfer." Coupling these two unrelated events, he adds, "Today's protest is notable more for its timing than for its size." From Beijing, he takes a train passing through several coastal and inland provinces to reach Hong Kong, as if to suggest metaphorically that Beijing were pulling the string from behind. The network frequently pegs the handover story to library footage of the Tiananmen bloodshed, not only creating an emotional déjà vu against Communist dictatorship but also foretelling life in the posthandover Hong Kong. Standing in front of the glistening skyline and the magnificent Victoria Harbor, Rather announces that Hong Kong's free enterprise is "going back to the old-line and hardline Chinese Communists" (June 25).

Wearing a safari outfit, the "war" correspondent Bob Simon comments, "A Communist regime gets control of a piece of real estate without firing a shot." Compared with the U.S. getting out of Vietnam, Simon praises the British for doing it with style, "without a tail between legs." The war metaphors abound.

Amidst the prevailing doom and gloom, however, some predict that capitalism will triumph. The *New York Times* columnist Thomas L. Friedman (July 3) characterizes China as "one country, no system"—having largely abandoned Communism but not fully embracing capitalism. If China fails to live up to its obligation toward Hong Kong, China "will be punished by that most brutal, efficient and immediate of diplomatic tools: the ATM machine." He refers to the more than $100 billion in foreign investment in Hong Kong, most of it in highly liquid funds. Former U.S. Assistant Secretary of Defense Chas W. Freeman Jr. also writes in the *New York Times* (June 22) that most people in Hong Kong clearly believe that China would honor its words, given the booming stock and real estate markets. He scolds Governor Patten for "jumping the gun" by staging elections in Hong Kong in 1995, defying what Deng Xiaoping had in mind for Hong Kong: "benevolent autocracy" that is economically libertarian but politically authoritarian. Obviously no fan of Hong Kong's fragile democracy, Freeman charges that "American politicians, suffering from apparent 'enemy deprivation' and calling for a new Cold War with China, unnerve Hong Kong more than they do Beijing." His view draws rebuttals from Patten's press secretary (June 22) and another letter writer, arguing that a flourishing market economy is "compatible only with a free society" (June 24). Of course, neither Friedman nor Freeman anticipated that an Asian financial crisis would erupt only a year later to prick Hong Kong's economic bubble.

The *Wall Street Journal* appears to be even more uncompromising toward China, both in the three editorials and in the invited commentaries (by Jessie Helms, Margaret Thatcher, and Martin Lee). The language used is generally stronger, more biting, and without pretense to fairness. An editorial (July 1) claims that "no amount of complaining from its citizens, or from Washington, London and any other capital can stop Beijing from behaving as it wishes" or from having "absolute control" in Hong Kong. Another editorial (June 26) invokes "Tiananmen bloodbath" twice to question if China's promised "high degree of autonomy" for Hong Kong would be turned into a mockery. A third editorial (July 2) condemns European leaders—including German Chancellor Helmut Kohl, French President Jacques Chirac, and the former British Foreign Secretary Geoffrey Howe—for kowtowing to Beijing, to the neglect of Hong Kong's rights.

The handover is an ocassion for the PRC media extravaganza to celebrate nationalistic triumph over western imperialism. To counter this, the British media emphasize that their small island nation has brought modern civilizations to the world and has left a good legacy—freedom, prosperity, the rule of law, and an efficient civil service—in Hong Kong. Margaret Thatcher uses Hong Kong to reaffirm herself as "an unashamed defender of the record of the British Empire in bringing the rule of law and the prospects for self-improvement to millions who would never otherwise have known them" (*Wall Street Journal*, June 27). Imperial nostalgia notwithstanding, she is eager to fend off the criticism that while as prime minister she "sold out" free people of Hong Kong to the Communists. Thatcher's rhetoric attempts to de-essentialize the virtues of Chinese nationalism and the evils of British colonialism, in ways that shockingly exemplify the caricature made by Said (1993) of the imperial construction of Orientalism: the notions that Britain brings civilization to primitive or barbaric peoples (p. xi) and that "you are what you are because of us; when we left, you reverted to your deplorable state" (p. 35).

While positive British legacy constitutes the main frame for the British media, it is treated only as a *secondary* frame by the U.S. media to bolster their own ideological contestation over capitalism versus Communism. A *New York Times* editorial (July 1) argues that even if Hong Kong's Chinese rulers will dwell on the evils of colonialism, a decent respect for truth "requires an acknowledgment that Britain's legacy also includes Hong Kong's yearning for democracy and its material prosperity." A story praises "Britannia's indelible mark" (June 29), quoting sources to say that colonialism brings "important benefits." Western media largely give prominence to Governor Chris Patten's (1997) rhetoric that Hong Kong is "an astonishing Chinese success story with British characteristics." Prince Charles summarizes British legacy this way: "Britain is part of Hong Kong's history and Hong Kong is part of Britain's history. We are also a part of each other's future" (*Chicago Tribune*, June 30). Few if any British or U.S. journalists have noted Britain's antidemocratic record in the colony, especially in the background of "the crude bluster regularly emanating from Beijing" (Chinoy, 1999: 397). Historian Maurice Meisner (*Los Angeles Times*, June 29) takes a rare exception by noting that all modern Chinese leaders have wanted to abolish colonial rule, but it was Churchill who opposed Roosevelt's support of Chiang Kai-shek to reclaim Hong Kong.

There is a strong media suggestion that "the whole world is watching" over China, an icon imported from the civil rights movement of the 1960s to imply putting international pressure on that authoritarian regime. The *Los Angeles Times* (June 23) quotes Christopher Cox, a member of the U.S. congressional delegation to the handover ceremony, and German Chancellor Helmut Kohl to that effect. A letter to the editor from a Taiwanese American (July 17) echoes the same sentiment. Even President Clinton vows to "keep a close watch" over Hong Kong's freedom (*Washington Post*, June 15).

The *Washington Post* doubts that "authoritarian China" can succeed in using Hong Kong as a model to bring "democratic Taiwan" back into its fold.

An editorial (July 1) argues that Taiwan is not a colony, as was Hong Kong, but a democratic polity entitled to decide its own future. Another story (June 27) reports that Taiwanese greet news about Hong Kong's handover with such apathy, ambivalence, or outright hostility that television ratings are consistently low. To counter Beijing's "one country, two systems" policy, Taiwan officially appeals to international media for sympathy by advocating "one country, one system—the better system," a reference to its own democratic reform.

Besides Taiwan, an assortment of countries or entities—ranging from Tibet, Vietnam, India, to Singapore—are implicated. Thus, international politicians and media fight an ideological battle in the site of Hong Kong on the occasion of its sovereignty transfer. Citing China's violation of agreements with Tibet, a consultant to Refugees International implores the free world to keep a "vigilant watch on Hong Kong" (July 2). Like CBS, the *Washington Post* compares the Hong Kong handover to Communist North Vietnam's takeover of the capitalist South, although the latter was a forced wedding after a long and bloody civil war (June 29). In reference to the Indian independence, Jim Mann of the *Los Angeles Times* (July 2) evokes the image of Nehru's famous speech: "At the stroke of the midnight hour, when the world sleeps, India will awake to life and freedom." Mann says that Hong Kong is already full of life, but its freedom "remains the big question mark." Having praised Nehru, Mann needles the wooden President Jiang, noting that his cliché-laden speech is not something to be remembered.

Next to the Tiananmen crackdown, Singapore and its authoritarian patriarch, Lee Kuan Yew, emerge as favorite media referents. First, Singapore's *Straits Times*, toeing the official line, reprimands "the British nation's surrogate mourner (in Hong Kong)—the western media, human rights lobbyists and crusading politicians in Washington and parts of the European Union." It claims that China "will no doubt again thwart the ill-wish of its detractors in the months and years ahead" (quoted by *New York Times*, July 3). The *New York Times* notes editorially Chief Executive Tung's fondness of Singapore's authoritarian system (June 29). Tung's praise of the Singaporean model in an interview with CNN is deemed as "wholly out of touch with Hong Kong's freewheeling reality" (Chinoy, 1999: 396). Kristof brings up Singapore twice in the same *New York Times* story (June 25) as a negative example of viewing press freedom as a luxury, not necessity. Richburg reports in the *Washington Post* (June 30) that Tung has appointed pro-China politicians, several of whom had been pro-British, to his advisory Executive Council, which "closely resembles the island-city state of Singapore, a place where political debate is muted, where government is authoritarian and paternalistic but efficient." The *Los Angeles Times* (June 28) opines that Beijing and Hong Kong's new leaders, drawn from the business elite, see Singapore as a model for different reasons. Finally, Governor Patten gets a lot of media mileage out of lashing back at Lee

Kuan Yew, his critic, as an "eloquent advocate of authoritarian government" not necessarily Asian or Confucian. He retorts: "Why do we assume that Lee Kuan Yew is the embodiment of Asian values rather than Aung San Suu Kyi or Martin Lee?" (*Washington Post*, June 25).

Erosion of Democracy and Freedom

The new Cold War is translated locally into struggles over the erosion of fragile democracy and freedoms. Reversing Britain's antidemocratic record in Hong Kong for 150 years, Governor Patten implemented the last-minute electoral reform in 1995 as a British legacy and as a preemptive measure against Communist abuse of power. While Beijing denounced him as a "sinner of the millennium" (Dimbleby, 1997), Bernard Shaw of CNN describes his farewell as "the protector of Hong Kong's fragile democracy sailing into the dark." As a *New York Times* editorial (July 1) declares, "By *habit* and *ideology*, Beijing is quite capable of quashing freedom in Hong Kong" (emphases added). The new regime is dissolving the assembly of elected legislators, supplanted by a "Beijing-handpicked" "puppet" (*Washington Post* editorial, June 24). A *New York Times* editorial (June 29) praises Secretary of State Albright's decision to skip the inaugural session of Hong Kong's provisional legislature as "rightly snubbing an undemocratic body appointed by Chinese leaders." It also proclaims that democracy supporters "may be harassed by the authorities if they stage demonstrations in the days ahead"—a scenario that did not materialize.

Many U.S. print journalists had requested interviews with Tung for weeks to no avail, although he did talk to CBS and CNN. Bernard Shaw asks Tung bluntly: "Are you a puppet of Beijing?" By and large, U.S. journalists are sympathetic to the outgoing governor, who rails against Hong Kong's business elite for switch of allegiance to Beijing. The *New York Times* writes that most wealthy executives "managed to secure U.S., British or Canadian passports as escape hatches before undertaking their pro-China proselytizing." These executives tell reporters not to pay attention to the "negative" democratic advocate, Martin Lee. The *Washington Post* also identifies prominent leaders who have given up British passports or knighthood (June 29) to pursue an award being created by Tung (June 30). If Tung is portrayed as a shipping tycoon with Beijing's backing, Martin Lee is hailed as democracy's hero. Lee recounts in the *Wall Street Journal* (June 30) how freedom brought his parents and their generation as refugees from the mainland to create Hong Kong's economic success, vowing that his generation should continue to fight for freedom. As a media icon, Lee knows that "the foreign press expected something will happen," and his speechwriter thinks it is a "good sell" for Lee to be packaged by foreign journalists as anti-China (Knight and Nakano, 1999: 43). But Lee always prefaces his public speech by claiming to be "proud to be Chinese, more proud than ever before."

Most western journalists have liberal access to the democrats being ousted from the provisional legislature. But in what seems typical of journalistic search for formal balance, the *New York Times* also interviews two pro-China legislators in an otherwise critical story (June 15): David Chu, a "positively ebullient" real-estate developer who claims that nothing will have changed; and Allen Lee, a Liberal Party leader harshly criticized by Patten for switching allegiance to Beijing (Dimbleby, 1997), who claims that the handover is "not the end of democracy." The *Washington Post* (June 29) also quotes a local police inspector, as an obligatory antidote to show journalistic objectivity, as saying, "We don't want to switch our loyalty and cannot serve the Communist government of China."

The "rolling in" (CNN) or "pouring in" of the "much feared" (CBS) People's Liberation Army is widely regarded "with trepidation" and "gives many people jitters" (*New York Times*). To CNN's Chinoy (1999: 400), "the imagery of military occupation, added to the weight of the Tiananmen history, was not . . . a particularly good omen for the new, postcolonial Hong Kong." A *Washington Post* editorial (July 1) criticizes that the PLA "makes something of a spectacle of itself, arriving at a time and in places where local residents and millions of watchers worldwide cannot fail to draw some unpleasant conclusions." On June 27, Bob Simon of CBS reports that the British "are going off with music" and the Chinese "are coming in by tanks." On June 30, CBS News once again calls up the images of the Tiananmen crackdown:

> Dan Rather: After 156 years of colonial rule that created the wealthiest city in the world . . . (Turning to Bob Simon, who was standing by and facing the camera.) First of all, let's talk about the army. I think the whole world is talking about that . . . 4,000 troops, armored personnel carriers. You're in Hong Kong now, folks are pretty saddened about that?
>
> Bob Simon: Yes, it is very sad. It brings back memories. For the folks here, the PLA means the Tiananmen Square. On June 4 in 1989, right after the massacre in Tiananmen Square, one million people took to the street here. That's one in six people in Hong Kong.

On the handover night of June 30, Rather introduces a "festive celebration" in Tiananmen Square and continues: "This is how the pro-democracy movement started in April, eight years ago." He reports, "Near dawn, a truckload of troops arrived (in Hong Kong). None of the soldiers appeared to be armed." The image is nonetheless cut to show the scene of June 4, 1989, in Tiananmen Square with soldiers holding rifles and firing in the background. The unsaid message, more powerful than said, suggests that Tiananmen II is possible in Hong Kong. Situating the image within such a political context, the media could "disseminate bias without serious reservations or opposition" (Said, 1981: 45).

Both CBS and CNN allude to the historical irony—and Patten's favorite rhetoric—that Hong Kong is the only decolonized place with less freedom and democracy (Patten, 1997). Patrick Tyler writes in the *New York Times* that Beijing may crush a "base of subversion" for about 100 mainland dissidents who were smuggled into Hong Kong after the Tiananmen crackdown with the help of the underground Operation Yellowbird (June 22). The *Washington Post* quotes the popular Chief Secretary Anson Chan as saying, "Minding our own business is the best guarantee of our autonomy" because China will clamp down hard "if it suspects we are allowing Hong Kong to be used as a base for subversive activities" (June 23). In retrospect, this scenario was born in a broadly anxious mood under Beijing's pre-handover bluster, which became so punishing that the colonial administration advised the dissidents to leave before July 1. In reality, as soon as the PLA entered into Hong Kong, the mood changed overnight: it retired to barracks not to be seen in public. Scenes of some crowds greeting the PLA along its parade route must have confounded journalists who had expected an explosive protest to occur.

Erosion of press freedom is forecast with frequency.[5] In a typical article (*New York Times*, June 25) Kristof predicts that China's critics will have "a major confrontation in the next few years with Communist hardliners who never met a publication that they did not like to censor." Beijing may exert pocketbook pressure on such outlets as Dow Jones and Reuters, he warns, and put Hong Kong's role as an information hub for all of Asia at risk. The *Wall Street Journal* reports that major media in Hong Kong "bend even before the winds starts to blow." Contradicting the "officially optimistic" mood, both papers (*Wall Street Journal* editorial, June 26, and *New York Times*, June 25) quote polls to show that 50 percent of the public and 86 percent of business executives fear the loss of freedom under Chinese rule. In a different story, however, Faison (*New York Times*, June 30) notes that "even at this climatic turning point in Hong Kong history, the bulk of newspaper fare consists of tales of robbery, sexual harassment and bizarre moments of human tragedy."

Trojan Horse

While it is common to see Hong Kong as the recipient of abuse and negative influence from China, the U.S. media also invoke a complementary frame—deriving from the famous Greek "Trojan Horse" mythology—to suggest that Hong Kong will be a harbinger of economic, even political, change for China. The media celebrate the myths of Hong Kong's continuing economic boom, replete with visual charts of the soaring Hang Seng Index and Red Chips Index (the PRC stocks sold in Hong Kong)—without, of course, expecting the subsequent Asian financial crisis to wreck them. As the *New York Times* reports, virtually none of the even most optimistic forecasters "foresaw this almost raucously bullish sentiment on the eve of such a precarious historical moment" (June 25). Characterizing Hong Kong as "the tail that wags the dragon," it states that 13 years of transition have made it China's money capital (June 27). Accompanying the article is a photo juxtaposing the Bank of China tower with the Hong Kong Club, as if to show a convergence of new money and old power in Hong Kong's capitalist way.

Kristof states: "The central question is whether Hong Kong amounts to a colossal Trojan horse: a prize so glorious that China's Communists cannot leave it outside the gates but which, once inside, will destroy those in power" (*New York Times*, July 1). He mentions Sun Yatsen, the founder of the Republic of China, as someone who had been inspired by British achievements in Hong Kong. He quotes a local columnist in comparing Hong Kong to a bran tablet: "These things are small and inoffensive as you take them, but they kind of invisibly expand in your stomach when they are in there, and have a beneficial effect." Red star over Hong Kong, it is concluded, may be the end of Maoism. Foreign affairs columnist Friedman writes on July 1, "Auld Lang Syne," accompanied by a drawing that depicts Hong Kong as the head of a dragon that is China. Drawing on the metaphors of speed and weight, he suggests that while China is big, old, and heavy, Hong Kong is young, light, and mature in the age of information technology. China is the past, and Hong Kong is the future of China "when it grows up."

Margaret Thatcher claims that a future generation will "look back on the ceremonies of June 30 not so much as marking the end of Hong Kong's colonial past, but as marking a new impulse toward freedom and democracy in China and the rest of Asia" (*Washington Post*, June 27). In responding to a question posed by CNN's Bernard Shaw, she emphatically stresses that the Hong Kong fever will spread across China. As "an example and a flagship of what Chinese can accomplish," she says, Hong Kong is "a small crystal ball for a big solution." Another article by Peter Stein (July 1) in the *Wall Street Journal* illustrates that Hong Kong's tycoons now bet their future on China's big market. Similarly, the *Washington Post* quotes a local tycoon who builds highways and hotels in China as saying that although the difference between the development in Hong Kong and China is "like France and Bulgaria," it might be more like "France and Spain" in 50 years (June 15).

Soft News and "Local" Perspective

Having examined the four ideological packages, we would like to pursue two more theoretical issues. First, in the inferential process, the "soft" news—be it light-hearted anecdotes, historical episodes, or the "mood" pieces—is likely to be as ideological as the "hard" news. Even a frivolous topic may well disguise the serious ideology embedded in it. Second, as we have argued, the "local" perspective in the age of globalization is likely to reproduce the "national" perspective. "Local" may not be subnational; in foreign news, local is national. Local differences either do not exist or are suppressed.

American journalists are committed to facts, but facts "lack a framework of theory or ideology from which to deduce evidence or infer explanations" (Carey, 1986: 167). Journalists can establish causes, consequences, and motives often through intuitively and spontaneously weaving selected facts, words, and images together. Generality is inferred from facts; personal tales build up a large claim about the contour of collective fate. These mediated realities are not as important to be demonstrably true as they are presented to be believable and offer "dramatic proof of one's expectations" (Nimmo and Combs, 1990: 9). Insofar as their stories conform to cultural expectations, journalists seem at liberty to impute causes and consequences without fear of challenge. For example, media spectacles prize on stories of conflict resolution with "good guys" beating "bad guys." A real conflict satisfies the elements of a melodrama: the actors, acts, a scenario, crescendos, and motives; in the absence of a real conflict, a contrived one can be staged. All U.S. elite newspapers have made all sorts of sharp constrasts in life experiences to make the basic point that many refugees have made it in Hong Kong compared with their relatives left behind in China. There are many similar stories of different permutations to portray that a "good Hong Kong" is being beaten by a "bad China." By so doing, they ignore contradictory stories and make all sorts of inferential leaps; their selection of interviewees is intuitive, unexplained, yet assumed to be "typical."

Even as benign and exotic as fortune-telling—a favorite western media topic—deserves scrutiny for its rich ideological meaning. Take for example a story by Faison in the *New York Times*, "Any Omens? Colony's Soothsayers Won't Say" (June 23). He starts by saying that Hong Kong people go to fortune-tellers because their future "remains firmly in the realm of the unknowable." With an ironical twist, even the fortune-teller cannot tell the future of Hong Kong. Although China bans fortune-telling stalls, nightclubs, and racetracks, he says that few fear such a crackdown after the handover, but he then launches into possible loss of civil liberties. Fortune-tellers say that many of their customers are visiting midlevel Communist Party officials who no longer believe in the system, and most vocally optimistic people in Hong Kong are not working-class people, but wealthy business people. Fortune-telling thus foregrounds media distrust of the new sovereign. Fortune-tellers are certified as critics of China with an aura of credibility usually vested in highly placed sources. This cutely written story is a classical example of "displacing the reality with a 'plausible explanation' of the reporter's own" (Said, 1981: 110).

Furthermore, journalists amalgamate the formally homologous (sometimes only ambiguously related) events or issues into a paradigmatic framework to build a narrative flow or to achieve thematic unity. News invariably evokes the past, the present, and the future, for it selectively implies "some of the probable causes, relevant contexts and possible consequences of the reported events" (van Ginneken, 1998: 110). In the process of news domestication, journalists "refigure cultural scripts" (Bennett and Lawrence, 1995) and reaffirm the core values with their public and sources. On July 4, Independence Day, a *Los Angeles Times* editorial says that the British handover of Hong Kong is at least "a voluntary, long-planned and bloodless passing of power," whereas the American Revolution, the first of British jewels wrenched away, was violent. "After July 4, 1776, there was no going back," the editorial claims, "In time, the dominoes toppled." In this cultural script, Hong Kong is not incidental to the commemoration of a highly mythologized Fourth of July, but—standing at the end of the line of steady British decline— a descendant of the American Revolution. Likewise, CBS uses the handover of Hong Kong as a "feeling good" factor for celebrating American democracy on Independence Day.[6] Thus the separately selected episodes of Britain's, America's, and Hong Kong's past are now coherently congealed into a grand historical narrative.

In some cases the internal connection between cases or events is tenuous or cursory. Typical is a story in the *New York Times*: even Bermuda gets into the act because, with Hong Kong gone, it is the largest in what little is left of the British Empire. Another story (July 1) says that Britons "find stronger reason for national pride in the current success of their tennis players at Wimbledon and rugby team in South Africa than for nostalgia over their imperial past." It proceeds to quote the *Daily Telegraph* as saying that British conquerors "benefited mankind." Hong Kong, mixed with sports, is nothing more than a ploy for rehashing British glory!

In other cases, this discursive practice of amalgamating does less to illuminate this internal tie than to reveal the interpreter's cultural framework. Typical is Karl Meyer's essay in the "Editorial Notebook" of the *New York Times* (June 28). He writes about Warren Delano, an ashamed American opium trader in China who returned to the United States and married his daughter to the father of Franklin D. Roosevelt. According to Meyer, the Opium War was denounced in British Parliament, and the same outrage was expressed in the pulpit and the press in America and England. Based on this experience, Meyer writes, Americans pulled out of the opium trade. He concludes: "It is precisely this conviction that underlies efforts to attach human rights condition to trading relations—to temper the amorality of the market—a point that, alas, seems to elude the Socialist soon-to-be masters of Hong Kong." Delano is not only of considerable historical interest but also of contemporary relevance as a precursor to western morality. In this perverted historical script, western opium traders have set themselves morally right, while China, the victim of the opium trade, has clung to the "amorality of the market." Journalism indeed becomes self-fulfilling prophecy when "opinion is metamorphosed into reality" (Said, 1981: 108). The nineteenth-century Chinese dynasty and the current Communist regime become an intermingled entity, historically invariant and temporally contiguous. How western opium traders became enlightened defenders of human rights is undisclosed.

Finally, we come to the point about the "local" perspective. Hallin and Gitlin (1993) argue that war coverage is a ritual of consolidating the community unity. Alexander and Jacobs (1998) similarly observe that media ritual, especially created by television, helps to sustain shared beliefs and a common cultural framework essential to the fostering of collective identities and solidarities. This kind of media ritual draws on cultural frames defined by the power establishment (Curran and Liebes, 1998: 6). We contend that the "local" perspective is mostly derivative of the *national* narrative on international issues. We checked the *Des Moines Register* and the *St. Louis Post-Dispatch*, only to find them relying heavily on the AP wire stories. The *Chicago Tribune* and the *San Jose Mercury News*, each sending correspondents to Hong Kong, do not differ ideologically from such quasi-national outlets as the *New York Times* and the *Wall Street Journal*.

The *Chicago Tribune*, like most local newspapers, looks for the "Chicago connection." Correspondent Liz Sly points to the gleaming Convention Center, "perhaps an appropriate commentary on Hong Kong's hopes for the future," as a product of partnership between a Chicago firm and a Hong Kong firm (June 29). With that architectural icon she surmises that the 1,000 U.S. companies (including 90 from Illinois, of which she singles out Caterpillar) based there remain stubbornly optimistic. Moreover, on July 1, a reporter writes about three Chicagoans of Chinese descent who bought tickets to watch Hong Kong "before it changed." The story is headlined, "For many, scene is well worth the ticket." The "many" in the headline actually refers to three people in the text. As expected, the paper reports about Chicago's Chinese community greeting the handover with pride and anxiety.

A sharper example comes from comparing the national network, CBS, with its affiliate, Channel 9 "Eyewitness News" advertised as "the most watched news" in the Washington, D.C., area. CBS sees the Hong Kong handover as a quasi-ideological war, albeit of elusive nature, that serves to renew the dominant consensus, whereas local media habitually create personal and geographical immediacy by sourcing laypersons from hometown who happen to be on or near the spot, no matter how little light they may have to throw. At noon on July 1, Channel 9 has been showing network feed depicting a sequence of ceremony activities. Then the local anchors cut in. They phone Lisa Spivey, the publisher of *American Technology*, who is at a hotel on the Kowloon side just across the Victoria Harbor and the Convention Center. The anchors field a series of six personalized and predictable questions, hardly deviating from the network's stereotypical frames:

- What do you see from where you are?
- How much concern is expressed about the presence of Chinese troops?
- Do businesses feel they will be back to business or (there will be) any changes?
- Do you expect to see things going back to normal tomorrow?
- I have to ask you personally: What does it mean to witness all this?
- Just want to know: Do you see any sign of protest?

Having finished the interview, the female anchor expresses awe at the "very impressive color and lights" and comments on "very interesting look on his (Prince Charles's) face." Apparently needing a crash course, she mentions that Prince Charles "wishes the *province* success in its transition" and that "the jewel is back to the *crown* of the People's Republic of China." With that remark, "now we turn to a very tragic story: drive-by shooting of a boy," followed by news about Mike Tyson biting off his opponent's ear. National and local news agendas converge, not diverge. This personalized interview, trivially enveloped in the conventional anti-Communist frame, is a "strategic ritual" (Tuchman, 1978) aiming to objectify the reality and to create a pseudosense of realism and intimacy.

Conclusion

Banging the democracy drum is an American tradition. In 1845 John O'Sullivan (1976) coined the phrase "manifest destiny" to define the spirit of American expansionism and to promote and justify the spread of democracy across the North American continent, especially with regard to the annexation of Texas, and later, Oregon. American and other western Christian proselytism in China was more than a religious movement but played a central role in the expansion of the West and the regeneration of China (Barnet and Fairbank, 1985). This chapter clearly shows that that U.S. media coverage of the handover reveals as much about Hong Kong's plight as about America's "manifest destiny." Throughout the 1990s, in the wake of the Tiananmen crackdown, there has been a prevailing mood of gloom and doom in Hong Kong, as reinforced by Sino-British rows, China's incessant threats, and Governor Patten's rhetorical eloquence (Patten, 1997). This ideological canon proves to have strong staying power on *Fortune* magazine, among others, which had prognosticated the death of Hong Kong months ahead of the handover.

As the only superpower left in the post-Cold War world, the United States and its media pay so much attention to the handover not simply because of their burning interest in this little island. Rather, the United States steps into Hong Kong as the chief voice of the West. Giving away Britain's last and most prosperous colony to the world's remaining socialist giant, albeit as its special capitalist region, is viewed as an assault on western-cum-universal values. The U.S. media rally around and behind the star-spangled banner to bang the democracy drum. They frame the event in terms of the U.S.'s self-perceived role as a "new guardian" in the context of another emerging Cold War, which is marked not only by an imminent erosion of freedom and democracy in Hong Kong under China's pressure but also by an eventual victory of Hong Kong's capitalist democracy over China's socialist authoritarianism. In an interview (May 6) with the *Los Angeles Times* columnist, Tom Plate, Chief Executive Tung implies that his job could become impossible if the United States and China constantly are at each other's throats. He argues that there are no truly major strategic fault lines between the two countries, and deplores how the West views China through CNN broadcasts from Tiananmen Square on June 4, 1989. He claims that the changes in China are so astounding that the Tiananmen massacre will not happen again.

The U.S. media privilege the frames of democray and freedom over others by drawing on elite consensus and cultural assumptions as articulated by national foreign policy. Thanks to ideological consonance, these frames seem to be naturalized by journalists—even in the face of what seem to be contradicting evidence—without meeting critical challenge from the (un)informed public. The universal validity of U.S. media ideology, unless compared against alternative national media narratives, is generally to be assumed and untempered. Media not only renew national consensus and the dominant values but also reinforce the foreign policy. We have demonstrated that the state, especially its foreign policy, remains central to defining international news, despite various postulations about "global modernity" (Tomlinson, 1999) or about the decline of the nation-state vis-à-vis international and local entities (Braman and Sreberny-Mohammadi, 1996; Featherstone and Lash, 1995; Waters, 1995). For the U.S. media rhetoric at least, also in contrast to Hallin's (1994) claims, the Cold War logic and metaphors seem very much alive and overwhelming. We find little ideological difference among various U.S. media, although television may have played a cruder and more naked role. Journalists have the reputation of being cynics, but in the deep structure of things, their worldview is unmistakably American.

In retrospect, the media may have covered a heightened pseudo-event, much ado about nothing. For various reasons, the handover turns out to be not as bad as anticipated. Under such circumstances journalists only have so many ways to outwit their competitors. Even if they only talk to the same slate of 20 to 50 people and to other journalists, they still have to give their stories "sweeping," but in many ways reductive, interpretations. By no means is the ideological contestation less intense. When the event refutes their hypotheses, journalists must do something to save the integrity of their news paradigmatic structure (Bennett et al., 1985; Chan and Lee, 1991). The U.S. media resort to "hyping up" (Aronson, 1983) their stories through staging the conflicts, amalgamating homologous events, localizing the news significance, and fixing visual presentation. The media ritual thus created does not result in radical abandonment of the original ideological tenets, but produces latent consolidation of them in different guises. Even the most lighthearted accounts are ideologically loaded—some subtle but many blatant.

Finally, the audience seems indifferent to foreign stories of this magnitude that are not unexpected occurrences within their ideological expectations, despite the media's best hyping efforts. Hong Kong news has quickly faded out of the radar screen of the U.S. media, which have moved on to look for other wrongs to be righted. Short of major calamities, it will be difficult to keep Hong Kong news alive, which has lost its unique identity and will be treated as part of the larger China story. For good or for bad, the transfer of sovereignty will prove to be the peak of world-media attention showered on Hong Kong.

Chapter 6

Essentializing Colonialism: Heroes and Villains

We provided the scaffolding that enabled the people of Hong Kong to ascend: the rule of law, clean and light-handed government, the values of a free society, the beginnings of a representative government and democratic accountability. This is a Chinese city, a very Chinese city with British characteristics.

> —Chris Patten, the last governor of Hong Kong, July 30, 1997

I feel like a child who has grown up under the care of a foster mother, but now it is time to reunite with my natural mother. I treasure the warmth I feel in the arms of my foster mother and worry my natural mother is a fierce woman. I feel anxious.

> —A Hong Kong citizen, *South China Morning Post*, June 20, 1997

History has demonstrated unequivocally that without the Chinese Communist Party, there would be no socialist new China, and there would be no smooth return of Hong Kong.

> —The *People's Daily*, editorial, June 30, 1997

"To thank the Opium War" is not an appropriate way of saying it, but to say thank you for what colonial rule has brought to Hong Kong would be consistent with the facts.

> —Lee Yee, a columnist, June 30, 1997

Great Britain lost its first colony with the American Revolution in 1776 and may have lost its empire with India's independence in 1947. Even so, turning over the "capitalist jewel" of Hong Kong (as the media call it) to Communist China in 1997—eight years after the crumbling of the Berlin Wall—symbolizes the end of global colonialism. If India's independence marked the beginning of dismemberment of the British Empire, by the time Britain bids farewell to Hong Kong, its world hegemony had already long receded. All Britain could do was to reminisce about its past glory and to grumble about the likely Chinese abuse, but it was totally powerless to sway the contour of history. It is significant to note that while Indians ousted the British with vehemence, Hong Kong people wistfully implore the British to stay, only to be repulsed by the PRC, whose rise on the international stage has been met with the West's consternation. Amidst the ending of the Cold War, the struggle over the closing of British colonial rule in Hong Kong is a center of global ideological theatre for almost two decades.

Under colonial domination, as Osterhammel (1997: 16–17) writes, the fundamental decisions affecting the lives of the indigenous people are made and implemented by a minority of foreign invaders, who convince themselves to have "ordained mandate to rule" and to pursue "interests that are often defined in a distant metropolis." Fanon (1968) characterizes colonialism as exploitation, manipulation, suppression, mistrust, racism, deceit, and imposition—definitely antithetical to the now universally accepted democratic values. The ugly arrogance of old British colonial officials and their discriminatory practices in Hong Kong was vividly caricatured by such renowned Chinese writers as Lu Xun. On the other hand, what the British managed to achieve in Hong Kong was said to have fathered Sun Yatsen's revolutionary thought that led to the toppling of the corrupt Manchu dynasty in 1911. Since 1949 Hong Kong has been a source of ideological construction as a "beacon of freedom" at the door of the "Iron Curtain" or as a symbol of colonial oppression against a people's revolution. Is British colonialism in Hong Kong markedly different from the characteristics of classical colonialism? Has British rule been continuously evil, inhuman, and ruthless for 150 years, or has it become "kinder and gentler" in its latest stages? What does "the end of Hong Kong" imply to China and to Britain? History is a Rorschach test. Picking certain aspects for selective emphasis at the expense or to the exclusion of other equally salient aspects is an inherently ideological process. We shall show in this chapter that as the PRC media seek to essentialize colonialism as something inherently evil, the British media seek to de-essentialize it as something that may bear positive results. Hong Kong media, however, find themselves caught in split loyalty and identity.

Like any form of foundationalism or fundamentalism, essentialism is a process by which the rich, complex, and even contradictory dimensions of a people replete with culture and history get reduced to certain oversimplified, innate, natural, or immutable properties (Said, 1993). These "fundamental" properties serve to "define what something is, and without which it could not be what it is" (Edgar and Sedgwick, 1999: 131). With this "something" so crudely defined, however, the interpreter tends to ignore the concrete processes of change, struggles, discontinuities, and internal contradictions. He or she may secure a discursive or ideological closure by freezing "the fluidity of meaning" (Hall, 1997: 245). The contemporary cultural politics has, for example, focused on the hegemonic implications of essentializing gender to sex and ethnicity to race. If gender is reduced to sex, a fluid discourse becomes a sterile concept:

the social processes of shaping the gender role are made irrelevant to (or buried under) the "constant and dichotomous," biologically defined sexual categories (Howard and Hollander, 1997: 28). To the extent that the difference between men and women is seen as "natural"—an act of God—then there is nothing that we can do about this difference because it is "beyond history, permanent and fixed" (Hall, 1997: 245). Nor is it desirable to tamper with "nature." Therefore, gender inequity gets perpetuated. Likewise, the concept of ethnicity—created through human action, and open socially and ideologically to multiple interpretations—should not be reduced to that of "fixed and inherent" race (Hall, 1996a, 1996b, 1997).

Essentialization stereotypes, naturalizes, and fixes the difference of others to a few simplified characteristics: American exceptionalism, British civilization, Japanese industrialism, German ingenuity, or Chinese (Confucian) harmony. A moment's reflection would prompt us to ask: How does the Confucian philosophical musing reconcile with the historical reality of the Cultural Revolution? This act of essentialization is crucial in international discursive contestation. Various discursive contestants decide on whether or how to essentialize a certain issue or symbol according to their situational needs and interests at stake. This process does not necessarily call for distortion of facts, but for selective accentuation or interpretation of them, thus is highly dependent on "who the interpreter is, who he or she is addressing, what his or her purpose is in interpreting, at what historical moment the interpretation takes place" (Said, 1981: 154). This process signifies "otherness," constructs exclusion, and tends to gloss over the internal difference within a group.

Edward Said (1978, 1993) documents in his seminal work how the oriental discourses have historically been orientalized *in* and *for* the West. The varied life of the billions of Islamic people scattered across various states, societies, histories, geographies, and cultures has been reduced to "one simple thing" by western media (Said, 1981: x). The Orient is essentialized "for" the West in that it is a shorthanded approach to otherness that often serves to legitimate the internal order and enhance the identity of the self. This otherizing process has more to do with the West than with the Orient. As Stuart Hall (1997: 258) puts it, essentialization enables the "bonding together of all of Us who are 'normal' into one 'imagined community,'" and "sends into symbolic exile all of Them—'the Others'—who are in some way different—'beyond the pale.'" For this reason, in the realm of international news, internal differences of a national perspective are usually insignificant by comparison to the differences between national perspectives. The media in Taiwan and South Korea have "otherized" China and North Korea to achieve internal cohesion against the Communists (Chung, 2000). British colonialism in Hong Kong, as this chapter will show, also is a living concept subject to social construction and reconstruction for ideological advantages.

Colonialism implies, according to Osterhammel (1997: 4), (a) "coloniza-tion" as a *process* of territorial acquisition, (b) "colony" as a particular type of sociopolitical *organization*, and (c) "colonialism" as a *system* of domina-tion. Domination is at the heart of a colonial relationship. The colonized peo-ple, often non-Europeans, were subject to unequal relationship imposed by their conquerors, often Europeans, with the installation of an undemocratic and exploitative mode of social organization. Colonialism assumes that the dependent and immature non-Europeans stand in need of guidance from the more civilized Europeans (Osterhammel, 1997; Said, 1993), who are given a universal and historical mission of messianic liberation. The British pushed this point to its fullest by permeating the feelings of "imperial nostalgia" in official and media discourses and by drawing a sharp comparison between the "advanced Hong Kong" and the "backward China" (Patten, 1997). This nar-rative was nothing but repugnant and racist to the PRC. British discourses seem to agree with Marshall (1996: 370) that the origins or intentions of colo-nial rule are not as significant as its (supposedly positive) consequences. Both China and Britain have brushed aside the issue of representation of Hong Kong people, who had no say over their own future and could do nothing but accept the fait accompli negotiated on their behalf by the two hostile sover-eigns (Chan and Lee, 1991).

Journalists Coming to Town

As many as 63 British media outlets and 688 journalists come to cover the handover of Hong Kong. For our study, the British sample includes BBC, ITV, the *Times*, the *Guardian*, the *Daily Telegraph*, and the *Financial Times*. All of them have Hong Kong news bureaus, which started their planning process one or even two years before the handover was to take place. They started filing sto-ries about various aspects of Hong Kong months before the handover and steadily increased their frequency as time neared, leading up to one page per day for newspapers in the week prior to July 1. Television ran documentaries or special series on a prescheduled basis. While the local bureaus provide main news contact and set the news agenda, their home offices also send in major re-porters as reinforcements to meet the journalistic competition.

Logistics—ranging from the satellite feed, the camera, the wires, to the crews—can be a journalistic and technical nightmare for television news, all requiring massive investment in equipment and human power. The BBC's huge operation that rivals the Gulf War coverage and surpassed the coverage of South Africa's 1994 election courts criticisms of overkill from some mem-bers of the British Parliament. To that charge, a BBC spokesman retorts: "This is an historical milestone and we feel it is entirely appropriate that the

BBC should cover it fully, both from a news-value point of view and under our public service remit" (*Times*, June 28).

The PRC authorities orchestrate a massive media mobilization to stage a "national event" of nationalism (chapter 7). For the Hong Kong media, the handover story started long before the conclusion of the Sino-British Joint Declaration in 1984 and had lived through eruption of conflicts between China and Britain since then (Chan and Lee, 1991; Lee, 2000a). Despite the handover fatigue, the media compare this event to a war mission. TVB alone commits 400 people. A total of 2,816 journalists representing 106 media outlets are registered to cover the story.

The Chinese Media: Essentializing Colonialism

British colonialism is often thought to have started in 1497 when John Cabot claimed "the New Found Land" for Henry VII (Marshall, 1996). At its height, before the Second World War, the British Empire covered territories ranging from Africa, Canada, South America to Australia and Asia. The empire virtually terminated in the late 1960s, with its ties to the colonies cut off during the war and with Britain's will and ability to rule the global reach considerably weakened after it (Darwin, 1988; Fieldhouse, 1966). The decline of the old British and French empires took place against the backdrop of the rise of the United States and the Soviet Union as superpowers and of the general decolonization process under the auspices of the Untied Nations.

Hong Kong, which China ceded in 1842 after losing the Opium War, was one of the last colonial acquisitions by the British Empire. For Chinese, the loss of Hong Kong, which spearheaded 150 years of national humiliation at the hands of western powers, has been (some say forever) scarred in history books as a "national shame." Having overturned the Manchurians in 1911, the Republic of China started to make claims on sovereignty over Hong Kong. While China succeeded in forfeiting most of foreign-held territories, concessions, spheres of interest, and extraterritorial rights in the late 1920s and 1930s, Hong Kong remained firmly in the British grip (Lane, 1990). After the Second World War, President Franklin Roosevelt supported Chiang Kai-shek in his attempt to recover sovereignty over Hong Kong, only to be aborted by opposition from British Prime Minister Winston Churchill.

Mao's rise to power touched off an acrimonious debate over "who lost China" in the United States. Sir Alexander Gratham, Governor of Hong Kong, said in a 1954 speech that Communist China was the most likely source of invasion, yet the "barbarous Communism" could not conquer civilized China. The Communists declared that they intended to reclaim Hong Kong *eventually*, but for pragmatic reasons they would maintain its colonial status quo *for a long while* (Chan, 1997; Jin, 1998). This was based on Mao's policy of "long-term calculation and full-scale utilization." In other words, the PRC was ideologically opposed to but economically compliant with the fact of Hong Kong as a British colony. A cross point city of strategic importance (a "bridgehead of the free world") in the Cold War, Hong Kong was a thorn in the eyes of the PRC, who prided itself on nationalism, patriotism, self-reliance, anti-imperialism, and support for national liberation movements in the Third World. In 1973 China asked the United Nations to remove Hong Kong and Macau from the list of the world's colonies and put them in "the category of questions resulting from the series of unequal treaties left over by history" (Lane, 1990). Facing international blockade, however, Beijing found itself absolutely having to rely on Hong Kong as a window to the outside world and as a source of trade and foreign exchange, to the point that Mao Zedong himself decided at several key junctures against removing British jurisdiction from the territory. In the 1960s the glaring division between China's high moral ground of anti-imperialism and its practical considerations of economic benefits came into Soviet lashings as "collaborating with British and American capital in Hong Kong" to exploit the working people (Lane, 1990: 65).[1] Even during a local riot in 1967 that erupted as a spin-off of China's radical Cultural Revolution, Beijing did not change the political status quo in Hong Kong. For this reason, Beijing refused to accept Portugal's offer to return Macau in 1974 after a leftist riot. (Macau was returned to China in 1999.)

By the 1970s and 1980s, Hong Kong began to be recognized as "by far the most lustrous jewel of the once-Imperial Crown's otherwise residual adornments," and one whose economic light outshone its nominal possessor's (Connell, 1998: 1). No sooner had China emerged from the ruins of the Cultural Revolution than Britain began to seek out Beijing to clarify the status of Hong Kong after the lease of the New Territories expired in 1997. Painful negotiations produced the Sino-British Joint Declaration of 1984, under which Hong Kong was to be absorbed by China as a capitalist special administration region in Deng Xiaoping's "one country, two systems" policy. From 1984 to 1997 both countries experienced rounds of diplomatic bouts; wars of words and insults became a daily media fare in the 1990s, when the British decided to undertake limited democratic reform in the final years. Polls, media accounts, and massive outflow of emigrants all pointed to a prevailing sense of doubt, distrust, and anxiety.

The handover narratives of the Chinese media tend to essentialize the evil and unjust British colonialism clothed in nineteenth-century imperialism. The media make preponderant references to the Opium War as an irascible icon of China's humiliated national psyche. Further, anticolonialism and anti-imperialism have been defined almost as synonymous with mobilizing Chinese nationalism and patriotism around the cause of national salvation. The PRC also acknowledges the weakness of the Qing dynasty for the loss of Hong Kong; this recognition exonerates the PRC from historical responsibilities and credits the Chinese Communist Party and Deng Xiaoping for righting the historical wrong (chapter 7). The media stop short of launching a full-scale attack on the present conditions of British colonial rule, for fear of contradicting China's policy of leaving Hong Kong's capitalism intact after the handover.

The Chinese media—quoting the authorities, or trying to provide a logic or argument in news and commentaries—often attribute Hong Kong's astonishing economic prosperity not to British rule, but to the hard work of the local Chinese (*People's Daily*, June 20) and the support of mainland China throughout all these years (*People's Daily*, June 3). CCTV produces features to show how the Chinese workers tried unselfishly to ensure that Hong Kong compatriots got their cheap water and food supplies from the motherland. These activities are not portrayed as business transactions but as supports out of national care, and the fact that Hong Kong provided the PRC with approximately 40 percent of its foreign exchanges is never mentioned. Whenever the PRC media stress the importance of maintaining the cherished social framework to protect Hong Kong's prosperity, they largely ignore the role of the British in establishing such legal and economic infrastructures.

In sum, by honoring the Chinese Communist Party and Deng Xiaoping for redeeming Hong Kong from British colonialists, the Chinese media have constructed a story and a history that are exclusive and reductive. In other words, they construct a totalistic narrative to tell a very partial history that has lost sight of at least five key points:

(a) The sovereignty reversion of Hong Kong is by no means as unique or unprecedented as the Chinese media have claimed. In view of the general and worldwide decolonization process, Hong Kong in fact stands as one of the last remaining colonies at the end of the twentieth century. It is particularly peculiar for a revolutionary Communist regime to tolerate the existence of a colony at its doorstep.

(b) A succession of Chinese leaders long before Deng had made failed attempts to reclaim Hong Kong. Instead of actively seeking to redress the colonial conditions in Hong Kong, the PRC's decision to "resume the assumption of sovereignty" (in official terms) over it was passively prompted by the expiration of the 99-year lease of the New Territories.

(c) Despite all the media's patriotic clamors, it should be not forgotten that Mao himself set the policy of preserving Hong Kong's colonial status quo in order to take advantage of its economic and political access. He did so even at the risk of Soviet ridicule.

(d)   Hong Kong people, more than half of whom are refugees from mainland China, reacted to the handover in an overwhelmingly negative fashion (Chan and Lee, 1991). Culturally proud but politically loath to be Chinese, they appreciated the British legacy and lacked confidence in the PRC to keep its promises. They did not want to kick the British out; nor do they want to welcome the Chinese in.

(e)   The Chinese media have not given due credit to Britain for establishing Hong Kong as the world's leading financial center with modern legal, bureaucratic, and commercial infrastructures. The PRC media credit Hong Kong's glistening success to the strong support of the motherland instead. Hong Kong did profit from being the switch point between China and the outside world and from the supply of cheap goods and labor from the mainland. The colony, however, has also had to bear the brunt of enormous pressure to keep pace with successive waves of mainland refugees in the provision of jobs, housing, and welfare in the past five decades.

The British Media: De-essentializing Colonialism

After the Second World War, Britain came to recognize that it no longer had the might or resources needed to maintain the global reach of its empire, and that the old conditions that favored colonialism had broken down. Nonetheless, if the process of decolonization was well managed, Britain could maintain its residual or extended politico-economic benefits in the former colonies. Hong Kong being the last leg of this decolonization process, Britain was predisposed to cooperate with China in the interest of securing a smooth transition. British interests in Hong Kong remain considerable: apart from more than 1,000 British corporations with billions of dollars operating in or from there, Hong Kong is Britain's gateway to Asia and China.

Equally important, Britain is determined to retreat from Hong Kong with honor and dignity. Retreat was not a defeat. Insofar as the colonial beginning was not justifiable, British officials and media prefer to concentrate on defining the positive legacies they left behind in Hong Kong against the deplorable record of the PRC. Governor Chris Patten is repeatedly quoted as lamenting that Hong Kong represents the first instance of decolonization in which the colony is to be handed over to a regime with much less freedom and democracy. Moreover, as frontline player in the western camp—and a staunch ally of the United States—in its attempt to contain Communism (Sanders, 1990),

Britain has defined its legacy as an integral part of the current geopolitics to advance its own interests in the world.

British Legacy

Prime Minister Tony Blair in 1997 apologized to Ireland for the nineteenth-century potato famine. But when asked whether Britain would apologize for the Opium War, Foreign Secretary Robin Cook says no. He adds that Britain could condemn the Opium War, but to go around apologizing for what Britain did in the last 150 years would take the full-time job of a prime minister (*South China Morning Post*, July 27).

"Imperial nostalgia" reigns high. Graham Hutchings of the *Daily Telegraph* thinks that although many British people may not able to articulate the feeling toward the empire, they still feel certain emotions about being reminded of how great they once were. Playing upon this emotion, his paper's headline reads on July 1: "Farewell to Empire." Of course, no British media or politicians would try to defend the Opium War, so they try to keep its historical origin at a distance or in the background. Among the little that is published on the subject, England is portrayed to have grabbed Hong Kong through gunboat diplomacy, the Opium War, and the need to force China to open international trade (*Times*, June 28). In introducing a television segment on "how did the British come here in the first place?" on the handover night, John Tusa, BBC's anchor, comments that "the answer is a great deal of uncertainty and plenty of guilt." But admission of guilt like this is far and few between.

The morality of the colonial origin is for the most part brushed aside. Instead of linking the "dark" Opium War to colonialism or imperialism, the British media focus on the current "bright" conditions of Hong Kong. On the day of his departure, Chris Patten urges all parties not to dwell on history. No one could condone either the Opium War, which led to Britain's acquisition of Hong Kong, he insists, or the upheavals in China that have led to mass exodus of population to Hong Kong (*Financial Times*, July 1). Apart from exonerating British imperialism from its guilt, this narrative also highlights the fact that British record has outshone the PRC. After all, how bad could British colonialists be? On another occasion, Patten asks rhetorically: "No one says what a rotten thing the Roman Empire was, do they (sic)? It gave us law, transport, public administration, and when it went, Europe descended into chaos." To him, the British Empire, at least in its later stage, was "an invariably honorable venture, conducted by honorable people. We don't need to creep around feeling guilty about it" (*Daily Telegraph*, June 30).

The British legacy in Hong Kong is only a part of the "we brought civilization to the world" theme (Said, 1993). Former Prime Minister Margaret Thatcher calls herself "an unashamed defender of the record of the British Empire" in a

Wall Street Journal article (June 27). "Because men who set off from our islands conquered the world," the *Daily Telegraph* asserted editorially (June 30), "English is now the world language of commerce, law, science, and a universal model for good government." It continues, "Hong Kong is Britain's creation." Likewise, the *Times* (July 1) states that many Hong Kong Chinese look back "with gratitude," and Britons could reflect "with pride" on what they and their ancestors have "contributed not only to Hong Kong but to those dominions and colonies over which the Union Flag once flew." "Even the Chinese, recalling more than 150 years of 'national humiliation', admitted this week that British rule was not all bad," the paper adds. Further, John Casey, writing in the *Daily Telegraph* (June 30), has not the slightest doubt that the postimperial world order was "less just, less stable and less civilized than what it succeeded." Like the *New York Times*, the *Guardian* (June 26) cites Dr. Sun Yatsen, the founding father of the Republic of China, as someone to have admired the "British-led Hong Kong efficiency and law, contrasting it with the chaos of the China in imperial decline." Patten's voice should have joined Dr. Sun's historical echo.

Emphasizing what Britain had done for Hong Kong and playing up the emotional ties between them de-essentialize colonialism in such a way as to strip Britain of its moral sin and to remind Hong Kong people how thankful they should be. Colonialism is given a positive overtone for bringing civilization and modernization to the backward people (Said, 1993). Patten says eloquently in his farewell address under the pouring rain on June 30:

> As the British administration ends, we are I believe entitled to say that our own nation's contribution here was to provide the scaffolding that enabled the people of Hong Kong to ascend: the rule of law, clean and light-handed government, the values of a free society, the beginnings of a representative government and democratic accountability. This is a Chinese city, a very Chinese city with British characteristics.

This "Chinese success story *with British characteristics*" theme, with the accent on the British part, pervades British media discourses. In a story broadcast on the night of June 30, BBC reiterates that Hong Kong—where "decency" and "fair play" ruled—was "the best-run" and the "most successful" of all the British Empire. On July 2, the day after the handover, the *Times* recites a list of British contributions in the colony. In a typical commentary entitled "Sealed with a Golden Kiss," Simon Jenkins reiterates that Britain had in 1997 left Hong Kong "not only stable, educated, prosperous, free and administered by its own indigenous civil service, but also represented by a publicly elected legislature of fellow-citizens." Jenkins concludes, "For all the carping, Britain has departed Hong Kong in better order than anyone dared to predict, blowing a golden kiss as it goes."

The media personify Governor Patten as embodying the British legacy, (Dimbleby, 1997) even though the Foreign Office had found him disagreeable. His chief critic among the professional diplomats, Sir Percy Cradock, attacked him on Channel 4 News for taking a belligerent approach to Beijing, which ironically led to the derailment of "the through train," or the wholesale transfer of the entire Hong Kong government on July 1. Siding with Patten, however, the media typically portray him as a fighter for liberty and democracy with "the intelligence to govern well, the faith in democracy, the courage to stand by the principle of liberty against the angry power of China" (*Times*, June 30). By personifying Patten, the media translate the abstract "British legacy" into something concrete and "empirical": his waving hands out of his car and shaking hands with people (ITN, June 18); the "best loved" and "best remembered" governor of all times who gave Hong Kong people "new confidence" (BBC). Jonathan Mirsky of the *Times* writes on June 25, "As the last British Governor leaves Hong Kong on Britannia next week, he bequeaths the colony a political legacy which Beijing can no longer throw overboard." Fergal Keane of the BBC (June 27) states that Patten's democratic reforms would "outlast the guns of China." Two stories in the *Daily Telegraph* (June 27) argue that "the seeds of democracy he has sown will grow" to constitute a "benchmark from which Communist China cannot deviate too far without attracting the wrath of the western powers." These profuse praises heaped on Patten, however, belie Britain's long-standing record of antidemocracy in Hong Kong.

Summing up the British scoreboard, the *Daily Telegraph* (July 1) predicts that the British influence—"an idea of doing things in a free, independent, creative, dynamic way"—would infect China rather than the other way around, however much Beijing may try to prevent it. ITV's Ian Williams similarly comments that Hong Kong has been influencing Southern China "not only in business terms, but in social terms, in political with a small 'p'" and "five years from now, probably we will say Hong Kong influences China and not the other way round." Andrew Higgins of the *Guardian* (July 1) has some reservations about how long the British legacy will last, in a big story entitled "Tung's cheerleaders may live to eat their rich words." It quotes Cheung Man-yee, the director of Radio Television Hong Kong, as saying: "People thought the tail could wag the dog. Then we realized we were dealing with a very big dog." After all, Hong Kong is too small as China is too big to sustain the "one country, two systems" for long.

Britain as Protector of Freedom

"Abandoning" Hong Kong affronts western triumphalism over Communism in the Cold War. The Tiananmen crackdown provided an impetus for

Britain to harden its policy toward China. Governor Patten decided to implement limited democratic reforms as a British legacy in the colony (Dimbleby, 1997). China was adamant about dismantling the changes in political infrastructure that Patten had instituted. All western media discourses concentrated in one way or another on the dubious prospect of freedom and democracy under Communist rule.

Prince Charles is widely quoted as telling Hong Kong people, "We shall not forget you, and we shall watch you with the closest interest as you embark on this new era of your remarkable history." In echoing British foreign policy, the *Times* (June 23) says that Tony Blair had secured a commitment from world leaders to defend Hong Kong rights by keeping China to its promises. On July 1, the *Times* runs a banner headline on the second page, "Blair Talks Tough with Beijing Leaders," with a subtitle, "Chinese Warned Against Abuse of Power." In the story, Blair claims that "Britain is the best guarantor of the liberties that the people of Hong Kong have." Right next to the report is an unusually large picture showing rows of menacing People's Liberation Army. The *Daily Telegraph* (July 1) notes that Blair had told President Jiang Zemin that Britain would hold China to account "at the court of international opinion" if Beijing should violate the Joint Declaration. Hailing Foreign Secretary Robin Cook as "freedom's watchdog in former colony," the *Times* (July 2) warns that Britain would consider referring any Chinese breach of the Joint Declaration to the United Nations. Similarly, the *Guardian* (July 1) editorializes that Britain should and could play a "vital future role" in Hong Kong through the Joint Liaison Group and by continuous monitoring of the Joint Declaration. To walk away quietly from Hong Kong would simply be "betrayal." While urging Britain to continue monitoring the progress in Hong Kong, the *Times* (July 1) features a protest led by the Democratic Party over its ouster from the Legislative Council, with its leader Martin Lee asking, "Why must we pay such a high price to become Chinese again?"

Patten is portrayed as a democracy fighter until the very end. A couple of days before the handover, Patten warns on the BBC that China could not snuff out Hong Kong's freedom despite the fact that Tung Chee-hwa has set limits for the advocates of independence for Taiwan and Tibet. Patten argues that China's plans to deploy troops in Hong Kong during the handover night would send an "appalling signal" to the people of Hong Kong, many of whom had marched in 1989 to protest against the Tiananmen massacre by the PLA (*Guardian*, June 28). The *Times* starts its leading story on the front page (June 28) by saying: "China last night sent shivers through Hong Kong by announcing that thousands of troops backed up by warships and helicopters would cross into the territory within six hours of the change from British sovereignty." Patten interprets the dispatch of Chinese troops as "bad signals to the world." (In fact, the army was unarmed and fewer in number than the press corp.) Andrew Higgins of the

Guardian concludes (June 27) in an interview that all the Chinese insults that had rained down on Chris Patten had turned "a humble failed British politician into a knight on a white charger" and Patten finally bowed out "with no regrets."

Dignified Retreat

According to Dimbleby (1997: xiv), one of Patten's primary missions was "to convince public opinion in the United Kingdom and internationally that Britain's withdrawal from Hong Kong had been accomplished with at least a modicum of dignity and honor." He appears to have well achieved this mission in view of the overwhelmingly celebratory, if also sad and sentimental, media characterization. "Dignified retreat" by the British is depicted with imperial nostalgia, with the emotional attachment between the colonizer and the colonized.

The media vividly exhibit pictures, stories, and tidbits related to British cultural icons or colonial symbols: a Black Watch soldier rehearsing a Highland dance for a Hong Kong farewell concert, the sailing of the Royal Yacht Britannia, the lowering of the old Hong Kong flag for the last time, and Patten bowing his head in meditation in a farewell ceremony. The pageantry was filled with colored uniforms, military band, regiment in formation, and the Union Jack. Besides, a central icon is the Royal Yacht. In covering the Britannia sailing away, BBC correspondent Eric Robson describes it with the tone of a romantic lover: "She is moving from the shore, . . . gliding through the glass canyon of Hong Kong, in the busiest water of the world, where thousands of various kinds of ships move through everyday, but none is as pretty as Britannia! After 80 state visits in her 47 years of service, she has not seen quite as emotional a departure as this one." Mixing history with attachment, the *Guardian* reports on the "uncertain fate of the emblems of British sovereignty in the packing up of an empire." Andrew Higgins writes, for example: "The mansion that since 1855 has housed 28 British governors—and wartime rulers sent from Japan—is to be handed over to Hong Kong's new proprietor entirely shorn of the colonial crests, royal insignia, regal monograms and all other emblems of British sovereignty. From Tuesday it will fly the red flag."

The *Times*'s bold front-page headline on July 1, "Final Farewell to Hong Kong," is subheadlined, "Tears Mingle with the Rain as Retreat is Beaten." The leading paragraph reads: "The party is over. The British rule in Hong Kong ended on the dot of midnight last night in torrential rain but with dignity and panache. The Last Post had been sounded, the retreat beaten." The story says that Patten "was cheered to the skies" for his role in introducing democracy and for standing up to China. The *Daily Telegraph* on the same day gives a one-page account of Patten's last day in Hong Kong. Entitled "Flag of Freedom is Lowered Forever," the report features a large picture of a solemn and sad Patten stepping forward to receive the Union flag from an officer. It goes on to explain that this is the "simple moment," amid the pomp and spectacle, that defines "a people's sadness." The only emotion betrayed by the governor is "deep, deep sadness." Robert Hardman, the correspondent, adds that if anyone was to be permitted a gentle sob, it was the governor himself, who had witnessed numerous "heartfelt gestures and piercingly moving sights."

The British media question how genuine the "jubilant" display of national patriotism in China and Hong Kong is. After showing the celebratory activities in Beijing, Katie Adie of the BBC (June 30) is quick to add that they are held in the shadow of the Tiananmen crackdown, noting the tight security and the "controlled" celebration by "happy but dutiful" people. ITV interprets such orchestrated celebration as a sign of Chinese nationalism (June 27) and as part of a "major propaganda coup" (June 26). Noting that Hong Kong people are only "loyal to themselves" and have a weak identification with China (*Daily Telegraph*, June 30), the media argue that the reunification "cajoled," "persuaded," and even "bullied" them into accepting that they are Chinese. The *Guardian* (June 18) cites a poll to say that "the gap between reality and propaganda" was a "blow to China's line on handover glee." The poll reveals "a phlegmatic population upbeat about making money, anxious about its liberties and far less patriotic and politically apathetic than China's propaganda portrait of the colony."

The British are "the best when it comes to ceremonies," says Marcus Eliason of the Associated Press, who used to cover royal weddings in London:

> They know how to do all the right little touches. The Governor departs with the family and with the girls weeping; he could simply easily have said: "Lavender, girls, get in the car and leave, I would handle the ceremony." They want to make it as human; they want to make the Pattens part of Hong Kong, to make it look like it is not just the Governor . . . The British did not leave here as hated oppressors; they were in fact quite missed. A lot of people feel quite sad.

By depicting human emotion, television imparts dignity to ceremonies. BBC's Brian Hanrahan (June 30) talks about the "tears in the eyes" of the Government House staff. As the band starts to play "God Save the Queen," Patten bows solemnly. It is raining, and a lone bugler plays the *Last Post*. The Union Jack is being slowly lowered. Patten stands straight, looking on and trying to hold back his tears. Raindrops start to wet his jacket, shining under the reflection of the late evening light. Holding the folded Union Jack, Patten lowers his head to the tune of "God Save the Queen." Then the band plays "Farewell, friends." Patten gets into his car and circles the Government House once before departure (he should have circled it three times according to the announced script). People from all walks of life come to witness this occasion, making it what Hanrahan calls a "family occasion."

At midnight British television broadcasts the formal handover ceremony live in its entirety. Given the solemnity of the occasion, the BBC hosts function merely as conduits, footnote providers, as well as aesthetic designers calling for preplanned shots of scenes. (The bureau chief of Japan's NHK echoes in an interview with us: "For such an important period, we say very little things. Saying too much will destroy the dignity of the ceremony. We will let people decide.") All these images project a dignified retreat. While official ceremonies carry solemnity, personal moments are most touching. For Fiona Anderson, the BBC bureau chief in Hong Kong, Patten's departure from the Governor's House, showing the staff in tears, is very moving. The departure of Patten and Prince Charles at the pier is equally "emotional and evocative" to AP's Eliason. The moment is so unceremonially "real"—just ordinary folks who come to hug them and shake their hands—that Patten and Charles are suddenly reduced to their human proportions.

No nostalgia could be complete without the reluctance of the colonized to accept the colonizer's departure. In a report entitled "Colony Bids a Reluctant Adieu to His Excellency," the *Daily Telegraph* portrays Patten as "smiling, affable and, at times, visibly moved" when he goes for "his final wander among the people, to the sort of reception that is often reserved for royal walkabouts." It says: "For weeks, Government House has been receiving a flow of letters and gifts from the public. These are complicated emotions, bound up in nostalgia for the old and fears of the new, but many will indeed miss His Excellency." The handover ceremony is scripted to the second for the media to reflect smooth transition and retreat in honor. The *Times*'s editorial on July 1, 1997 says it well:

> Emotion flowed freely in Hong Kong yesterday. . . . But for the departing British it was also a moment of nostalgia and regret, sadness and a sense of loss. Not only was the Union Flag lowered for the last time on a colony that was the last substantial remnant of an Empire that once covered the globe; but in their speeches, ceremonies and parting gestures, representatives of the Crown, the Government and the Armed Services recalled an almost forgotten sense of duty and responsibility, good government and dedication to the peoples over which Britain once held sway.

Hong Kong Media: In Search of Identity

The handover does not bode well for a land of refugees who have swarmed into Hong Kong in several waves to escape from turmoil and oppression in China. Even though they were denied a voice throughout and after the Sino-British negotiations, Hong Kong people and their media clearly sided with the British against the PRC in overwhelming majority (Chan and Lee, 1991; Lee,

2000a). They have little illusion about the PRC-style nationalism or patriotism: many elite members stock foreign passports in their back pockets, while more than half a million professional people have emigrated overseas. During the 1989 democracy movement in China, more than one million Hong Kong residents took to the streets to support the students, only later to be denounced by Beijing. National identity is fraught with contradiction and ambivalence, as the *South China Morning Post* (June 21) quotes someone as saying:

> I feel like I am torn between a foster mother, Britain, and my natural mother, which is China. I feel like a child who has grown up under the care of a foster mother, but now it is time to reunite with my natural mother. I treasure the warmth I feel in the arms of my foster mother and worry my natural mother is a fierce woman. I feel anxious.

Similarly, the *Post* columnist Fanny Wong writes on the second day after the handover:

> Embracing the future, many of us share that rationally, rejoining our compatriots in the mainland and to be part of the family again is joyous. But psychologically, we also feel apprehensive . . . Will the "one country, two systems" concept work? Will Beijing really honor its promise of "Hong Kong people running Hong Kong"? Will the central government genuinely commit to granting Hong Kong a high degree of autonomy?

Quoting a University of Hong Kong poll, the *Apple Daily* indicates that 47 percent respondents said they felt proud to be a Chinese national, and 46 percent said they did not. Forty percent said if Hong Kong continued to be ruled by the British, Hong Kong's future would be better; only 15 percent said it would be worse. In tracing the longitudinal polling data on public confidence (July 1), *Ming Pao Daily News* singles out the Tiananmen crackdown as the worst nightmare for Hong Kong people.

Most mainstream papers laud British contributions to Hong Kong's success and bid farewell to the departing sovereign with sadness. Despite the shameful colonial beginnings, the *Apple Daily* editorially praises (June 30) that the British have "integrated Hong Kong people's strength to create a world wonder" and that their retreat would be "in glory." Patten is a hero of democracy, not a "sinner of the millenium." TVB's coverage of the dignified ceremonies, tearful eyes, sentimental tunes, and enthusiastic crowds could not help being nostalgic. A *South China Morning Post* report (July 1) shows a group waving a sign, "We will never forget you, Mr. Patten." A freelance columnist, To Kit, goes further to quote two major satirists in Taiwan who thank British imperialism and the Opium War for making Hong Kong what it is today (*Ming Pao*, June 30). The *Ming Pao Daily News* (June 30), afraid of being seen as unpatriotic or as journalistically timid, editorially gives all parties involved—Britain, China, and the toiling and sweating local people—equal share of the credit for Hong Kong's success.

Conclusion

Hong Kong is the place where the histories of China and Britain have intertwined to create a culture that is supposed to be "hybrid, heterogeneous, extraordinarily differentiated, and unmonolithic" (Said, 1993: xxv). As these histories are full of contradictions, ambiguities, and struggles subject to ideological construction, each side strives for historical clarity by smoothing out rough edges to provide a mythical narrative to suit one's advantages. In its long colonial history of 150 years in Hong Kong, Britain was at best a very late convert to the cause of democracy. Patten's democratic reform was taken up with commitment and political expediency under rancorous circumstances. But the British media behave as if Britain had always been a guardian of freedom and democracy, only to sidestep pages of inglorious record. They also accentuate the positive legacies of British colonial history while downplaying its negative origin. On the other hand, the Chinese media elevate nationalism to the status of inherent and sacred virtue against colonial evil, to the neglect of Mao's opportunistic moments to prolong that evil, and of Hong Kong people's embrace of colonial rule vis-à-vis Beijing's imposed hegemonic nationalism.

The significance of nationalism and colonialism, instead of being reduced to a "pure and simple" characteristic, should be open to interpretation in a multiplicity of social and historical frameworks. The ambivalent Hong Kong media find it difficult to take one side exclusively from this intertwined history. They praise the British while feeling uncertain about the prospect of being reunited with the motherland. Inasmuch as British colonists receive credit for providing the "scaffolding" that enables Hong Kong to succeed, the media place the spotlight on how to maintain that colonial "scaffolding" to ensure continued postcolonial prosperity. The implications of colonialism are thus interpreted anew. Further, the media from the U.S., Canada, and Australia all recognize the British legacy in Hong Kong as the endorsement of generalized western values rather than sentimentality for British hegemony.

There are different discursive constructions of colonialism by the British, PRC, and Hong Kong media. No one was in a position to offer an explicit defense of the Opium War—the British prefer to call it the "Trade War"—that led to the British acquisition of Hong Kong. But the significance of historical events varies. The idea of British legacy is the strongest in the British media, often echoing the perspectives of British officials by way of personifying Chris Patten. Imperial nostalgia—about the empire, the British legacy, and Patten's withdrawal—becomes all the more heightened in the face of the PRC's nationalistic challenges. Chris Patten is portrayed as the freedom and democracy fighter who persists in the face of immense pressure from China.

Who are the heroes or villains? To the British media, the heroes are the British, Patten, and local democrats (his allies). It is sentimental for the British to finally give up such a successful crown jewel to China, which may not know what keeps the jewel shining. The villains are the Communist leaders and the PLA who killed prodemocracy students. On the opposite side, the Chinese Communist Party, Deng, and the PLA become heroes who reclaim the lost land. British imperialists, the villain, ushered in more than a century of national humiliation. Patten is a "sinner of the millennium," harboring ulterior motives against China. They simply ignore the voice of local democrats.

As mentioned, the British media narratives fail to acknowledge the dark side of history: the colonial beginning, bad administration, and corruption prior to the mid-1970s, antidemocratic record, suppression of social activists, British privileges in Hong Kong, and the Nationality Bill, which disenfranchised the Hong Kong people. As an exception, William McGurn writes in the *Daily Telegraph* (June 29), accusing the former Foreign Secretary Geoffrey Howe and his colleagues of submitting to pressures from China and colluding in restricting the growth of democracy in the mid-1980s. Besides, Patten (1998) condemns these conservative British officials for compromising on democratic ideals, but reserves the greatest scorn for the Hong Kong business elite, the Tory politicians and Whitehall mandarins who argued in favor of a softly-softly approach towards Beijing.

Akin to the pattern of imperial construction of Orientalism (Said, 1978, 1993), the PRC media have tried to "occidentalize" the West as "imperialistic, capitalistic, exploitative, decadent, materialistic." The official Chinese discourse is noted for its stress on the difference between "us" and "them" (including British colonists and western imperialists) to support nationalism that helps to integrate the Chinese nation-state and overseas Chinese. The western "other," as construed, is not meant for the purpose of domination, but for disciplining and ultimately dominating the Chinese Self at home. In the more open mid-1980s, a group of Chinese dissident intellectuals produced a TV documentary series, *He Shang* (River Elegy), to essentialize the West as culturally more open, risk-taking, and thus superior to the closed and oppressive culture of the imperial Communist China (Chen, 1993). The exaltation of the West, in this context, is an indirect but powerful way to render "alternative" or "oppositional" readings to official truths. Philosophically, we should adopt an antiessentialistic and antiotherizing approach to discourses, but in certain contexts articulating an essentialized discourse may have a politically liberating role to play. While the PRC discourses on the handover cast western colonialism in bad light, the "other" can be painted in beautiful colors in order to promote it as an ideal for transforming the existing authoritarian system.

Chapter 7

Defining the Nation-State: One Event, Three Stories

Bonding the Chinese blood eternally is a historical destiny.
—The *People's Daily*, June 16, 1997

If Hong Kong is good, the country is good; if the country is good, Hong Kong will be better.
—Tung Chee-hwa, Chief Executive, 1997

Say No to China.
—The *Liberty Times*, Taiwan, June 29, 1997

Nationalism is the fruit of idle pens and gullible readers.
—Ernest Gellner (1997: 10–11)

The handover of Hong Kong strikes different chords in the conscience of the three Chinese societies: the People's Republic of China (PRC), the Republic of China (ROC) in Taiwan, and Hong Kong itself. It raises core issues about the meanings of China and Chinese as well as the relationships between a nation and a state. These issues are particularly sensitive in the post-Cold War era, as national and ethnic identities have stepped forward to become a prime locus of struggle. As a nation struggles for its discursive representation in the globalized mediated culture, the state is its chief authoritative voice, and the media play a central role in constructing political and historical narratives of what Anderson (1983) calls the "imagined communities." Against this backdrop, the handover of Hong Kong becomes a site and moment for the media in these three societies of the "Cultural China" (Tu, 1991) to discursively contest their visions of China and Chinese.

China has been called variably a "nationless state" (Fitzgerald, 1995) or an "empire-state" (Bockman, 1998). It is a civilization defined by a set of cultural practices and shared symbolic resources, often in service of state unity. The definitions of China and Chinese have never been unproblematic. Historically, successive dynasties sustained the unity of the Chinese Empire State, but the

127

criteria for inclusion in it were fluid, ambiguous, and changing constantly. Each dynasty chose its favored attribute—ethnic, geographic, social, or cultural—to attain the goal of state unity. Neither ethnicity nor residency within certain territorial boundaries is sufficient to define what Chinese people are. Today's PRC continues this historical trajectory by staking its political media discourse on claims of state unity and national sovereignty in the context of rising nationalism.

At the historical moment of Hong Kong's handover, the three Chinese societies in the Cultural China, situated in different systems, ideologies, and historical sentiments in the international political economy, clash in their articulation of the Chinese nation and state as three different, discursive communities. How to define the Chinese state has important bearings on the political legitimacy of the PRC and its claim of sovereignty over Hong Kong and Taiwan. The tension between nation and state is a source of anxiety in Hong Kong and has flared up internal politics in Taiwan. The discursive clash is most likely to occur at what Levi-Strauss (1966: 259) calls "hot moments" that may draw out different symbolic resources to interpret historical events in such a way as to exert critical influences on the dynamics of struggle over political and cultural identities. Therefore, we have to analyze this discursive clash within "the communities of competing producers, of interpreters and critics, of audiences and consumers, and of patrons and other significant actors who become subjects of discourse itself" (Wuthnow, 1989: 16).

This discursive struggle has to be placed against another backdrop: the rising nationalism in the PRC, partly bolstered by economic achievements and partly prompted by the perceived need to dispel domestic challenges and to fortify national boundaries against the globalizing forces of free markets and democracy (Snyder and Ballentine, 1997). Nationalism fills the gap left by widespread public disillusionment with Communist ideology in China. Official discourses often pit the national strength of China against the dismemberment of the Soviet Union to prove the "correct" policy of harnessing economic reform as an engine to realize China's "dream of prosperity and strength." The "receiving end" of PRC nationalism has very different reactions. As we shall show in this chapter, while the PRC media celebrate the integration of China as a nation-state, Taiwan's media seek to delink nation from state, and Hong Kong's media are ambivalent about being incorporated as part of the Beijing-defined Chinese family-nation. In this process, they have all tried to selectively "domesticate" aspects of the handover of Hong Kong to renew their own ideological boundaries.

The PRC: Celebration of the Family-Nation

The PRC's media coverage is organized temporally and spatially by a "master frame" (Snow and Benford, 1992) that conceives of the Chinese nation as an extension of the family. Temporally, the handover of Hong Kong is placed in a much larger historical framework of the Chinese nation redeeming itself from past humiliation. This historical "script" enables the PRC media to collate various seemingly isolated episodes, the historical nuggets and present celebrations at home and abroad into coherent stories, and impute a distinct causal sequence to these stories. In doing so, the media link two different "modes of interpretation" (Zelizer, 1993), placing the "local" (or micro) reports of the handover in the "durational" (or macro) context of Chinese history. Spatially speaking, the family-nation narrative is organized by congealing different events and different people and the interrelationships between them into a coherent whole. Through such structuring, the master theme of family-nation runs through four discursive packages (Table 7.1): national achievement, national festival, nation family, and brighter prospect for the future. These four discursive packages are woven into media narratives in special time-space configurations.

National achievement: This package glorifies the "homecoming" of Hong Kong as a national achievement, ending 156 years of colonialism and humiliation at the hands of western powers, and as protecting territorial integrity of the

Table 7.1
Discursive Packages of the PRC Media

	Frame	Position	Signification Devices
National achievement	National strength of China washing away past humiliation.	National strength under the Communist Party brings international respect.	National flag, the Great Wall, President Jiang, Deng, Hong Kong coming home.
National festival	A long awaited moment for celebration by all Chinese.	All Chinese share the same pride.	Sea of joys, fireworks, the countdown clock, songs, drums, flowers, and lights
Nation family	Chinese are members of the same family.	Family members share the same blood and attachments.	As affectionate as bones and flesh, blood is thicker than water, children of the Yellow Emperor, the Yellow Emperor tomb, common language and ancestry, "four waters converge to one"
Brighter prospect for the future	Hong Kong's return opens up opportunities.	Hong Kong as bridge between China and the world.	Hong Kong skyline, "tomorrow will be even better."

nation. Such catchy phrases as "national strength," "international respect," and "washing away of the national humiliation" abound, together with canonization of the supreme leader (Deng Xiaoping's pictures and recorded voice), geographical/historical icons (the Great Wall, the Yellow River), and the political authority.

National festival: The handover marks a historical moment of celebration among all Chinese who are said to feel "happier than on the New Year's Day" (as quoted on TV). Our informants in the *People's Daily* and CCTV confirmed that they had been told to use the theme "happy festivities"(xiqing) to organize their coverage.

Nation as a family: All ethnicities at home and all Chinese abroad are depicted as members of the same "family-nation" linked by blood and culture, all happily rooting for national grandeur. "Family" is, again, a master metaphor: "children of the Yellow Emperor" are as "affectionate as bones and flesh" in the "big family of the motherland."

Brighter prospect for the future: CCTV shows President Jiang Zemin presenting his calligraphy, "Hong Kong's tomorrow will still be better," to the newly formed Hong Kong Special Administration Region government at its inauguration ceremony. The media depict Hong Kong as a bridge between China and the world, providing capital investment and know-how for modern management. Visually showing a cargo train carrying food supplies from the mainland, CCTV attributes Hong Kong's economic prosperity to the unselfish support of the motherland. Now that Hong Kong and China will live under the same family-nation roof, they will be ever more prosperous together.

Historical Script

The following historical script threads these discursive packages with a clear designation of heroes and villains:

- Western powers inflicted national humiliation on China, and China was too weak to fight back foreign aggression.

- British imperialists stole Hong Kong away from China by force, and Chinese people had always wanted to dispel national humiliation.

- Only the Chinese Communist Party can bring independence and strength to China, thus saving the state from demise and the nation from extinction.

- National strength, bolstered by economic reform, enables China to reclaim Hong Kong according to Deng Xiaoping's "ingenuous" "one country and two systems" device.

- Under President Jiang's leadership, China will score greater achievements, and Hong Kong will have a brighter prospect.

This historical narrative entitles the Chinese Communist Party to its claims as a savior and the solely legitimate political representative of the Chinese nation as well as the heir to Chinese civilization. A *People's Daily* editorial on the eve of the handover (June 30) is illustrative:

> Ever since its founding, the Chinese Communist Party has regarded independence, unity, democracy, and strength of the motherland as its goals. . . . History has unequivocally shown that if there had not been the Chinese Communist Party, there would not have been socialist New China, and there would not have been a smooth return of Hong Kong (to China).

All other papers are required by the Party to carry this editorial in full on their front page. This official rendition of history permeates all news reports, commentaries, and even the celebration performances. It serves to connect the nation's past and present, ensures a "hegemonic reading" (Hall, 1980) of the handover coverage, and guides media selection of events, symbols, and icons. Among the most prominent images are the invading western troops who set the old Summer Palace in Beijing on fire; the "Eternal Warning Bell" (*jingshi zhong*) in Jinghai Temple in Nanjing[1]; and Commissioner Lin Zexu who burned British opium in Humen in 1840. Besides, a group of senior citizens, all more than 100 years old, were called upon to condemn the dark past and praise the bright present.

All official media outlets go out of their way to reinforce this official narrative. The *Guangming Daily* (June 27), a paper devoted to intellectuals, artists, and professionals, prints the National Anthem on its front page, with a commentary entitled "Singing the National Anthem and Marching to the Future." It starts with a quote from Deng, "Chinese people have stood up thanks only to the Chinese Communist Party and socialism." The *People's Liberation Army Daily* stresses that it is the "strong backing" from the "powerful people's army" that enables the Party-led struggle to regain territorial integrity (July 1, editorial). From June 16 to 23, in a series of six long articles analyzing the significance of Hong Kong's return, the paper repeatedly drums up the message of "strong national defense." On June 27 the paper argues in a full-page article urging "patriotic education."

Using family celebration to personalize the political event, the media strive to enhance the "empirical fidelity" of this official history. Official interpretation of this historical narrative is thus resonant with the existing "meaning systems" in the Chinese culture (Fisher, 1984; Snow and Benford, 1992). On the night of June 30, CCTV shows stroller-pushing parents watching the fireworks and celebratory performances in various major cities who exclaim to be "happier (today) than on Chinese New Year!" The *Guangming Daily* publishes a special column recounting personal experiences of Chinese celebrities who had once lived in Hong Kong. The *Guangzhou Daily* publishes a series of long feature articles to highlight that many people in Guangzhou have relatives in Hong Kong, and both places speak the same dialect.

CCTV also airs a special report of a *family* memorial, attended by more than 300 descendents, in honor of Commissioner Lin Zexu, the Qing official who ordered the burning of British opium, an incident that triggered a war leading to the loss of Hong Kong. His descendants hang a huge banner on the memorial site, "A Family Tribute to Welcoming (Hong Kong's) Return and to Condoling the Ancestor's Spirit (*ying huigui wei yingling jiaji dianli*)." The most "senior" member of the family—not the oldest, but the most prestigious, or China's former representative to the United Nations—first reads a eulogy. Then, someone from the youngest generation recites what the CCTV reporter calls a "patriotic pledge" (*aiguo juexinshu*). In another televised *family* event, Commissioner Lin's descendents display his letter instructing them to devote themselves to the goal of reclaiming Hong Kong. Now their distinguished ancestor, they proclaim, can rest in peace. The *PLA Daily* (June 27) features an offspring of Xu in military uniform making patriotic remarks. National affairs are interspersed with family activities because blood unites the family and the nation. Traditional family ancestral worship extends to a political ritual for the nation, and family hierarchy corresponds to the party-state hierarchy.

Members of the family-nation, based on a common ancestry, are supposed to share past humiliation and today's redemption. The *People's Daily* reports on June 27 that a "Hong Kong Return Monument" has been erected near the tomb of the Yellow Emperor (*huangdiling*), the alleged origin of the Chinese nation and civilization. Even though ethnic minorities have never shared the myth of the Yellow Emperor, the paper claims, "Erecting a monument to record significant events at the ancestral burial site is part of Chinese tradition." CCTV's special reports also prominently show footages of various activities held at cultural icons of Chinese civilization: the Yellow Emperor's tomb, the Yellow River, and the Great Wall. This family-nation, built by descendants of the Yellow Emperor, extends to global Chinese communities, all enthusiastically celebrating the big family reunion. On July 1 the anchors of CCTV's Evening News introduce the program by announcing that "Hong Kong has come home" and "family members of the same blood are united!"

The idea of Hong Kong coming back to the family of the Yellow Emperor's offsprings is a potent cultural symbol with which the political authority *essentializes* the Chinese nation, revealing a key characteristic of the perennial nationalist discourse. Invoking the image of global ethnic Chinese communities bound by "flesh and bones" (*gurouqing*), President Jiang declares at an official mass gathering in Beijing that "history has proven that a country's strength requires the leadership of a progressive political party." Then various speakers, all officially picked, vow one after another that China will unite around the Communist Party with Jiang at its core.

Social Taxonomy and Geographical Configuration

If the historical script provides a temporal flow for causal attributions of the historical event, the family-nation metaphor calls for a spatial configuration in the constitution of the Chinese nation. The time-honored practice of the Party propaganda is to highlight that the Party wins the hearts and minds of the broadest segments of the population. Therefore, the media arrange a parade of nominal "representatives" from different social, ethnic, and occupational groups as a show of unanimous support for the Party. Whenever there is a major political event (such as the first launch of a satellite in 1970 and the fall of the "Gang of Four" in 1976), there would be many "representatives" from different sectors taking turns to praise how farsighted the Party is in the *People's Daily*. These "representatives" bear group labels, never identified as individuals. In line with this tradition, an associate editor of the *People's Daily* writes an article on July 3, 1997, which, after quoting the chief executive, "empowers" many "ordinary people" to recite their feelings of national pride. To be inclusive, these "ordinary" people are said to represent all walks of life; the report starts to note each of the sectors one by one: the commerce sector, the science and technology sector, the agricultural sector, the education sector, the medical sector, the arts and entertainment sector, etc. Even a Xinhua report about joyous celebration within the armed forces (carried by the *People's Daily* on the same day) gives a full list of all major divisions and the military rank and file (students, teachers, and experts). Again, no one is identified as an individual.

Similarly, the *PLA Daily* (June 27) devotes one page to celebratory activities of the military and another page to "patriotic passion" of various military units from across the country. The *Guangming Daily* (June 28) takes the same approach to show the jubilance of university students. The *Economic Daily* (June 22) publishes a special page of seven articles to highlight nationalistic activities in various official "bases for patriotic education": Tiananmen Square, Humen Opium War Museum, the tomb of the Yellow Emperor in Shaanxi, and the birthplace of Deng.

Media representations of ethnic minorities comprise an array of anonymous individuals, who represent "brother ethnic groups" (*xiongdi minzu*) to welcome Hong Kong back to "the motherland's big family" (*zuguo da jiating*). They praise the Communist Party in their own ethnic languages and perform their folk songs and dances in traditional costumes—as if they spontaneously shared the Han majority's pains and joys. The ethnic "plural-ity" decorates the "whole" of the political community; the cultural and ethnic differences are obfuscated.

In addition, the PRC media construe a particular political geography in which the blood tie of ethnic Chinese transcends territorial boundaries. The media repeatedly announce that "the whole country" and "the whole world" are overjoyed in celebration. The spatial construction of the "global Chinese" cre-ates the impression that the whole world supports and celebrates Hong Kong's return to Chinese sovereignty. In particular, it connotes the unity of Chinese peo-ple worldwide, steeping themselves in the crown achievement of the Chinese state. This spatial construction also subtly suggests that as a member of the third world, China shares the common fate of past and present oppression from the West. On July 2 and July 5, the *People's Daily* fills its international page with re-ports of celebration and excerpts of official congratulations from carefully se-lected cities and countries from all continents. By the same token, CCTV dispatches 22 news crews to major cities, within and outside China, to "record" the "global Chinese connection," integrating national and international spaces.

The center of this geographic web is located, however, in the Tiananmen Square at the heart of Beijing, where a countdown clock presumably synchro-nizes all the activities around the globe. In a two-part CCTV special program called "When the Hundred-Year-Old Dream Comes True" (*bainian mengyuan shi*), the anchor claims that the countdown clock has become an "eternal mon-ument in people's heart." The camera shot starts with the countdown clock and then pans over to show a sea of the masses gathered in front of it. Then comes the voiceover exclaiming, "This is a huge festival for the Chinese nation, an im-portant celebration in the hundred-year history." After that, the camera moves to live images of the June 30 midnight celebration in Tiananmen Square, and a CCTV reporter shouts to a massive crowd around him, "Friends, let's count down, 10, 9, . . . 0! Hong Kong has come home!" The crowd chants, "Hong Kong has come home!" The giant TV screen in the Square shows CCTV's live coverage of the national flag rising at the handover ceremony in Hong Kong; the sound track plays the national anthem amidst sounds of fireworks. The sound and images are mixed with the thunderous chant, "Hong Kong has come home!" Ditto, from one city to another. A special page of the *Economic Daily* on July 1 carries ten stories and two pictures showing the masses, who watch televised ceremonies of the handover. The paper claims that Chinese people are "connected by the millions of TV screens."

Mobilization and Orchestration

This media celebration of national festivity is officially orchestrated through mobilization. In early April the CCP's Propaganda Department began to organize a series of workshops, urging chief editors from Party newspapers and directors of radio and TV stations in the country to create a "more hospitable opinion atmosphere" for Hong Kong's return to the motherland. In its wake, the Propaganda Department and the Office of Hong Kong and Macau Affairs of the State Council issued a guideline stipulating the principles of media coverage and the political terms of language to be used. The policy is to be implemented down to the very basic unit of the propaganda system. Together, these offices mobilize the officially sanctioned resources to facilitate the work of the Party organs, which prominently display interviews with pro-Beijing figures in Hong Kong.

Of the 16 media outlets chosen to cover the handover, the big three—CCTV, the *People's Daily*, and Xinhua News Agency—account for a lion's share of the 610-member entourage. The Big Three also establish command centers at their Beijing headquarters; CCTV's operation is particularly on a grand scale. The director of CCTV heads a special team set up in 1996; in March 1997, it opened a Hong Kong office. Altogether CCTV involves 1,600 people, including 289 people in Hong Kong and 100 people sent to cover 8 different cities in China and 15 foreign cities. Xinhua's handover team consists of 89 reporters in Beijing and 25 from the Hong Kong bureau. The five reporters in the Hong Kong bureau of the *People's Daily* work with 27 others sent from Beijing. Before departure, these skilled Beijing journalists were required to go through lengthy training sessions, in which they reviewed Deng's speech on "one country and two systems," the Basic Law, and the general conditions of Hong Kong.

The official orchestration involves a careful division of media responsibilities. Xinhua is solely responsible for reporting official sovereignty transfer activities. All media but the *People's Daily* and CCTV must carry Xinhua's reports. With Xinhua reports as the mainstay, other papers cover events within their own special spheres: hence, the *PLA Daily* shows the celebration within the military; the *Guangming Daily*, among intellectuals, artists, and professionals; the *Worker's Daily*, likewise, among industrial and manufacturing workers.

The CCP harnesses national ceremony for expressing patriotic emotions but, mindful of historical precedents, is determined to contain mass euphoria within limits. Its tightly controlled extravaganzas are visually appealing for live television, covering events said to be taking place simultaneously in eight cities, all strategically selected.[2] Moreover, to create the semblance of unity, the party-state mobilizes its enormous resources to facilitate the work of the Big Three. The Office of Hong Kong and Macau Affairs in Beijing and the Hong Kong Branch of the Xinhua News Agency organize "exclusive" media interviews with pro-Beijing figures.

Some wealthier media outlets in China have increasingly ventured to defy state restrictions, forcing the authority to yield certain grounds. For example, both the *Guangzhou Daily*, the top newspaper advertising earner in the country, and Guangdong TV are excluded from the official journalist entourage, but both managed to send reporters and crews to Hong Kong on either business or tourist (rather than official) visas. This is also true of their peers in Beijing and Shanghai, those with strong connections to high-ranking officials. Instead of covering formal ceremonies, they concentrate on what Guangdong TV journalists call "side shows" to enrich the official spectacular. They relish on doing "enterprising reporting" (Sigal, 1973) by interviewing people in parks, street corners, hospitals, and corporate headquarters; these items are largely missing from the news map of the Big Three. Barred from sending a team to Hong Kong, the *Economic Daily* publishes special pages with by-lined stories of celebratory mania, interviews with business people, and reports about the new railway service connecting Beijing and Hong Kong. Through the combination of political and market mobilization, the Chinese media blanket the country with a nationalistic blast.

Taiwan: Say No to China

The lifting of martial law in 1987 has invigorated the media in Taiwan, with the power of government censorship in retreat amidst a rearticulation of the press-state-market relationships (Lee, 2000c). The handover of Hong Kong puts Taiwan in an awkward position: it can only watch on the sideline because the territory is returned to Beijing, not to Taipei, and yet Taiwan is also Beijing's next target of national reunification efforts. It also brings to light Taiwan's precarious international status and its fundamental conflict with the PRC—a situation that is complicated by the search of identity as the island nation democratizes. The *United Daily News* (June 24) rightly characterizes this state of mind as "identity ambivalence." Reflecting this ambivalence, the mainstream *China Times* endorses the end of national shame but expresses concern about the condition of democracy in Hong Kong. The anchor of the Taiwan Television (TTV) narrates the live coverage on June 30 as "complete withdrawal of British colonial forces from the Chinese territory," then adding his democracy concerns. Says Liu Kunyuan of the Central News Agency: "A child snatched away for 150 years should rejoice at returning to the family but he is now afraid of facing an abusive father with a bad record. The father is behaving better now, but when he gets drunk, he can strike again."

The *Central Daily News*, the weakened organ of the Kuomintang (KMT), sends in a small team of reporters, but the team leader heaves a sigh of relief after discovering that the event is so flat as to do little damage to her understaffed paper. The *United Daily News* and the *China Times*, the Big Two that control two-thirds of Taiwan's newspaper circulation and advertising revenues, extended their news battleground to Hong Kong in full swing. Both papers editorially endorse "ending the national shame," but focus their primary concern on what will happen to Taiwan. The up-and-coming *Liberty Times* is the only paper able to establish a market foothold strong enough to challenge the Big Two in the postmartial law era. The paper owes its growing popularity largely to staking a claim as "standing for the voice of the 21 million Taiwanese" vis-à-vis the "pan-Chinese sentiments" of the Big Two. The paper advocates Taiwan's secession from China and firmly supports the first popularly elected president, Lee Tenghui (Li Denghui), in pursuing Taiwan's de facto independence. The paper, usually indifferent to the PRC, this time sends in a ten-person team and collaborates with foreign media to cover the news ground. The financially difficult, proindependence *Minzhong Daily* decides against sending in reporters to reinforce its stringers in Hong Kong.

The wide ideological span and different levels of resource commitment show up in the handover coverage. The media see the handover of Hong Kong as a sign of the PRC further extricating Taiwan's "international space." They are concerned about the erosion of Hong Kong's traditional role as a mediator and bridge between Taiwan and the PRC. All political parties reject China's "one country and two systems" scheme, but differ in their commitment to cultural, historical, and ethical identification with the Chinese nation. This difference divides the discourse of the rejection into two separate discursive packages: the mainstream media advocate "one country, one system—the better system," whereas the proindependence media emphasize "say 'no' to China."

Historical Script

Official histories in Taiwan and the PRC overlap partially in laying the blame of China's century-old national humiliation on British imperialism, so much so that the *China Times* (June 30) editorially hails the return of Hong Kong to "the Chinese territory" as "a proudest moment of the Chinese nation." In a news analysis, the paper's president writes that regardless of how one feels about the future of Hong Kong, at the "blinking moment of history" when the British royal yacht sails away, it marks "an unshakable historical fact: the borrowed land must be returned." On the eve of the handover, the paper quotes Taiwan's emissary as saying that he will attend the "historically watershed event with a sense of relief and solemnity." All the mainstream media outlets prominently report the celebratory extravaganzas from Beijing.

For Taiwan's media, however, praising the PRC as a historical victor is more difficult than cheering for the more abstract "Chinese nation," thus differentiating "cultural China" or "historical China" from "political China." Both the *China Times* (June 19) and the *United Daily News* (June 16) point out that Chiang Kai-shek tried to recover Hong Kong after the Second World War, in vain only because of Churchill's objection and Communist insurgence. The *China Times* reports (June 30) that the civil war between the Nationalist and Communist parties deprived the Chinese nation of "the fruit of victory in the war against Japanese invasion." On the same day, the paper editorializes Hong Kong as proof that a weak nation loses its sovereignty, and only a strong nation can recover its lost land. The proindependence *Minzhong Daily*, however, points out that the only way out for Taiwan is to abandon the "one China" policy and to build a Taiwan state. TTV (June 30) quotes a Taiwanese tourist in Hong Kong as saying, "Now China gets Hong Kong back, and Taiwan establishes an independent country."

To counter Beijing's pressure, the government of Taiwan holds an exhibition of the original copy of the Nanjing Treaty that ceded Hong Kong to Britain. The *China Times* (June 28) quotes Foreign Minister John Chang as claiming that the Republic of China (ROC) government, not the PRC, holds the "legitimacy and historical continuity" to represent the Chinese nation. If Britain had negotiated with the democratic ROC, according to him, Hong Kong people would have had no worries. Such remarks should be seen as a passive defense against Beijing rather than an active claim over Hong Kong sovereignty. The *China Times* reports (July 2) that as the world media zoom in on Hong Kong, President Lee and Vice President Lian Zhan also appear on TV repeatedly to balance "world opinions."

Political Geography

The PRC developed the "one country, two systems" concept as a solution for unifying mainland China and Taiwan, but it applies to Hong Kong at first instance. Taiwan media generally see the handover of Hong Kong as another significant event that muffles the island nation's international breathing room. Echoing the government position, they mount a strong rhetorical defense in pitting democratic Taiwan against the authoritarian PRC. The *United Daily News* (June 26) argues editorially, "When Hong Kong's freedom is in crisis, Taiwan needs to develop its democracy more fully." Media narratives exhibit a number of key features of spatial structure in their attempt to define the island nation's new relationship with Hong Kong, with the PRC, and with the international community:

DELINKING NATION FROM STATE. All media outlets anchor their coverage of Hong Kong from the vantage point of Taiwan's status, interests, and future. The *China Times* runs a three-part interview its president conducts with Zhou Nan, the PRC's de facto representative, highlighting that it will be more convenient for the Taiwanese to visit Hong Kong after July 1. The remainder of the interview is printed in two installments on the Hong Kong '97 Special Report section. Overall, the media focus their attention on concerns over Taiwan's status and the Taiwan-Hong Kong relationship. From June 30 to July 1, TTV's live coverage pays special attention to the future status of Taiwan's de facto consulate in Hong Kong (euphemistically named "The China Travel Agency"), travel arrangements to Hong Kong for Taiwan citizens, protests in Taiwan, and the song-and-dance celebration in Beijing.

A consuming interest of Taiwan's media is whether the talks with Beijing, suspended after President Lee's high-profile visit to the United States in 1995 and after the PRC's ensuing missile intimidation off Taiwan waters, would be resumed. As soon as the news is leaked out that Gu Zhenfu, Taiwan's negotiator, is among the 60 Taiwanese invited to attend the handover ceremony, the media begin to speculate on various scenarios. For days, both the *China Times* and the *United Daily News* carry items on the latest progress concerning Mr. Gu's itinerary and his seating at the ceremony. The *China Times* asks on June 16: How will Taiwan respond now? It then reports official approval of the acceptance of invitation to "show our respect for the return of Hong Kong to the Chinese nation," adding that the ceremony must be attended "with dignity" and with sensitivity to "any attempt to lower the status of Taiwan." Finally, the media report with relief that Mr. Gu is to be seated in the VIP section, together with other foreign dignitaries.

Both the government and the media are quite unified in rejecting the PRC's attempt to apply the "one country, two systems" formula to force Taiwan into Beijing's fold. The media prominently report the interviews Vice President Lian Zhan gives to CNN and NBC. On June 22 the *China Times* for example quotes Lian as telling Tom Brokaw of NBC: "Taiwan is part of China, but not part of the PRC." On CNN Lian rejects the PRC's "one country, two systems" and instead proposes "one country, one system—the better system," presumably Taiwan's democratic system. The interview, conducted in English, is dubbed with Chinese voiceover and aired in full on TTV. Moreover, all media report President Lee as saying that Taiwan should complete its constitutional amendment before July 1997 to show that "Taiwan is Taiwan, Hong Kong is Hong Kong, the two are different." This amendment was meant to establish the Republic of China as the political identity of Taiwan, renouncing Chiang Kai-shek's old sovereignty claim over the whole of China and the PRC's current sovereignty claim over Taiwan.

The media also quote the head of the official Mainland Work Committee approvingly as saying, "The Hong Kong model of the 'one country, two systems' is not acceptable for national unification because Taiwan is an independent sovereign state." He adds, "We shall never accept any attempt to reduce Taiwan to being a local government of China." On June 30 TTV interrupts its live coverage of the handover ceremony with President Lee's article in the *USA Today*, arguing that the handover gives "pride to all descendents of the Yellow Emperor," and Taiwan will be committed to "peaceful reunification of a *democratic* Chinese nation." Locked in diplomatic isolation, Taiwan appeals to the international media, especially those from the United States and Japan, as key venues for reaching out to the world community.

REORIENTING THE TRIANGULAR RELATIONSHIPS. Anchoring the news perspectives in Taiwan is a discursive strategy to reconstruct the triangular relationships involving the PRC, Hong Kong, and Taiwan. There is much concern that Hong Kong may lose its "buffer" role between the PRC and Taiwan. The *Liberty Times* (June 16) even speculates that Taiwan's customs may not be able to prevent the PRC from using Hong Kong to dump its cheap goods on Taiwan. The paper (June 20) further hypothesizes that Taiwan may have to trade with Hong Kong through indirect, rather than direct, routes, much like the indirect flow of trade between Taiwan and the PRC now. (These scenarios have not occurred.)

Politically, Taiwan's government and media have long called for "two states within one nation," so both Beijing and Taipei would share national sovereignty on an equal basis. Failing to gain Beijing's concession on that basis, Taiwan opts to play the "democracy" card against the PRC's "nationalism" card. Interrupting its live coverage on June 30, the TTV anchor again reads an official statement calling on Beijing to "give up its unrealistic intent over Taiwan." The *United Daily News* (June 26) editorially cites the polls to surmise, "Not only should the government (of Taiwan) renounce the 'one country, two systems' model as unsuitable for Taiwan; we should recognize that Taiwan now is the only democratic window for Chinese."

DRAWING POLITICAL BORDERS. Taiwan's media are fond of drawing contrasts between the oppressive PRC and the democratic Taiwan on the one hand, and between the poor PRC and the rich Hong Kong on the other. The eagerness to dissociate from China is strongly reflected in news analyses, editorials, official comments, and particularly in the revealing "mood" pieces. The *United Daily News* (June 21) notes that the commander of the PLA in Hong Kong will be making four times as much as President Jiang, but still at a meager US$1,540 per month. The *China Times* (June 15) quotes an unnamed Hong Kong psychiatrist to warn that the "handover hysteria" can cause psychological disorder, but all public hospitals are prepared to deal with this potential. The *Liberty Times* (June 21) interprets a "bad omen" in the Handover Giant Caldron breaking a leg while in transport from the mainland. On June 30, the *United Daily News* reports many signs of public apathy: people travel abroad en masse and profess no interest in learning pro-Communist songs, leaving only mainland Chinese visitors to fill some of the empty hotel rooms.

The proindependence *Liberty Times* (June 24) publishes a column article: "Chinese leaders, please listen to the voices of Taiwan people." The author claims that Taiwan was returned to China "against Taiwanese's will" after the Second World War, and Chiang Kai-shek ruled Taiwan as "one country, two systems" more brutally than Japanese occupiers. This time, the article argues, if China imposes its brand of nationalism on Taiwan, there will be another tragedy of historic proportion. On June 29 the paper reports a huge "Say No to China" rally with a headline, "Opposing Chinese Annexation, The Whole Taiwan Expresses Its Wish." Alongside is a large photo of protesters carrying signs, "Say No to China, the Whole Taiwan in Unison."

In sum, the reactive measures of the government and the oppositional groups against Beijing's nationalism shape media discourses. The democratic ferment shows certain ideological pluralism in media discourses, in that the mainstream media follow the government's attempt to delink the Chinese nation from the PRC state, while the proindependence papers pursue the goal of unifying the *Taiwanese* nation and state. The marginally important pro-unification group, which shares Beijing's nationalism, is also admitted into media representations.

Hong Kong: Ambivalence and Uncertainty

Unlike the foreign media, Hong Kong media have been wrestling with the ups and downs of the sovereignty transfer for almost two decades (Chan and Lee, 1991; Lee, 2000a); everything that needs to be told has been told. The handover is, to them, both a climax and an anticlimax. Some journalists suggest that the handover is a cause for Beijing, not for Hong Kong, to celebrate. "The day of the handover is a big show," as a reporter states, "but the day after will be the real story." Lurking behind this spectacle is deep-seated distrust of the PRC's ability to keep its promises. Despite the seeming boredom of the big show, news competition drives all media outlets to put in massive resources to capture it—sometimes in the name of "documenting the history." An editor from the populist *Apple Daily* puts it this way:

> Our editorial staff accepts the premise that people are happy about getting rid of colonial rule. Now we want to document whether the Joint Declaration and the Basic Law will be observed after July 1 . . . We want to record everything—what Hong Kong is like now, what expectations people have, what promises have been made to us—before July 1. We want to establish a baseline for future comparisons.

As if planning a "war mission," the *Apple Daily* suspends holidays from May onwards and deploys more than 100 people to cover the handover ceremony. The Oriental Press Group, its chief rival, has more than 170 reporters and editors to cover the story, even declining to accept any advertisement offer in the news section on July 1. The chief news editor of the *Oriental Daily News* remarks: "Our big boss does not care about spending money; anything you ask will be granted."[3] To start its field operation early, the *Apple Daily* called the GIS almost daily in the final three months before July 1 for information about the details of the events, but Beijing did not finalize the arrangements until the last minute. The local media could only publish the "countdown page" to heighten a sense of urgency and immediacy. This historicist approach—commissioning polls to "monitor the trend of public opinion" and recording all sorts of detailed schedules of official and nonofficial events with street maps—empirically reifies both journalism and history.

For the most part, media planning is focused on logistics and allocation of organizational resources; television's primary concerns are signal transmission and live coverage. To prevent jamming of telephone lines, a local newspaper even rents an ISDN high-speed telephone line inside the PBC for transmitting photographs (*Apple Daily*, July 1). From June 28 to July 3, local television stations rent three helicopters, at a cost of US$39 per minute, to provide aerial shots (*Ming Pao*, July 7). From June 16 on, the dominant Television Broadcasts (TVB) devotes 40 percent of its half-hour prime-time news to the handover-related stories, culminating in the 48 hours of nonstop live coverage of the formal ceremony on June 30 and July 1. Mobilizing a staff of 400, TVB's approach is to "let the audience witness everything" by providing a blanket coverage of events.[4] The resource-poor Asia Television (ATV) relies heavily on official "core feed."

Of course, not all journalists approach the handover with a conscious intent to "document the history," but most of them regard it as part of an ongoing story about Hong Kong in transition. While most journalists claim to be "neutral and objective," media narratives clearly display tremendous ambivalence and uncertainty about the handover.

"ONE COUNTRY, TWO SYSTEMS." The primary media concern is whether local autonomy can be protected from Beijing's interference. On July 1 the *South China Morning Post* (SCMP) prints the full text, in both English and Chinese, of President Jiang's speech at the handover ceremony with a headline, "Pledge on Rights and Non-interference." The *Ming Pao Daily News* (June 26) stresses that Hong Kong, as an international metropolis, must preserve its systems. The media spotlight Chief Executive Tung and his cabinet members, who are holdovers from the colonial team, and other new pro-PRC luminaries. The *Hong Kong Economic Journal* (July 5) notes editorially that former Chinese Premier Zhao Ziyang, an architect of the handover who had assured that Hong Kong people had nothing to "fear," is absent from the handover ceremony. He was purged for supporting the democracy movement in 1989. Given this, the paper asks, "How can Hong Kong people not be afraid?" Radio Television Hong Kong (RTHK), in providing the "core feed," has to juggle between British and Chinese perspectives.

QUEST FOR DEMOCRACY. The media credit Patten for installing limited democracy in Hong Kong, which "must be quite attractive to mainland Chinese" (according to the outspoken *Hong Kong Economic Journal*, July 5), but they also criticize the British for not establishing democratic institutions earlier (*Ming Pao*, editorial, June 30). All but the pro-China newspapers routinely give prominent coverage to leading prodemocracy legislators, who became household names during Patten's reign. The prominently covered protest staged by the democrats is, as the *Apple Daily* quips, "an alternative way to celebrate the reunification." However, some people criticize TVB for not giving enough coverage to the Democratic Party's protest.

BRITISH LEGACY. Media endorsements of—and pride in—what Patten (1997) calls "a Chinese city with British characteristics" accompany their distrust of Beijing. The *Apple Daily* (June 30) editorially praises the British for creating a "world wonder." It publishes a poll conducted by the University of Hong Kong, in which 40 percent of the respondents believe that Hong Kong would be better off under British rule, versus 15 percent who say that it would be worse off. The *Ming Pao Daily News* (June 30) publishes another poll showing that if time could be reversed to 156 years ago, more than 65 percent of the people would prefer British rule. The media, especially television, sentimentally remind people of the glory of the British Empire with all kinds of icons, while showing Patten in "hugs, kisses and tears all around" (for example, *SCMP*, July 1). The *Apple Daily* (June 30) captions one of its huge photos, "Long Live Chris Patten!"

MIXED FEELINGS. Ambivalence is expressed by a typical editorial in the *Apple Daily* (July 1) that claims that Hong Kong people are "emotionally identified with Chinese culture" but "rationally critical of China's authoritarian system," and thus "psychologically unsettled about the handover." A columnist (June 24) asks, "In saying goodbye to colonial rule and returning to the motherland, why do so many people feel unsettled and even alienated?" The media question the celebration hoopla as based on "fake sentiments." Reporting a poll conducted on the eve of the handover, the *Apple Daily* (June 30) indicates that only 24 percent of the respondents feel excited about it. A Buddhist monk writes in the *Ming Pao Daily News* (June 30), using a string of adjectives to describe Hong Kong people's feelings toward the handover: complicated, excited, eager, fearful, anxious, pessimistic, passive, abandoned. Days later, on July 5, the *Ming Pao Daily News* uses "anxiety, pray, and hope" in its headline to sum up a full-page review of the handover.

SMOOTH TRANSITION. The most important sources of the smooth transition package are quoted pledges from Chinese leaders, including President Jiang and Chief Executive Tung, and the officially organized festive celebrations with all the parties and fireworks. Despite the heavy rain, the *SCMP* (July 1) reports that more than half a million people saw the two firework displays, which combined are "enough to bring 40 of Hong Kong's greatest buildings to the ground." In addition, the laser guns for the spectacular are "powerful enough to shoot beyond the moon and light up a 20-storey office block." However, a hidden subtext emerges in the celebratory coverage of the festivities and fireworks as the *Apple Daily* (July1) claims in its editorial, "The real test and challenges begin today."

Historical Script

Hong Kong media, serving a land of refugees, focus their attention on the present and future rather than the colonial beginning of Hong Kong. Only the China-controlled papers in Hong Kong keep condemning the evilness of the Opium War that caused national humiliation. This does not mean that history is completely lost (*Ming Pao Daily News*, for example, prints a full-page feature on June 23, showing a map and photos of the British takeover), but the local media lose little time in saying that the colony has grown into a modern international metropolis. This is a story of a city cut off historically from China. Most media outlets echo Patten's eloquent defense of the British record (chapter 6).

What is important to Hong Kong media? Their prosperous "Chinese city with British characteristics" has been developed from a barren fishing village, in the background of decades of turmoil, starvation, and persecution in China—most recently, the horrendous Tiananmen massacre in 1989. The *Apple Daily* (June 28) suggests editorially that Beijing should "import" the good tradition and the "rational and modern system" that the British have established in Hong Kong. The paper takes Beijing to task for treating Patten with incivility and ingratitude. "After a century-long race," a columnist concludes in the *Ming Pao Daily News* (June 30), "it proves that being colonial subjects is better off than being slaves of a domestic regime." As if eager but unable to blot out the checkered past of the PRC, a columnist (June 25) writes tentatively in the *Ming Pao Daily News* that even though the televised images of horror remain vivid, "the most shocking and stormy days *might* have been over." The *Apple Daily* (July 3) says that unification marks a major event for Beijing, but for Hong Kong people, the handover ceremony is only "firing the first gunshot to open a new battlefield."

The media probe many new luminaries in government and legislature on their association with the Communist Party; a member of the Executive Council refuses the question on grounds that it implies a party member as "a bad person." There is much concern about continued political roles of the Communist Party and the Xinhua News Agency (the PRC's de facto representative that the *Apple Daily* characterizes as the "patriarch emperor")[5] and their implications for Hong Kong's autonomy. An article in the *Ming Pao Daily News* (June 23) states, "Hong Kong is going back to China, but not going back to socialism." The media express the fear that the "arrogant" and low-paid PLA may "abuse power" in Hong Kong under "material seduction." It is suggested that China may even send in the Tiananmen "butcher," former Premier Li Peng, if Hong Kong people step out of bounds.

Using polls is an effective "strategic ritual" (Tuchman, 1978) for the media to express their implicit ideological frameworks. Contrary to Tuchman's (1978) use of "strategic ritual" as a device of legitimizing the power structure, however, Lee (2000a) argues that polls and diversity of opinions hold populist appeals and are conducive to defending professional norms against political interference. The topics polled range from public evaluation of the outgoing and incoming regimes, political and cultural identities, to the prevailing mood. The *SCMP* and the *Ming Pao Daily News*, both owned by Malaysian-Chinese tycoons with considerable investments in China, have been accused of self-censorship. To cope with the cross-pressure between political concern and business interests, the *Ming Pao Daily News* has externalized its news treatment by creating several "public forum" columns to apportion a balance of opposing views. Disclaiming to represent the paper's position, these columns would express more unrestrained and more diverse views than its wishy-washy editorials, thus shifting editorial responsibility of the paper to the mystified "marketplace of ideas" (Lee, 2000a). One of the columns reprints the texts of popular radio talk shows, many of which are critical of Beijing. The paper (June 26) also carries another poll showing that most schoolteachers object to adding loving the Party and socialism to the proposed new curriculum.

Geographical Configurations

Hong Kong media view the handover as a local event in the global geopolitical context. The primary concern is protection of local autonomy under global watch from Beijing's interference. The media proudly depict Hong Kong as a meeting point between East and West, a window to the world for the PRC, and a bridge between the PRC and Taiwan—an international metropolis role that should be allowed to continue without damage. Beijing is thus an unwelcome central authority, to be checked by the western world.

With the British withdrawal, the United States is recognized as the superpower that could shoulder more responsibility toward Hong Kong (chapter 5). The *South China Morning Post* (June 30) reports that the United States and Japan have vowed that they will "protect Hong Kong's freedoms when the party's over." The paper quotes U.S. Secretary of State Albright as saying, "The United States is, and will remain, a friend to democracy in Hong Kong and elsewhere." The geographical construction of the media has put Hong Kong squarely within the world capitalist system, suggesting that, short of international support, it will be an orphan under an uncaring Communist mother. TVB focuses its coverage on Hong Kong, but it also spreads its resources to cover Chinese reactions in major cities like London, Beijing, Shanghai, Shenzhen, and New York.

Defining the Chinese Nation-State

Therefore, one event is being told by three different stories with contrasting—and contesting—historical interpretations, collective memories, and ideological visions. Let us compare the historical scripts and discursive structures of these three media narratives.

Historical Scripts

History is an epistemology for a group of people to imagine themselves as a community; it is also constructed to serve the present context (Duara, 1995). As is clear from Table 7.2, the Opium War as the colonial beginning is not contestable, but its significance is. While both the PRC and Taiwan media hold British imperialists accountable for causing national humiliation, Hong Kong media tend to discount the relevance of the "historical accidents" and emphasize today's prosperity and freedom. The culturally and ethnically Hong Kong Chinese are said to have developed a "way of life" based on transcendental values, very different from the "motherland."

The PRC media achieve their interpretative coherence by adopting family-nation as the master frame. But such a narrative is shy from people's everyday life and is officially controlled to present a distorted image of "national achievement" (chapter 6). Taiwan's media pay lip service to an abstract "Chinese nation," while rejecting the Beijing-imposed definition of nation-state. Defending discursively against Beijing's hegemony, they even suggest Taiwan's fledging democracy as a model of emulation for Beijing and Hong Kong.

Settling different starting points of the historical scripts enables the media to assign heroes and villains. Presenting a linear and continuous view of history, the PRC blames western imperialists for starting the trouble and praises the Communist Party for ending it. Taiwan's media both vilify British imperialists for the inglorious colonial beginning but blame Communist insurgence for hindering the early recovery of Hong Kong and for threatening Taiwan's democratic existence. The mainstream media in Taiwan seek to delink nation from state, whereas the proindependence media advocate severance of Taiwan from China as both a state and a nation. To Hong Kong media the heroes are the hard-working people who prosper under the British as personified by Patten and local democrats, who have the courage to stand up to Beijing's harassment.

Interpretations of the past are then linked to those of the present and future. The PRC sees the handover as a cause for national celebration and a further impetus to the prosperity of Hong Kong under "one country, two systems," totally oblivious to the feeling of local people. Both Taiwan and Hong Kong media are skeptical about the future of Hong Kong.

Table 7.2
Features of the Historical Scripts of the Three Media Narratives

	The PRC	Hong Kong	Taiwan
Starting point	The Opium War in 1840	Historical accidents that occurred 150 years ago	The Opium War in 1840
Hero	The CCP, Mao, and Deng Xiaoping	British legacy, Patten, Hong Kong people, and the democrats	Chiang Kai-shek, Taiwan people
Villain	Western imperialists, typified by Patten	Chinese Communists, the PLA	Western imperialists, Chinese Communists
Historical flow	Linear and continuous	Linear and punctuated	Linear, interrupted and restarted on a separate cause
Historical present	National pride and celebration; "One country, two systems" works	Hong Kong's future uncertain; Chinese identity in flux	Hong Kong's future uncertain; Taiwan's status unclear
Historical future	Greater national achievement, brighter future	Uncertain	Uncertain

The handover brings the meanings of Chinese and the tensions between China as a nation and China as a state to the forefront. The PRC media politically fold the nation into the state, which subsumes cultural and ethnic identities. Taiwan media stress the continuities of cultural and ethnic identities but dispel the politically mythologized nation-state. Hong Kong media are highly ambivalent toward the disjuncture between cultural nation and political state; they emphasize mixed ethnic and cultural ingredients of Chinese and the "unique" identity of Hong Kong.

The Discursive Structures

Any historical narrative pursues its inner logic of coherence, with chosen elements, specially accorded significance, and causal connections to form an overall theme. It is structured into a discourse of a given community by manipulating cultural symbols according to certain conventions and rules of textual composition, usually biased in favor of the power that be (Foucault, 1972; Gilbert and Mulkay, 1984; Tolson, 1996; van Dijk, 1988). Table 7.3 summarizes such structural features of the three media narratives.

Global Media Spectacle

Table 7.3
Features of Discourse Structures of the Media Narratives

	The PRC	Hong Kong	Taiwan
Vantage point	The PRC/Beijing	Hong Kong	Taiwan/Taipei
Ideological anchorage	Essentialized nationalism	Capitalism and freedom	Ethnic and cultural Chinese identity; democracy
Nexus of the news net	Beijing	Patten, Beijing/SAR	Taipei
Contending groups	Chinese vs. all others	Hong Kong Chinese vs. Mainland Chinese	Taiwanese vs. Chinese
Master frame	Family-nation	Hong Kong distinction	Democratization
Central issues	National unification and territorial integrity	Will the promises be kept?	Taiwan's legitimacy and identity
Appeal	Emotions and the essential features of Chinese	Exemplars	Emotions and principles
Mode of address	Interpellation	Experience sharing	Interpellation

The first four rows of Table 7.3 follow the theoretical proposition that news is constructed based on the "enduring values" and issue priorities of a society and that these shape the "news net" of a media organization (Gans, 1979; Tuchman, 1978). Guided by the essentialized nationalism, the PRC media depict an all-inclusive image of "Chinese" based on fixated ethnicity and a mythological historical origin. The news net is centered in Beijing, which organizes media discourses. In contrast, Hong Kong media emphasize the distinction of Hong Kong society, based not on ethnicity and cultural heritage but on the capitalist, free "way of life." The ambivalent identity of Hong Kong seems to be reflected in the two ideological centers of the news net: one in Beijing, the other in the western capitals. Nationalistic feelings and more transcendent values of democracy comprise Taiwan's handover discourse; the mainstream media differentiate Chinese from people of other nationalities, while the proindependence media separate Taiwanese from Chinese.

The other four rows of Table 7.3 show the methodological approach to the handover coverage. These features are based on both the "framing analysis" of themes and key issues (Gamson et al., 1992; Pan and Kosicki, 1993; Snow and

Benford, 1992) as well as the structuralist analysis of the appeal and "mode of address" (Althusser, 1971). The "mode of address" refers to the way in which speakers attempt to relate with their audiences through specific ways of talking to them. It is based upon and performs a power relationship between a speaker and his or her audience. Althusser (1971) observes that political authorities address their subjects as "interpellation." In this mode of address, audiences are spoken to, hailed, commanded, and demanded rather than being involved as partners of sharing and exchange, as may be the case in a ritual mode of communication (Carey, 1989). Interpellation places the media in a command position that coincides with and is built upon the high political authority. The "sharing" mode of address places the media as a community conduit to rejuvenate a bond and as a stage for performing cultural rituals.

The constraint of logical consistency (van Dijk, 1984) pulls these features in line with those more general structural features shown in the first four rows. The PRC media resort to heightened emotions in narrating a story of festivity of a family-nation. Its mode of address is "interpellation." In contrast, Hong Kong media single out their society and way of life as rooted in capitalism and international cosmopolitanism, distinct from the new sovereign. Using examples of individuals or groups and specific incidences, the media present the handover as a society in doubt about whether Beijing will keep its promises. Relative autonomy enables Hong Kong media to adopt "experience sharing" as the mode of address. The media converse with the audience and enact public anxieties. The Taiwan media use family separation to defuse the PRC's mythical family-nation; in more radical forms, they insist that Taiwan and the PRC are two "distant cousins" and "close neighbors" but "different countries," and that the PRC expansionism must be repulsed. Both the "family separation" and "anti-China's expansion" stories resort to emotions and principles, with the former to Chinese sentiment over national unification, while the latter to Taiwanese nationalism. The mode of address is also to hail and command the audience as the subjects, except now the subjects are both the domestic audience and the international community.

In sum, these comparisons on historical scripts and discursive structures show the clashing of media narratives by the three Chinese societies at a defining moment. The meanings of China and Chinese have been contested. In this contestation, the PRC initiates the theses and issues for Taiwan and Hong Kong to react. This discursive power imbalance is rooted in the political power imbalance in the broader international political economy. Will increasing participation of the PRC in the globalized economy lead to the infusion of more generalized values of freedom and democracy to pluralize China's identity discourse? It is too early to tell.

Chapter 8

Human Rights and National Interest: From the Middle Powers

Hong Kong is a domestic story for us. I sometimes feel like I could do the daily traffic reports in Hong Kong and it would get printed in my newspapers.
> —Jonathan Manthorpe, the Hong Kong-based
> Asian correspondent for Canada's Southam News

Why can't *our* Communists be like that?
> —An Australian newspaper commenting on China in the
> aftermath of the Tiananmen massacre, with reference
> to the events in Eastern and Central Europe

Gone are the days when Australia does just what Washington and London want us to do.
> —Alexander Downer, Foreign Minister of Australia

We come to Hong Kong to make a profit.
> —*Sankei Shimbun*, quoting a Japanese businessman, June 24, 1997

For almost 50 years the Cold War framework has provided an easy and simplified formula to look at the world. With the end of the Cold War, a veteran journalist contends that we have lost "the clarity of our coverage" and "the strategic imperative" (quoted in Freedom Forum, 1993: 47). According to Wallerstein (1993), the primary objective of the Cold War for the western alliance was to contain the Soviet Union, to maintain the unity of the free world and a united home front led by the United States, and to induct a steady, non-radical political and economic revolution of the Third World. Policy differences between western allies were downplayed for the sake of a larger common enemy. After the collapse of the Soviet camp, however, centralized dualism becomes decentralized pluralism. The junior partners in the western alliance may

151

find it easier to air their differences with the United States and see a different playing field without the staged East-West struggle. It is also getting more difficult for the United States to use the United Nations to cloak its own foreign policy and dress up the American initiative as multinational mandates. Can the western ideological united front survive? The rise of China, along with the handover of Hong Kong, would be an important test case.

The Cold War is over, and it has been argued that the foreign policy of the United States is one of trade diplomacy. National interest consists of vital existence, special interests of friends and allies, and general interests of international order (Von Vorys, 1990). If national interest is defined in terms of ideological, territorial, and economic dimensions, then it seems clear that economic interests have risen to challenge the supremacy of ideological interests. In fact, economic interests of securing the best possible terms of exchange within the world economy may become a preeminent ideology. The nation-state is the most important instrument and agent of pursuing national interest. Touraine (1997) argues that if democracy is to survive in the post-Communist world, it must somehow protect the power of the nation-state at the same time as it limits that power, for only the state has sufficient means to counterbalance the global corporate wielders of money and information. When western ideology and national interest (principally but not limited to economic interest) clash, what would the media discourses be?

Cohen (1963) paints the press as a watchdog, an independent observer, an active participant, and a catalyst of the U.S. foreign policy. Opposite to that is the view that the media are "no more than a pawn in the political game played by the powerful political authority and establishment in Washington" (Chang, 1993: 7). The media and policy makers sometimes form coalitions, and national news may very well reflect national policies, cultures, and institutional interests. For Ramaprasad (1983: 70), media diplomacy is "the role the press plays in the diplomatic practice between nations." There is a strong incentive for the state to use the media to articulate and promote foreign policy, to promote national image, to "trial balloon," to confer recognition, and to generate pressure on the opponent (Frederick, 1993). Herman and Chomsky (1988) even consider the media as a propaganda arm of the state.

The handover of Hong Kong takes place in the post-Cold War context. Will the chill of the Cold War remain? Will the traditional Cold-War bipolar mode of thought and language—us versus them, good versus evil, winners versus losers—still dominate media narratives? To what extent will the three junior partners of the western camp—Canada, Australia, and Japan—cast China's reclamation of Hong Kong in terms of the U.S.-style ideological tug-of-war? To what extent will the redefined spheres of their national economic and strategic interests temper such ideological discourses? This chapter will address these questions.

Canada: Special Ties

Canada and the United States, as neighbors and political allies, do have a lot in common, but Canada has always been trying to get out of the U.S.'s shadow and establish its own identity. Canadian cultural nationalism has seen its rises and ebbs for decades. After all, Canada is not a major power in global politics, and Canadian culture is a "marginal culture" vis-à-vis U.S. culture (Robinson and Theall, 1975). While successive government efforts have been made to protect Canadian identity from relentless U.S. assaults, the problem is that Canadian identity tends to be defined defensively not in terms of what Canadian culture is, but more in terms of what U.S. culture is *not* (A. Lee, 1997; Smythe, 1994). The identity of Canadian broadcasting (especially the Canadian Broadcasting Corporation) has been particularly central to this unhappy cultural struggle (Hallman, 1977).

Attallah (2000) argues that the notion of "American culture" is increasingly being displaced by the recognition of a "highly permeable, frequently diasporic, fundamentally democratic North American culture." Even so, Canadian journalists believe that their journalism is a bit less ideologically driven than American journalism. They share the westernized-cum-universal values of democracy and human rights, but seek perhaps not very successfully to assert a "Canadian perspective." Jonathan Manthorpe of Southam News is critical of Americans for carrying "the Holy Grail of human rights and democracy" as the only interpreters of how these values should be applied. CBC's Eric Rankin echoes: "Canadians don't think of themselves as being at the top," with more "realistic" and less judgmental views rather than American egoistic and patriotic fervor. He accuses the Americans of being only interested in Hong Kong in terms of how it would affect the United States, not how it could affect Hong Kong or China. How this philosophical difference is translated into media discourses is, however, much less obvious. By and large, the Canadian media seem to portray, as do American media, that Hong Kong will see the end of democracy and loss of press freedom under Communist threat, although its economy may continue to prosper. The major difference is that Canada does not claim to have a "guardian" role toward Hong Kong, but instead stresses its special linkage to Hong Kong.

The End of Democracy

Concern for Hong Kong's democracy is prominent, roughly in the same order of other western media. Our content analysis (Table 3.1) shows that 28.6 percent of Canadian stories predict democracy likely to change in Hong Kong; of which, 58.3 percent believe that it will change for worse. The other concern is about the possible deterioration of daily life in Hong Kong. This should be seen in the context that Canada played a special role in helping the colonial regime to strengthen democratic institutions in Hong Kong. It offered advice on electoral practice, the drafting of the Bill of Rights, the protection of privacy and freedom of information, and also by maintaining parliamentary links with the Legislative Council of Hong Kong. The PRC dismantled or threatened to dismantle many of these institutions.

The Tiananmen Square massacre is the dominant media reference. In reporting the three-day holiday in Beijing to celebrate the handover, the CBC (June 28) describes it as "the biggest gathering in Tiananmen Square since the massacre in 1989." Another CBC story mentions that western nations could not forget the Tiananmen Square massacre. The deployment of the PLA in Hong Kong is constantly linked to the Tiananmen massacre. In reporting a march of 2,000 people in Hong Kong, the *Globe and Mail* (July 3) describes it in a front-page lead story as "possibly the largest antigovernment protest on Chinese soil since the doomed student democracy campaign in Tiananmen Square eight years ago." Jan Wong, the paper's Beijing correspondent in 1989, admits to having a very dark view of China: "I can't see China tolerating freedom of expression here (in Hong Kong). Beijing's priority is control and stability, and even though in terms of business it is a thriving place, they don't care, that's not the main priority." Among many of the pieces she writes is a story (July 1) about the gay bars in Hong Kong, which have "most to fear" because China regards homosexuality as "a crime of perversion." The story found its way through syndication into the pages of the *San Jose Mercury News*.

The media favor Chris Patten and leaders of the Democratic Party vis-à-vis the Chief Executive Tung and his endorsers in Beijing. CBC (June 19) reports that Chris Patten, in reply to Martin Lee in the last Legislative Council session he attended, claims that "the single most important thing Patten would do for Hong Kong but could not do" would be to convince the Chinese leaders in Beijing to trust Hong Kong. CBC repeatedly interviews Martin Lee and Emily Lau. Lee's popularity, according to the *Globe and Mail* (July 1), is "rooted in defense of freedom and personal integrity."

Like their western counterparts, the Canadian media are positive about Hong Kong's economic vibrancy but negative about its political future. They are suspicious of China's promises to maintain a high degree of autonomy for Hong Kong. The *Globe and Mail* (June 25) and CBC (June 27), quoting a local woman, a teacher, a local press editor, and the Canadian Commissioner in Hong Kong, all express worry about the loss of democracy and press freedom under Chinese rule. The paper (June 18) quotes polls to say that people feel they have to accept the handover against their wishes and worry about corruption and lack of democracy. In a CBS piece aired on CBC, the American TV correspondent Bob Simon remarks: "Control, that's what it's all about. That's what people here have never had. Like the countless millions who would be tuning in to the festivities, Hong Kong people will be spectators too. Once again, watching their own history march right by."

In a different twist, the *Globe and Mail* (June 26) quotes Tim Reid, the president of the Canadian Chamber of Commerce, who praises the economic liberalization in China and economic integration between Hong Kong and China. A helicopter ride to the booming South China, he adds, "couldn't tell where Hong Kong ended and China began." He quips, "Politics is playing catch-up." CBC describes Hong Kong's economy as "euphoric," as reflected by the Hang Seng Index, and continuing to perform well. In its Pacific Rim Report, after China's minister for Hong Kong and Macau affairs Lu Ping gives a speech, a local businessman rebuts, and the host remarks wryly that "the rights to make money will be protected, but not sure about human rights." Finally, the economy is also seen as the best political solution as the *Globe and Mail* (July 1) states: "The Trojan horse of freedom is inside the gates . . . The hope is that Hong Kong can teach (market economy, pluralism, rule of law) to the motherland. Instead of China changing Hong Kong, Hong Kong would change China."

"Special Ties"

Even if many Canadians still hold a Eurocentric vision of the world, more trade now goes across the Pacific between Canada and Asia than across the Atlantic between Canada and Europe. Six of Canada's top ten trading partners are in Asia. For Canada, in 1997 China and Hong Kong respectively ranked fifth and sixteenth in terms of its imports, and sixth and eighth in terms of its exports. This does not begin to take into account the tremendous traffic of people and capital between Hong Kong and Canada. When things are good in Hong Kong, there would be an outflow of money and "returnees" from Canada back to Hong Kong. If the reverse happens, we shall see a new flow of money and immigrants to Canada.

Chinese have a long history of settlement in Canada; early settlers helped build the cross-Canada railroad. Canada and Hong Kong share the same British colonial heritage; some 40 years ago the Canadian flag was very much like a Hong Kong flag. Because of a vague Commonwealth linkage, Prince Charles and Queen Elizabeth II are familiar to Canadians and Hong Kong people in ways that they are alien to Americans. Since the early 1980s Canada has been the most favored country for Hong Kong immigrants, most of them wealthy and well-educated members of the professional and managerial classes who have uprooted themselves to escape the prospect of Communist control. Some estimated 200,000 Canadian citizens live in Hong Kong, one million people from Hong Kong now live in Canada, and another half a million have the right to live in Canada because of citizenship or family reunion. Even if many of them return to Hong Kong afterwards, these migrants become "a permanent human bridge" consisting of "sentiment, investments, and a shared pool of talent" (Luk, 1994: 22).

Cantonese is now the third language of Canada after English and French, and it is hard to miss the Chinese flavor in Vancouver and Toronto. The Hong Kong press covers daily events in Canada. Both the *Ming Pao Daily News* and the *Sing Tao Daily News* publish local editions in Canada, in addition to the Canadian Chinese Broadcasting Corporation, which runs radio and television networks across Canada offering both Cantonese and Mandarin programs.[1] Canada is strongly represented in Hong Kong.[2] *Maclean's*, the national magazine, publishes a Chinese edition. Canada is arguably Hong Kong's most important link, and what happens in Hong Kong has a very direct bearing on what happens in Canada.[3] It is easy to get the impression in Hong Kong that there is "no one who does not have a relative in Canada" (Lary, 1992: 109). Hong Kong has become something of "a mid-sized Canadian metropolis in its own right" (GIS, 1992: 30).

Chris Wood of *Maclean's* claims: "This (the handover) is not just Hong Kong people's story, this is in some respect our story." Jonathan Manthorpe describes that he sometimes feels that he is "in the Richmond West bureau of the *Vancouver Sun*." Jan Wong of the *Globe and Mail* says that she does not look for Canadians to interview, but "it's impossible to avoid Canadians" because "so many Hong Kong people are now Canadians." CBC interviews famed local personalities with Canadian passports. Fairchild Television plays up the sentimental linkages between Canada and Hong Kong in many of its programs, showing how much Canadian stuff there is in Hong Kong. Many media outlets, like *Maclean's*, are keen on recounting the history of Canadians who fought for and died in Hong Kong during the Second World War.

The Exotic Orient

On the other hand, to most Canadians, Hong Kong remains an "Exotic Orient." To make something unfamiliar more interesting, the *Globe and Mail* uses traditional icons—the fishing junk, rickshaw, sampan, fortune-telling, and Chinese temple—to give the city an imagined taste of the "Exotic Orient" despite Hong Kong's modern international character. Several articles guide the readers through the old and new Hong Kong, the rural and urban areas, the familiar and the exotic scenes. The Star Ferry across the Victoria Harbor is "the 40-cent ride of a lifetime" (*Globe and Mail*, July 1). Quoting travel managers, the paper (June 28) notes that neither the flights nor the hotel rooms (with both prices given) are full; most events are held behind closed doors—"It is not a royal wedding." Other stories predict a slump in tourism after the "handover fuss dies down." Also on June 28, the *Globe and Mail* has a full two-page story in the Travel section entitled "A Survival Guide: Hong Kong Now" (subtitle:

"How to Eat, Sleep, and Spend in Hong Kong"). Even its international affairs journalist, Marcus Gee, writes a piece (June 25) advising travelers to first go up to the Peak and enjoy the great sight of skyscrapers, the hill-hugging apartment towers, and the ferment of the harbor.[4]

Another favorite topic of media portrayals is various kinds of fortune-tellers (palm-reader, or a bird picking out cards). CBC (July 1) shows Tung Chee-hwa praying for good luck with Buddhist monks in a soccer field. It (June 30) airs a CBS piece contrasting worshippers burning incense sticks with those on mobile phones. Jan Wong (June 30) writes in the *Globe and Mail* about the traditional Chinese "cheongsam" as the gown of choice for the handover in the grand Hong Kong tradition of excess. Wong notes that the wife of a local celebrity will attend seven functions, and she has to change a cheongsam (with a price tag from US$700 to $5,000 or more) every single time. Another story (June 24) is on "Shanghai Tang," which sells Chinese chic to people with identity crises. Owned and operated by westernized local Chinese, this shop blends the traditional Chinese pop art with modern people's desire of old Chinese goods. Another story in the *Globe and Mail* (June 28) says that condom manufacturers believe the handover feel-good factor and a five-day holiday could boost sales by up to 20 percent.

Australia: Independent Policy?

The Australian media appear to share the generalized western-cum-universal values of democracy and human rights, painting as dark as the U.S. media (Table 3.1) a picture of Hong Kong under Chinese rule. However, they also strive, perhaps not always very successfully, to pursue a foreign policy more independent of Washington and London. They seem eager to reassert their Asian identity and adopt certain Asian values, hence enabling them to sing variations on the chorus of the western tune. Australia's interest in China as the ultimate concern in the Hong Kong handover is similar to Japan's: economic benefit and regional security. Both countries have their eyes on China and view Hong Kong as a test case for China to show the world that it can behave. To Australians, the handover, notwithstanding its problems, marks an opportunity to adjust its economic relationship with China via Hong Kong.

As a middle power with no significant part to play in the strategic balance in the Pacific, Australia is in an ambivalent position of being part of the British ties and U.S. defense system while wishing to be an Asian country. Once stridently Eurocentric, Australia was said to inherit "an image of the world held by the British foreign service," or a footnote assumed to "replicate American or British patterns" (Strahan, 1994: 11–12). Australia, along with New Zealand, was "the most isolated fragment of western civilization in the world" (p. 317).

Australia sided with the western camp during the Cold War. Not until the 1980s did it begin to shift its foreign policy paradigm from the Cold War to the East Asian economic miracle, pulling away from its Eurocentric orientation.[5] China was no longer to be perceived from the old view of oriental despotism as an inherently autocratic and expansionist threat and a source of chaos. Instead, China was to be recognized as a potential great power, with economic opportunities for Australia, to be brought into the world on an equitable basis. The Tiananmen crackdown brought backlashes, but economic links soon recovered (Mackerras, 1996). (But it should be noted that the imprint of the Tiananmen massacre is hardly erased from Australian journalistic mindset, as we shall show.) The 1991–92 *Defense Report* states that Australia had adopted a security policy of "forward defense," which is for "defending Australia with and in Asia rather than against Asia" (O'Connor, 1995: 87).

Australia continues to value human rights but tends to separate it from trade and economic relations. The Australian government has promised that it would engage in "constructive dialogue" with both China and Britain in order to help maintain Hong Kong's stability, prosperity, and human rights after 1997. Despite its nostalgia toward Britain, Australia has bluntly criticized "Britain's failure to create representative and responsible government in Hong Kong and to create a democratic ethos" (Joint Standing Committee on Foreign Affairs, Defense and Trade, 1997: xxi). The Parliamentary report urged the government to give human rights "equal weight with trade issues and strategic issues in any ministerial or official contacts with China." But it does not advocate a conditional or punitive linkage between trade and human right matters (p. 119). There is a view that Australia should continue to adopt a "cautious but friendly approach rather than an ideologically based approach to China" (Harris, 1996: 18–19); it is better to influence Beijing's political reform than undermine it.

Australia has considerable interest in Hong Kong.[6] More importantly, some people would argue that Australia should use Hong Kong as a base to target the China market. Dunn (1985: 20) advocates that: "We would be best advantaged by a China whose major deterrent was a strong and self-sustaining economy coupled with a stable and confident political environment." The Parliamentary report cited above clearly states that Australia has at stake business in Hong Kong and the access to the markets of the Southern China crescent (p. 103). Australian business people and the Australian government are generally optimistic about Hong Kong's future economic prosperity.[7]

Australia has absorbed an influx of 88,000 immigrants from Hong Kong, but the bonding between Australians and Hong Kong people has never been as strong as that between Canadians and Hong Kong people.[8] While the Canadian media regard a Hong Kong story as part of a "domestic" story (which is part of the dominant values), it is for Australians a "domesticated" story (which is interpreted according to internal dominant values) at best. Besides, the Australian portrait of the "Exotic Orient" is based more on various fascinating achievements of Hong Kong, unlike Canada's treatment of it as a sample of traditional and exotic Chinese culture.

Demonic China

Our content analysis (Table 3.1) shows that the Australia media are almost as pessimistic as the U.S. media about Hong Kong's democracy and civil liberties, and also tend to portray Beijing negatively. On June 30, the *Australian* printed on page one the headline, "Back off, Beijing Warns Canberra." Federal Parliament issues a 120-page report on Hong Kong's human rights, denouncing China's abolition of the elected Legislative Council and the installment of the Provisional Legislature. It calls for continued monitoring of Hong Kong's situation and publishing an annual report in Parliament. The media make ample references to the "Tiananmen massacre" and "brutal crackdown" to "prove" the evil nature of Communist China and to back up their own pessimism about Hong Kong's future. The *Australian* (June 21–22) quotes an author to characterize Beijing's plan as calling not for decolonisation, but recolonialisation. In response to our interview, Richard McGregor of the *Australian* rejects the accusation of the foreign press "demonizing China" as a propaganda system on the part of China to put journalists on the defensive. ABC reporter Jane Hutcheon observes, "The (Chinese) leaders do not want to accept responsibility or apologize for things that go wrong. If something goes wrong, it is covered up." She adds, "If foreign media demonize China, it is because China hasn't come clean yet." With the memories of the Tiananmen massacre still vivid, she observes that for China to talk about the handover "as the end of the national humiliation saga" reflects a "strong inferiority complex."

In a feature story, the ABC reporter (June 17) mocks some members of Hong Kong's business elite who stay put and "work with their new Communist bosses rather than run for cover with their second passports." The reporter raises doubts about whether Hong Kong's economic dynamism can "survive the first of July." Speaking of "China's 'one country, two economic systems'," the reporter comments, "Logically no one can see why the new rulers should want to wreck so valuable a property. Emotionally no one wants even to think about China's long history of self-inflicted and logic-free economic catastrophies." In the second special feature, ABC (June 30) shows Tiananmen footage of armored tanks. The reporter asks whether it "bothers" businessmen that "Hong Kong is going to be ruled by a brutal Communist dictatorship." The reporter also comments: "CH Tung's administration will hold its first meeting at 2:45 am, the very first act of the new Beijing-appointed legislature will be to restrict demonstrations, ban overseas funding for political parties, and outlaw subversion." In the third special feature show (July 1), the introduction declares: "Tonight, China's prize—Hong Kong—returns after a century and a half of British rule. But does the red flag signal a new game plan for organized crime and its export to Australia?" Exporting organized crime to Australia as China's new game plan seems rather far-fetched.

Economic Trojan Horse

China, the *Australian* (July 1) says, gets the "greatest prize of the century." "China will resume control of Hong Kong," The *Weekend Australian* (June 28–29) argues in an editorial, "but Hong Kong will have a big and positive impact on China's future." Hong Kong is but a lightning rod, and the real significance of its future is really about China. The best-case scenario is that China would become more like Hong Kong. Jonathan Fenby (the *Australian*, July 1) writes that Hong Kong can even play a key role in defining the relationship between China and the world in the next century. A *Financial Times* article (*Weekend Australian*, June 28–29) states that Hong Kong may serve as a catalyst for change on the mainland—relative press freedom and relative freedom of speech and association, if not the emergence of opposition parties—and as an increasing hub for China's relations with the outside world.

The worst-case scenario is, however, that Hong Kong would sink into a mainland mire of corruption, disrespect for the rule of law, and restraint on press and other freedoms. As a journalist (*Weekend Australian*, June 21–22) remarks, "Deng's edict [one country, two systems] is fine for business, but when it comes to politics, 'one country' is the rule." An ABC feature story says: "If Benny still looks happy five days before the handover, it's because like millions of others he's learned how to grin and bear the inevitable." Hong Kong's liberties will depend on "nothing more than a promise made by China." A quarter of ABC's 48 news stories mention Taiwan because the handover of Hong Kong is seen as a pretext to the negotiations and manipulations between China and Taiwan. Two Taiwan officials are even found among the top ten sources of the Australian media (Table 3.5).

Independent Foreign Policy

Australia does not have an international role to play and thus does not have the same superpower mania about China as there might be in the United States. However, Australia is anxious to show its independence from the United States and Britain in terms of foreign policy. Earlier in 1997 Australia refused to support the United States, Britain, and a number of European countries in condemning China's human rights situation at a United Nations forum in Geneva. Now it decides to attend the swearing-in ceremony in Hong Kong, breaking ranks with the boycotting United States and Britain. Foreign Minister Alexander Downer (*Weekend Australian*, June 14–15) puts it bluntly: "Gone are the days when Australia does just what Washington and London want us to do."

A round of exchange on this issue in the *Australian* is revealing. It starts off with former Prime Minister Malcolm Fraser (June 16) accusing the United States and Britain of "self-interest and hypocrisy" in Hong Kong. He criticizes Americans for believing that "the U.S. is right and knows best." The British promote local democracy in Hong Kong in the name of advancing human rights, but Fraser thinks what Britain has done "has the potential to do much to damage human rights in Hong Kong." He argues, "British and U.S. attempts to establish a western-style enclave in Hong Kong and to impose western conditions on China will contribute nothing to stability in East Asia and the western Pacific." He calls for an urgent and open appraisal of western policy in this region. Fraser appears to put Australia as a member of the East. A historian argues (June 20) that Australia's position on attending the swearing-in of the new Hong Kong Provisional Legislature does not "place it on a higher moral ground than the United States and Britain; merely that it has a different set of national interests to pursue in the international arena." Another scholar (July 2) writes, "The western assertion that individual human rights are universal has been challenged in East Asia by states emphasizing their rights to conduct their domestic politics free from external criticism."

Paul Kelly, the *Australian*'s international editor, observes (June 25) that the Hong Kong handover signifies something important in the future path of Australia-U.S. relations. In spite of similar basic values shared by the traditional allies, Kelly argues that Australia's interests do not necessarily coincide with the United States or the United Kingdom. "Hong Kong betrays the deepening tensions for Australian foreign policy between values and national interest and they will only intensify." In another article, he (July 2) asserts that "Hong Kong is a city in Asia; Australia wants 'one country, two systems' to work, but it doesn't expect Hong Kong to become a model democracy." The *Australian* (June 28–29) points editorially to Australia's interests at stake in Hong Kong. About 350 Australian companies are based in Hong Kong with investments of AUS$3.2 billion (US$1.9 billion) as of 1995; more than 30,000 Australians live and work in Hong Kong, and the combined Hong Kong and China will be Australia's third most important export market. In 1997, of the top ten export destinations, the United States ranks the third and the United Kingdom ranks the tenth; the rest are in Asia (Japan ranks first, South Korea second, New Zealand fourth, Taiwan fifth, China sixth, Singapore seventh, Hong Kong eighth, Indonesia ninth). ABC (June 30) comments that history will judge both China and Britain harshly against "the deception, secrecy and hostility that characterize their dealings over Hong Kong."

Amazing Hong Kong

Although Hong Kong is the first take of Asia for many Australians, their general knowledge of Hong Kong is low. To render the place more intelligible to the audience, the media have characterized Hong Kong as a "helluva China-town" and "the Manhattan of the East." It is a place "where East meets West, East meets East, North meets South, developing nations meet industrialized nations and mainland China meets everyone else," a place crowded with tycoons and gangsters (*Weekend Australian*, June 21–22), and a city of dreams, dragons, fortunes, and romance. The editor of the *South China Morning Post*, Jonathan Fenby, describes it as a "world-view colony" (The *Australian*, July 1).

Hong Kong people are Chinese by blood, according to ABC News (June 24), but citizens of the world by training and by inclination. Journalists (*Weekend Australian*, July 5–6) even note that Tung uses Mandarin, Cantonese, and English to give speeches to an international business audience. Hong Kong is a town of economics, not politics, so Tung is a businessman true to Hong Kong's deepest instincts, unlike Patten who is a born politician (The *Australian*, June 30). Greed is the secular religion in Hong Kong, where people are money crazy and superstitious (The *Australian*, June 27). Countering misconceptions, Greg Sheridan (The *Australian*, July 1), however, observes that Hong Kong people are not, as alleged, only interested in money instead of politics or arts; that Britain and Patten, contrary to claims, have no interest to give democracy to Hong Kong people; that Martin Lee is still a force to reckon with after the handover.

Japan: Money, Security, Not Democracy

Ezra Vogel (1979), worrying about the United States losing its competitive advantage, once pointed out that Japan is arguably the most information-conscious country in the world, having built elaborate and thorough business intelligence apparatuses and networks. According to his account, journalists play an important role in providing business intelligence for the Japan, Inc. As befits their international image, the Japanese media are intent on preserving much of Japan's economic benefits in the region without showing much concern for local democratic yearnings. It has been observed that elite integration between the Japanese government, commercial-industrial conglomerates, and the media is so powerful—much tighter than in the United States—that the media tend to echo the government-corporate views (Pharr and Krauss, 1996). Japan's "pack journalism" is notoriously characterized as being one of political elites speaking mostly with one voice.

As the only Asian member of the exclusive G-8 club, Japan has an identity problem: according to a survey (Fukuda, 1998: 105), only 38 percent of the

Japanese acknowledged that Japan belongs to Asia, and 39 percent thought of Japan more as a member of the industrialized West. The trilateral relationship between China, Japan, and the United States is a key to regional comprehensive security. After the Second World War, constitutional constraints and international opposition have kept Japan from assuming any major security responsibilities commensurate with its economic status, even within the Asian-Pacific region. Under the protective umbrella of the United States, Japan has developed its relations with foreign states through economic means of trade, aid, and loans (Wong, 1991). Japan's "least offensive" policy has placed economic benefits above ideological interests in foreign diplomacy (Ozaki and Arnold, 1985). Based on hard-headed calculations, Japan takes a long-term approach towards investing in China and knows how to make use of loans and credit and to deal with China as a market and as a security concern. Japan and China are both friendly trade partners and potential rivals for regional leadership. Mutual ambivalence notwithstanding, both powers expect to profit from a closer relationship, especially in stemming western protectionism (Fukuda, 1998: 109). For the sake of economic and security interests, Japan also knows the importance of integrating China into the regional and world economic systems.

Inasmuch as human rights are not a guiding spirit of Japan's foreign policy, its leaders have questioned the idea of applying western standards of democracy to countries like China (Kesavan, 1990). During the Tiananmen crackdown, the U.S. media zealously sided with the protesters as if to score ideological victories, but the Japanese media were reluctant to challenge the Chinese authorities in order to protect Japan's economic gains (Lee and Yang, 1995). Deeply involved in China's government-initiated development plans, Japan had little desire to enrage the Chinese rulers. Japan's role as an aggressor nation in China in the Second World War also prevents Japanese from being morally righteous about China's human rights problem or too censorious of Chinese leaders. Japan was the last among industrial democracies to impose economic sanctions against China after the Tiananmen crackdown and was the first to lift them. In fact, the Tiananmen incident did not lead to major fluctuations in Sino-Japanese trade but led to a remarkable increase (Yokoi, 1996).

Most western media that had been based in Hong Kong to report about China moved up their offices to Beijing after the PRC normalized its relations with the United States in 1979. But the Japanese have continued to maintain a large contingent of reporters in Hong Kong quietly, if also efficiently, gathering economic intelligence about South China. They do not get excited about China's democracy or human rights unless politics means money and trade. Since 1988 Japan has overtaken the United States as the second largest foreign investor in Hong Kong, the first being China (Taneja, 1994).[9] To cover the handover of Hong Kong, Japan sends in the largest international media contingency, with

1,300 journalists from more than 40 media outlets, who register with the Government Information Services for press accreditation. There are twice as many Japanese journalists as either British (688) or PRC (611) journalists. We know that NHK alone has a news and technical staff of 80 and five anchors; TV Asahi also has a significant presence, and the major newspapers (the *Asahi Shimbun*, the *Yomiuri Shimbun*, the *Sankei Shimbun*, and the *Nihon Keizai Shimbun*) each have 15 to 20 journalists, adding to those of the Kyodo News Agency. Japanese television stations prefer to work with their own huge staff rather than with local stations. Their generally low profile prevents any published sources or our informants from providing the exact distribution of this news army.

Japanese media coverage of the handover appears to be thorough and comprehensive. Their reportorial style tends to stay close with detailed facts; most stories are short, straightforward, and uncolorful accounts of activities without much interpretive depth or contextualization (Lee and Yang, 1995). Comparatively speaking, Japanese journalists seem to act more as noncommitted "observers" rather than British participants or American protagonists. This factual or event orientation does not, however, imply an absence of values. The Japanese media seem to share—with seeming timidity and reservation—the generalized western values of democracy and human rights, and cast their share of negative light on the political life of Hong Kong. Almost all the topics on the handover found in other countries, including many trivial "mood" pieces, also appear on the Japanese media agendas in a truncated form. They are authority-oriented, following Patten's official line to castigate the installation of the Provisional Legislature by China. They ridicule the influence of the "hand-clapping culture from the mainland" on Hong Kong and caricature the strong "Chinese Hong Kong appeal" with "the Beijing way" in Tung's mandarin speech (*Yomiuri Shimbun*, July 1). But as a matter of editorial policy, Japanese media put economic issues above political issues and try to avoid human rights concerns to the extent possible. NHK has a considerably briefer coverage of the protest staged by the Democratic Party than do western media. In many cases the democracy concerns are depicted as a conflict between China and the United States, rather than a conflict between China and Japan. In this equation, the United States also figures more significantly than Britain, the old sovereign of Hong Kong. Japanese media seem noncommittal on the issue of democracy, and (despite individual journalists' sympathies) definitely not committed to supporting local democratic yearnings.

No coherent master frame of East-West ideological conflict stands out in Japanese media discourses. The democracy and human rights concerns are outshone and subsumed by a more pragmatic metanarrative that highlights Japan's economic and security interests. The *Sankei Shimbun* (June 25) reports that that the Japanese government's approach to Hong Kong is economically active but politically passive. Many Japanese reporters we interviewed seem to be more concerned about the future of democracy and press freedom in Hong Kong than their editors care to accommodate. A *Yomiuri Shimbun* reporter confides that his editor would have scolded him for wasting the space if he dwelled on the themes of democracy. For this reason, when he requests an interview with Democracy Party leaders he is given a cold shoulder. Several of his Japanese colleagues have provided corroborated accounts. A Kyodo News reporter takes western journalists to task for playing up the human rights issues at the expense of economic issues; he contends that the human rights issue is important but does not symbolize the handover of Hong Kong. Every Japanese news team includes business reporters; one of the three business reporters on the *Asahi Shimbun* team points out, "After the Cold War is over, politics and economics are inseparable."

The Japanese media see the handover of Hong Kong from the perspective of its economic relationship with China. In 1997 China is Japan's second largest importer (next to the United States, with 12.4% of Japan's total imports) and fifth largest exporter (with 5.2% of Japan's total exports.) Japan does not import much from Hong Kong, but Hong Kong is Japan's third largest exporter (next to the United States and Taiwan, accounting for 6.5% of Japan's total exports). Moreover, Japan has U.S.$48 billion of assets in Hong Kong. In 1996 a record 2.4 million Japanese visited Hong Kong, putting Japan as the most important foreign country on the tourist list. In 1997 the figure decreased to 1.4 million, still ranking third. A Japanese magazine specializing in Hong Kong matters is published in Hong Kong and sold in both Hong Kong and Japan. This does not begin to take account of the potential influences China may have on Japan's future. Therefore a Kyodo News Agency reporter concludes, "Hong Kong economy has intensified its relationship with China's economy so much that every time Japanese reporters write about Hong Kong economy they must refer to China's economy."

For that matter, the *Nihon Keizai Shimbun* (June 28) notes that Japan is very cautiously maintaining a political balance between the United States and China. Like Australia, Japan refuses to join the United States and Britain in their boycott of the inauguration of the Beijing-installed Provisional Legislature. An *Asahi Shimbun* reporter finds U.S. and British views on this issue rather strange and "too theoretical," saying that as an Asian he understands Beijing's attitudes.

As a whole, the Japanese media are ebullient about China's economic reform and express hopes for the future of Hong Kong economy and closer cooperation with China. The *Nihon Keizai Shimbun* (June 27) states that closer ties with the mainland will stimulate business expansion in Hong Kong, and that Japanese financial interests are taking advantage of the new opportunities. NHK airs two special programs, highly positive on the economic prospect. Its crew travels more than 18,000 kilometers visiting eight different Chinese cities. The programs mention the entrance of more than 2,000 Chinese companies into Hong Kong, quoting the CEO of the Hong Kong-based Bank of China to offer a view of prosperous economy in 1998 and beyond. They report Chinese

Vice-Premier Chen Qichen's assurance that Hong Kong will continue to be an international economic center with the support of the motherland, while dwelling on China's state enterprises getting listed in Hong Kong's stock market. On June 30 TV Asahi also airs a special program, light on politics and heavy on economy. It shows its reporter traveling to inner provinces of China to survey various aspects of economic development. He interviews local people, Japanese entrepreneurs in China, as well as a manager from Singapore, who predict that the next century will be a century for the global Chinese.

Media exuberance about Hong Kong's economic future does not, however, betray a tinge of uncertainty. The media are concerned about Hong Kong's political culture to the extent that it may affect business climate and operation. The *Sankei Shimbun* (June 26) quotes Japanese business people's worry over Hong Kong's political future, which may create economic turmoil. "We come to Hong Kong to make a profit," a businessman is quoted as saying, "If we can't make a profit, we'll leave." In view of the risks associated with the change, the *Nihon Keizai Shimbun* (June 28) argues for diversifying Japanese investment in Hong Kong (from which to expand into China) and Singapore (from which to expand into Southeast Asia.)

Another related concern for the Japanese media is regional security. China as a rising regional, if not world, power is a source of security concern for the international community. As a demilitarized nation Japan needs the protective umbrella of the United States, but as an Asian neighbor it cannot afford to agitate China. The Tokyo headquarters of Kyodo News Agency prepared some stories long before the handover about how the return of Hong Kong to China would affect the U.S.-Japan Security Treaty and the security of Northeast Asia. The *Yomiuri Shimbun* (June 25) notes the U.S. concern regarding the ability of its battleships to call port in Hong Kong under Chinese rule; the next day it writes about the potential that China may use Hong Kong as a card to pressure countries into severing ties with Taiwan. The *Sankei Shimbun* (July 1) reports that Japan's Defense Ministry emphasizes the importance of preventing China from pushing its sea rights southward, also noting that the entry of the PLA into Hong Kong to show China's rising military status "causes unhappiness of the United States." Another story on the same day says that Taiwan is concerned with China's possible use of Hong Kong to do espionage operations and launch a military threat against Taiwan. The *Nihon Keizai Shimbun* (July 1) reports that Hong Kong will add 30 percent to China's GDP, which may renew the talk of "China threat" in Southeast Asia.

One Theme, Several Tunes

Overall, Canada, Australia, and Japan can be classified as singing the theme song with different tunes. They have little confidence about the "one country, two systems" under an authoritarian regime. Unlike the Americans, however, none of them fancies itself to be the new savior or guardian of Hong Kong. In one way or another, they have all criticized the U.S. media for being egotistic, self-righteous, rude, and imperialistic. Despite such criticisms, on the issue of democracy and human rights the vaunted "national perspective"—be it Canadian, Australian, or Japanese—does not seem to stand out differently from the United States.

At the periphery of the western alliance, human rights concern is the master script of the camp; national interest is the cause for the variations. The end of the Cold War lessens the ideological and political bonds for these second-tier countries, and they are more willing to show their differences with the United States when their own national interests are at stake. The traditional bifurcated view toward international relations has given way to a multilateral approach. The United States is still the leader of the western world, but China (and Hong Kong) is a closer-to-home neighbor with high potential in business opportunities and benefits. Universal ideals are desirable, but economic interests are irresistible. The media performance in the Hong Kong handover is but another illustration.

The cases of Canada, Australia, and Japan illustrate ideological contestation at two different levels. At the external and global level, these three countries—members of the periphery in the western alliance or, alternatively, what Wallerstein (1976) would call "semi-peripheral countries" in the world capitalist system—clearly side with the United States and other western allies in the ideological warfare against China. They use democracy, freedom, and human rights to glue the coalition front in their fight against the common ideological enemy. Internally, at the second level of analysis, the western camp comprises different factions of countries pursuing different national concerns and interests. They may not agree with all the ideological underpinnings and strategies taken by their allies, nor would they want to strictly follow the leadership of the camp. With so much economic and security interests with China at stake in the post-Cold War milieu, national interests of the western periphery are likely to come to the fore, even if this implies a minor or moderate clash with the agendas of the center in the system.

Chapter 9

Media Event as Global Discursive Contestation

In some way echoes from China reverberate in every American county
and town.
—Dan Rather, CBS News anchor (Buerk, 1997)

"Ceremonial politics" expresses the yearning for togetherness, for fusion.
—Daniel Dayan and Elihu Katz (1992: viii)

The global in the local, the local in the global.
—Annabelle Sreberny-Mohammadi (1991: 122)

By any yardstick, a world of 8,000 news hunters has created a big "media
spectacle" in a faraway small island of Hong Kong, a ritualized media performance for the consumption of a global audience from Vermont to Sydney,
from Shanghai to Liverpool, or from Hong Kong to Vancouver. Globalization
touches our everyday lives in so many ways, yet it is also illusory to us. Although the media increasingly gain their global reach as part of the globalized
economy, the discourse of a global event remains essentially processed
through national-cum-local prisms. In this volume, we have tried to show that
the *global* news event is staged, domesticated, and hyped to produce various
media discourses that express different preferred *national* identities, values,
and order as much as they disclose the real and imagined conditions of Hong
Kong. In a metaphysical sense, is the whole of these discourses larger than the
sum of its parts? These discourses may be juxtaposed to form a totality with a
rather wide spectrum of conflicting perspectives that does not, however, necessarily reveal the whole story. International politics is in part an identity politics; international journalism is in part a struggle over national identity. Each
national media system may claim to have certain solid historical bases for constructing its identity discourse, but each discourse is bound to be partial,
sketchy, and self-serving. Thus viewed, the media event is a key site and moment for staging global discursive contestation, which is nonetheless

grounded in unequal power and resources of the international political economy. Despite the glowing rhetoric of globalization, this is neither "the end of history" (Fukuyama, 1992) nor "the end of ideology" (Bell, 1962).

In this closing chapter, we would like to summarize and extend our themes and arguments in the form of propositions.

The Structure of International News

Power and money make news. It has been said that in the contemporary age and today's world, the global is the local, and the local is the global (Sreberny-Mohammadi, 1991). Global events have local consequences, and local events have global roots. But make no mistake about it: the global and the local are not created of equal power. If the handover of Hong Kong had not been billed as the first major clash of global systems and ideologies after the crumbling of the Berlin Wall, it would not have attracted any world media attention and concern. Despite the absence of his network from Hong Kong for two decades and the declining audience interest in international news, Dan Rather of CBS imparts global significance to the handover of Hong Kong in an interview (Beurk, 1997): "We at CBS try to put it in the context of the ongoing story of China striving to be a world superpower... The world is an increasingly smaller place, and the echoes from China reverberate everywhere. In some way they reverberate in every American county and town."

His colleague and competitor, Jim Laurie, senior correspondent of ABC News, asks rhetorically: "Whither Hong Kong? In the minds of many Americans, so what!" (Knight and Nakano, 1999: 154). The answer, which he stops short of providing, seems quite simple and clear: whither China does matter. Structurally speaking, international communication takes place in the descending order of center-to-center, center-to-periphery, and periphery-to-periphery relationships (Galtung, 1971). This has at least six major implications for the international news structure.

1. The "media event" (Dayan and Katz, 1992) is staged at the global level for the global media to enact their cultural values in discursive contestation between nation-states. We shall return to elaborate on the nature, consequences, and limits of discursive contestation in the following sections.

2. Hong Kong is too peripheral to cross the threshold in the structure of foreign news (Galtung and Ruge, 1965). In the final analysis, Hong Kong only represents foreground skirmishes for the world media in their continuing, deep-seated background

battles against China, the remaining Communist giant and a rising economic and military power on the world stage. Negativity
is a key factor: Hong Kong news will fade out if the transition is
smooth, or else it will continue to be on the radar screen of the
world media. The degree of media attention it begets increases
in direct proportion to the tumultuousness and explosiveness of
the place.

3. This battle of media discourse is taken up between the most important Communist country and what Wallerstein (1976) calls
"center" nations of the United States and Britain as well as
"semi-peripheral" nations of Canada, Australia, and Japan in the
world capitalist system. They all compete for legitimacy and
recognition on the global stage via media discourses, but the
common interests of western alliance may conceal, mix up with,
and sometimes struggle against specific national interest.

4. The peripheral nations are at best bystanders to this media spectacle, either too apathetic, too impoverished, or too powerless to
be serious players in the battleground. Moreover, given their
globalized economy of scale and the national strength behind it,
the media in elite nations control the terms, condition, and content of media discourses in peripheral nations through the diffusion of words and images. Galtung and Vincent (1992: 8–9)
conclude, "Reporting about the periphery countries will be not
only scant and quantitatively insignificant, but also highly negative, and even more so for news about periphery people in periphery countries." Hong Kong is not likely to interest people in
Somalia, for example. If for any reasons poor and weak nations
are interested, they can ill afford to mount their own journalistic
operation and often have to rely on the supply of stories from
such global-scale outlets as the BBC, CNN, Reuters, and the
Associated Press. Even if they "domesticate" the messages to fit
national needs, we would argue that the range of their agendas
remains broadly and strictly dictated by the global-scale media.

5. The unequal center-periphery relationship is also characteristic
of the world within "Cultural China"; the media in Hong Kong
and Taiwan take defensive and reactive postures toward the
PRC's offensive pressure. While Beijing basks in national glory
on the global stage but seeks to shield the handover as an issue
of national sovereignty from external intervention, the weaker
parties of Taiwan and Hong Kong prefer to elevate it to the level

of international concern. The latter have little recourse but to appeal to the international community, via the global-scale media, for sympathy and understanding and to repel the hegemonic pressure of the center power.

6. The logic, mechanism, and news net of domestic and international journalism are integrated with and dependent on institutional rhythm and visions of the power structure. But as Table 9.1 shows, there are also crucial differences. Domestically, both state and nonstate sectors (including dominant classes and groups) may play an important role, and the news plurality is also broader to cater to more diverse constituencies. In an anarchic international order, the state is the chief voice of the nation, and the media agendas are more attuned to the elite conceptions of the world, as codified by the state-articulated foreign policy and the dominant ideological and cultural assumptions. Nonstate sectors are less important. Moreover, the world order sets the parameter for media discourses on international affairs, but no single centralized authority has the ultimate power over others. Nation-states participate in international organizations on a voluntary basis by ceding part of their power and submitting themselves to agreed-upon rules, but this voluntary submission can be broken or withdrawn, even though possibly at a price. Given these constraints, the media are more likely to collaborate with the nation-state than with the international authorities.

Media Events and Hyping

The handover of Hong Kong is a quintessential "media event," which defines the nature and outer boundary of the filtered global news. But the event also turns out to be lacking in blockbuster, something that the world media that had committed tremendous attention and resources to it discovered much too late. As a result, the media hype the news.

1. Instead of seeing "media events" as fitting into one of three discrete categories (Dayan and Katz, 1992)—contests, conquests, and coronation[1]—we emphasize their *interactive* quality that may possess combined attributes. The handover of Hong Kong is altogether a political and symbolic *contest* between China and Britain conducted according to negotiated

Table 9.1
Domestic News vs. International News

Dimensions	Domestic News	International News
Interest base	Class-based, sector-based or community-based interest	Nation-state
Locus of ideology	Less discretion for journalists' interpretation because the claims are more readily falsifiable and the issues are more familiar to the target audience; ruling ideology is often taken for granted; contestation over the articulation of ruling ideology is possible	Greater discretion for the journalists' interpretation because the issues are more distant and less familiar to the home audience; lack of global ruling ideology; engaged in dialogue with home ideology; contestation with ideologies of foreign countries
Core audience	The elite and general public within a nation	The elite within and across nations
News net	Primacy of government officials at various levels and other social agencies; international forces are secondary; domestication is not necessary	Primacy of the nation-state and international forces; other domestic social agencies are secondary; domestication is essential
Competition	Competing with other national media and less so with other local media	Competing with global, national, or local media (depending on the nature of the media outlet itself)
Discursive community	National authorities, journalists, representatives of social groups	State officials and diplomats, correspondents, representatives of international and national groups
Consequences/functions	Media serving more of a forum for the domestic social forces; building consensus and legitimacy; maintaining the status quo	Projection of preferred identity and image; legitimizing and binding the home system; articulating foreign policy

rules, schedule, and rituals; a historical *conquest* between charismatic leaders of both sides who get tested in the diplomatic and media ordeal; and a *coronation* for the rites of British retreat with honor and of Chinese nationalist victory. These elements get intertwined.

2. Furthermore, we emphasize the *transformative* quality of the media event. During its life cycle, a media event is likely to go through the three stages of contests, conquests, and coronations. Despite being a "calendar event," the world media endow the handover with special ideological significance and invest huge resources into covering it. But the event is not quite up to its billing as a major (violent) showdown for the world media. Instead, it was transformed during the course of its life cycle, with contest and conquest gradually receded and coronation coming to the fore. The event is robbed of its expected excitement as dictated by the entertainment logic of news.

3. The handover of Hong Kong, given its choreographed nature, fails to reach the critical threshold of a media event, with many defining characteristics of a unique news genre. As a live, preplanned event, perhaps presented with reverence and ceremony, it attracts a large horde of journalists but does not seem to interrupt the flow of everyday life or to electrify large global audiences. To compensate for the lack of theatrical excitement or dramatic surprises, the world media resort to "hype up" the news. Hyping is both a set of techniques for covering a media event and an integral part of news discourse. Both television and newspapers seem to apply similar "hyping" strategies of certification, visualization, mystification, and amalgamation.

4. Professionalism is the cardinal principle of western journalism (Schudson, 1978). It has increasingly established itself as a quasi-universal standard of journalism despite a huge gulf that remains between idealized beliefs and the actual practice (Weaver, 1998). Even among the state-run media in China, struggle for professionalism has been valiant and rancorous at times (Lee, 2000b; Polumbaum, 1990; Zhao, 1998). We argue that discursive contestation is conducted through the enactment of professional norms, which is nonetheless predicated on implicit commitment to the established order; journalists can only be fair and impartial when they subscribe to fundamental social

assumptions without challenge. In international news, this commitment to maintenance of systemic stability is often translated into honing journalistic canons to foreign policy-cum-national interest as well as cultural repertoire.

5. We argue that the globalized media in a globalized economy has infused the entertainment logic into newswork, making hyping increasingly an imperative to pull in audience interest and attention. The ideological underpinnings of newswork are often expressed through—or behind—the techniques of hyping, and this practice has come to be widely accepted, assumed, and unrecognized. The use of hyping techniques is particularly important when the event is perceived to be bland, flat, and not newsworthy, or when its historical significance is not concretely or graphically accessible. Jim Laurie of ABC News, among others, admits to audience apathy as a major reason for television to pursue ceremonies over substance (Knight and Nakano, 1999: 154). The light-hearted pieces, "color" and mood stories, and human-interest reports flaunt as much ideological premises as the conventional, serious, "hard" news.

6. In hyping the news, the media, especially television, may substitute drama and rituals for "facts" in order to satisfy the "pleasure" principle of the news-entertainment logic, thus eroding the positivistic epistemology and methodology of journalism. Journalists are not only observers and storytellers; they are "star" performers, annotators of events, and makers of attractive myths. They draw on, circulate, and feed back into the prevailing cultural and ideological reservoir—tending to reinforce the status quo in a dramatic way.

7. We argue that when journalists encounter enormous gaps between their hypothesized and perceived realities, they are more likely to "repair" part of their news perspective in order to save its overall paradigmatic structure, instead of abandoning their journalistic paradigms. Beneath the veneer of staged coronations and against the disconfirming evidence, they treat the ideological background as the foreground. To "repair" the paradigms, they may cull more evidence to support the old themes, explain away discrepancies as exceptions to the rule, introduce more stringent criteria for judgment, or invent ad hoc hypotheses. In the summer of 1997, the western media had predicted a vigorous economy and a repressive polity for Hong

Kong. A year later, surprised at politics-as-usual and a sick
economy, they nonetheless largely adhere to the old explana-
tory canons (see epilogue).

8. The illusion or disillusion of history-making draws the world
   media to Hong Kong. Their hyped narratives, in line with
   home-base orientations, give world audiences a pseudosense
   of participating in the history of the moment. Media events
   privilege the role of television as a "live broadcasting of history" (Dayan and Katz, 1992; Scannell, 1995). Compared with
   the linguistic and technological barriers of the print media,
   television is a high religion of today capable of bringing rich
   images from remote locales simultaneously to large numbers
   of audiences in the context of time-space distanciation (Featherstone, 1995; Tomlinson, 1999). But emphasis on vivid images may pressure television to produce stereotypical and
   hyped realities in place of reasoned analysis.

9. We agree with the integrative role of media events portrayed by
   Dayan and Katz (1992: viii), who state that ceremonial politics
   "expresses the yearning for together, for fusion." Media events
   tend to present the authorities, which organize the event, with
   solemnity and reverence. Alexander and Jacobs (1998) echo this
   functional perspective when they argue that media events construct "common identities and universal solidarities" that "erase
   the divide between private and public" and "narrow the distance
   between the indicative and subjunctive," thus legitimizing the
   powers and authorities outside the civil sphere.[2] In this volume,
   we have tried to show that the processes of staging, domestication, and hyping all serve to produce national narratives in confirmation of the political and economic system.

10. We are somewhat skeptical when Dayan and Katz (1992)
    overempower the audience as the agents capable of negotiating
    with the media over the meanings of the discourses and of de-
    coding hegemonic definitions of the political establishment.
    The active role of an audience to question the meanings of *in-
    ternational* news is particularly dubious, given the fact that the
    audience is generally apathetic to and ignorant of foreign hap-
    penings and thus tends to accept the media interpretations un-
    critically. Whether the integrative role of media events in
    "narrating the sacred" can be sustained on a long-term basis is a
    topic of further inquiry.

Media and Authority

Political authorities are primary definers of reality, and the media are secondary definers of reality. The media rewrite the second-order script based on, and within the limits of, the first-order script written by political authorities, which usually are event organizers.

1. We argue that a hierarchy of political authorities exercises different degrees of power and influence on the course of the event and, consequently, on news narratives. In our case, the Hong Kong government, as the event organizer, is in fact answerable to the higher powers of China and Britain. Both powers, having concluded the terms of sovereignty transfer in 1982 and having fought openly and rancorously over their interpretations in the two subsequent decades, have set a general atmosphere for media gloom. They also negotiated the agenda and procedures of the handover ceremonies to their minutest detail, heightening them to the level of national face and sovereignty. Both powers hotly contested over the joint rights of the BBC and CCTV to provide "common feed" before they reluctantly relinquished it to a local television consortium at the last minute. In its interim, the Hong Kong government as a not-entirely-autonomous event organizer is at a loss to meet media requests for the schedule because Beijing does not release it until the final moment. Anything having to do with matters and presumed symbols of sovereignty is beyond the jurisdiction of the event organizer, which only has "operational control" over the event within the set parameter.

2. We argue that within these larger boundary constraints, the event organizer has the capacity to limit and facilitate newswork through provision and arrangement of the physical infrastructures in addition to controlling the flow of events and information. To mark the occasion, the Hong Kong government has built a magnificent convention center for the ceremony to take place; in its annex sits the gigantic press center, where the world media operate as the nerve center to emanate stories to the entire world. Media sociology is thus organized as a centralized activity, with which the media cooperate and compete to develop reportorial strategies for tapping their sources and mapping the geography.

3. We argue that through carefully planned administrative routines, the event organizer may exert structural influences on the constitution of the "news net," access to news and news sources, and the

scheduling of journalists' daily work. The Government Information Services (GIS) issues media accreditation to the global media; the number of accredited media outlets and journalists seems to be in positive correlation with the political and economic positions of the countries they come from (with many small and poor nations largely absent from the scene). It provides a stream of background information and daily briefing, and arranges "package tours" participated in by a large number of visiting (especially parachute) journalists, leading to the production of many similar stories around the world. These organized activities of routine and "soft" nature are particularly effective in influencing the news agenda when journalists do not "smell blood" in the street or fail to find erupted conflicts and violence to enthrall their audience.

4. Centralized control of information production and distribution, such as the "common feed" and news pool, promotes content homogeneity in favor of the event organizer and is not conducive to "enterprising journalism."

5. In an open news environment the media are subject to the cross-pressure of various prominent pressure groups in their effort to sway the direction of news agendas and public opinion. The media are, however, sometimes capable of subverting the intentions of such groups, especially when the latter run counter to the interest and ideology of media outlets. The extent to which this happens is also related to the logic of media competition and to the perceived credibility of event sponsors.

Globalization, Domestication, and National Prisms

Modern media have a global reach. They bring events in the once remote places into our homes and thus make them in some ways familiar to us. Tomlinson (1999), following Anthony Giddens, argues that modern media, especially television, "stretch social relations in new forms of time-space distanciation." Both time and space are compressed by media technologies. Through the mediation of journalists and modern media technologies, the handover of Hong Kong is presented, often live, in front of the world audiences regardless of geographical distance. The globalization process "deterritorializes," in the sense of liberating symbolic exchanges from spatial referents (Featherstone, 1995; Tomlinson, 1999; Waters, 1995). The significance of the event thus goes far beyond the immediate experience of local inhabitants.

1. Globalization does not mean universal inclusion. We argue that globalized news operation, like domestic news, is suspectible to the law of power and money. The strong nations control media resources, news agendas, and ideological fora, often to the exclusion of the poor and the weak. There continues to be an unequal flow of news between nations. Nor do nations speak as equals. The populist and postmodern celebration of the marginal, which leads to the hypothesized de-centering of the nation-state and re-centering of the international civil society and grassroots movements (Hamelink, 1993), has not found sufficient evidence for support. We also take exception to the claim by Waters (1995) that economic exchanges localize, political exchanges internationalize, and symbolic exchanges globalize. His romantic formulation that the territorial boundaries are coterminous with nation-states whereas globalized culture is liberated from spatial constraints, may be technologically valid but ideologically problematic. Inasmuch as the media construct meanings and significance, the cultural is the political, and the meaning tends to be of "national" character even though there is a possibility for the development of a transnational culture unrelated to any particular nation-state.

2. Inasmuch as all global news is local, the globalizing phenomenal worlds we inhabit must be filtered through "local knowledge" (Geertz, 1993). We argue that this is often done sociologically through the process of "domestication," thus bringing distant, unfamiliar events to home audiences as if they were an extension of domestic news (chapter 3). Culturally, the media enact a performance to enthrall a large audience, mobilize the domestic "attention resources," and put the domestic power hierarchy on stage (chapter 4). Ideologically, the media essentialize the complex and contradictory reality into core attributes of a nation and history to construct a reductive constrast between "us" and "them" (chapters 5–8). It is valid for Featherstone (1995: 118) to argue that the global and the local are fused to make a blend, which he calls "glocal." Thompson (1995) describes this relationship as between "globalized diffusion" of images and "localized appropriation" of their meanings.

3. We agree with Sreberny-Mohammadi (1991) that in the arena of international newsmaking, the "local" often is the "national," while the truly "local" is ignored or suppressed. As chapters 5–8 show, different media systems have domesticated the handover of Hong Kong from the essentialized perspectives of *national* prisms

(American democracy, British imperial nostalgia, Chinese nationalism, Japanese economism, and so on) in consonance with each country's dominant ideology, coherent myths, sentiments, cultural repertoire, and collective memories. Such prisms reflect the relative position of each nation-state, along with its central interests, in the international political economy.

4. We argue that the media domesticate the news within the constraints imposed by the larger political economy and respond to the "staging" effort of the event organizer. News is a foreground story pegged to recognized occurrence of an event in accordance with the background assumptions of top domestic (national) concerns and priorities. The domesticated foreign news favor domestic (high-ranking national officials) and ideologically compatible sources, and give the event inflated political or historical significance with culturally lucid metaphors.

5. We argue that even the global-scale news organizations (such as CNN and the BBC) are, contrary to their claims, not exempt from the process of domestication according to the prevailing norms of "center" countries in which they are based. They serve the affluent markets of "center" countries and the elite sector of semiperipheral or peripheral countries in the world system.

6. In the domain of international news, we are frankly skeptical about some versions of the globalization theory that have hypothesized the erosion if not the demise of the nation-state, which is said to be ceding its power to supranational and subnational entities (see Sreberny-Mohammadi, 1996). It is argued, for example, that the British nation-state has been in retreat by yielding part of its sovereign power to the larger European Union and the smaller Scottish Parliament. But as we have tried to show, in the anarchic international order, the nation-state acts as the "prime definer" of mediated culture, for it provides a "quasi-religious sense of belonging and fellowship" (Featherstone, 1995: 108). The nation-state codifies its visions, interests, and myths in terms of foreign policy, which has strong historical continuity that incorporates the enduring and consensual interest that the nation has abroad, and thus nourishes journalistic paradigms as an integral part of the international discursive war.

7. We argue that the national prism, often in the name of national unity, may suppress *"local"* dissent, differences, or struggles. By selectively knitting together an ensemble of celebratory images,

for example, the PRC media present a mythical globalized Chinese nation in which people, regardless of ethnic and geographical differences, cheer for Beijing-imposed and Han majority's cultural definition of nationalistic triumphalism. Media representations have thus rubbed salt into the historical wound of ethnic minorities in their unsuccessful struggle against hegemonic myths, memories, and interests. When a "local" perspective is presented, it is often derivative of the national narrative; the "local" perspective is likely to support, not to challenge, the established ideological framework. U.S. local media love to boast of presenting "local perspectives" by featuring eye-witnessing "people from home" (those who happen to be on the spot), but their bland perspectives are more often than not based naively on a stock of clichés and stereotypes rather than on expert knowledge or cultivation.

8. International newsmaking is a "national" project. We argue that national prisms, in making what what Featherstone (1995: 111) calls "external presentation of the national face," tend to subsume *internal* partisan or ideological differences in international news discourses. When national attention turns to actions and interests abroad, internal partisan rifts give way to national identification. In the United States, this is manifested in the rhetoric of a "bi-partisan foreign policy" and the syndrome of "rallying around the flag." Its elite media may occasionally criticize President Clinton for his alleged "softness" toward China, but their ideological common ground toward U.S.-China ties is far more significant than any technical criticism of this kind. Similarly, the Labor-oriented *Guardian* and the Tory-oriented *Daily Telegraph* pretty much amplify the same "British voice" over the handover of Hong Kong.

9. As a metaphysical totality, the globalization process may serve to relativize and pluralize various national media narratives; even if each narrative articulates a partial facet of the reality, we argue that narratives of the hegemonic powers are more dominant than those of the peripheral nations. China's "one country" is not Taiwan's "one country"; China's emphasis on "one country" is antithetical to Hong Kong's emphasis on "two systems," but the fact remains that China's discourse, backed by its stronger power, carries greater weight. The relativized and pluralized media representations that constitute "complex connectivity" in the global communication system (Tomlinson, 1999) are a tug of ideological war.

10. We argue that the clashing of perspectives may force each national media system to consciously clarify, articulate, and defend its ideological position vis-à-vis that of its friends or enemies alike. Therefore, the Canadian, Australian, and Japanese media affirm western ideology and yet show a neurotic anxiety in search of their identity niche. By the same token, China imposes a centralized discourse of "hot nationalism" (Billing, 1995), denying its citizens access to "complex connectivity" through which the foreign media may offer alternative interpretations with new vistas and new ways of thinking. Through routine and steady reinforcement of "banal nationalism" (Billing, 1995) in everyday life, in contrast, citizens in western countries are in all likelihood apathetic to, and thus ignorant of, alternative or oppositional discourses of other countries as well. No wonder Anderson (1983) calls a nation "the imagined communities" constantly in need of constructing and maintaining its own identity.

11. We argue that media prisms are often constructed by recalling and activating symbols of national and cultural tradition to incite a sense of imagined grandeur and common sentiments. The PRC media unproblematically amalgamate traditional cultural figures (the Yellow Emperor), landscapes (the Yellow River, the Great Wall, the Tiananmen Square), historical myths (General Lin Zexu), and ethnic songs and dance to construct the unity of national glory. Likewise, the British media mobilize a repertoire of cultural icons (the Royal Yacht, the Union Jack), personalities (Patten), songs (Elgar) to mystify imperial grandeur of historic proportion. Media celebration is part of the civil ritual, selectively essentializing the complex histories of national triumphs and losses, joys and sorrows, conflicts and contradictions into simple and ageless qualities. Localization, through domestication, is in this sense globalization.

International Discursive Contestation

We have argued that media events represent a site, form, and moment of international discursive contestation between nation-states. Media narratives represent national interest, face, identity, culture, and ideology. They certify the authority structure with purpose, prestige, and legitimacy. They solidify the internal cohesion of the system by drawing sharpened differences with "the other" (Coser, 1957; Said, 1978). The implications are as follows:

1. We argue that not all media narratives assume equal power, visibility, or influence in the stage of international contestation. Winners tend to be countries that assume a central position in the international political economy. In the western camp, there seems to be a clear hierarchy of influence, with the central countries' narratives setting the major tone and their followers going along with and yet rebelling against them. We don't believe that defensive Australian or Canadian media narratives (middle powers) would ever be given the same discursive voice as their U.S. counterparts (a superpower). In the same vein, Taiwan and Hong Kong are as defensive as the PRC is offensive.

2. We argue that globalized media discourses may produce "mediated quasi-interaction" (Thompson, 1995: 85) for world audiences, sometimes so significant as to affect the course of the news event, moblizing some degree of interdependency such that "localized activities situated in different parts of the world are shaped by one another" (Thompson, 1995: 150). Knowingly or unknowingly, the world media in many ways have structured the style and mode of interaction between various political actors in international politics. For example, western leaders, notably President Clinton and Prime Minister Blair, take the lead to trumpet "the world is watching China" theme, both for domestic and international media consumption. The G-8 leaders, meeting over the global economic issues, feel obliged to interrupt their agenda and pledge their support for Hong Kong before the camera. Their pledge immediately hits the world media headline in a chain-like reaction.

3. We argue that the mediated global communication may change the local dynamics. The media perform before and for the world "bystander public," who watch the play of the power game on the sideline without much say, but whose support is nonetheless crucial to the players' legitimacy. Coupled with (or in the absence of) regular diplomatic channels, various principal national actors use the media as "a looking-glass mirror" to gauge one another's intentions that provoke further reactions and counterreactions (Lang and Lang, 1983). Local people in Hong Kong are openly gazing at and being gazed at by world journalists in a gigantic news stage. Opinion polls and media commentaries indicate that the global media watch seems to have boosted public confidence among Hong Kong people, for they feel that international pressure may help to discipline the PRC's behavior. Asked by CNN if he is Beijing's "puppet," the new Chief Executive Tung emphatically

denies the charge, waving an impatient gesture. In the depth of structural uncertainty, Anson Chan, Patten's Chief Secretary (to be retained later by Tung in the same position), went public with an interview with *Newsweek* weeks before the handover was to take place, to express her concerns through the media to her future boss, Beijing, and the world. She chose an international news-magazine for the interview because it gave her a credible platform and a sense of gravitas that a local paper lacks. Media publicity has also emboldened local democrats to challenge Tung's author-ity and policy. The fact that Beijing blamed the international media for causing the Tiananmen unrest in 1989 is an implicit ac-knowledgment of the central media role in exacting a colossal price for its international diplomacy. Mindful of the PLA's "killer" images during the Tiananmen bloodshed, the PRC is intent on staging a good media show by sending unarmed elite troops into Hong Kong before the world's television screen (who, however, still come across on U.S. television as menacing as they were in Tiananmen Square eight years ago). Nice media rhetoric and cel-ebratory images are important for domestic audience consump-tion to reinforce the legitimacy of China's party-state.

4. It is tempting but untenable to put a postmodern spin on our find-ings: to empower the marginal, as Thompson (1995) seems to suggest that the domesticated "national prisms" are so diverse as to present a formidable challenge to the generality of "media im-perialism." Thus, it is argued that the recipient (usually weak) na-tion may derive alternative or even oppositional meanings from western-dominated news rather than accept its intended mean-ings. But we believe postmodern exaggeration of the national "agency" power fails to answer this question: To what end? Many of the *national* narratives are antidemocratic and suppressive of dissent. Moreover, it may unduly overlook the structural con-straints of domination and power in the international political economy of news and information.

5. By the same token, we believe that there also is a danger to exag-gerate the potential of international discursive contestation in transforming the hegemonic order or the existing rules of the game. Discursive struggle is linked to, but different from, substa-tive institutional struggle. In the latter, social movements fight against the centralized agencies to obtain favorable policy out-comes often involving tangible material resources. The discursive struggle may not be directed to specific and well-defined institu-

tions; it gains and loses not in terms of material base but in terms of symbolic expressions of preferred values and legitimacy. We are generally sympathetic to Gitlin's (1991, 1997) sharp criticism of the current tendency in cultural studies and postmodern theories to displace more illusive cultural politics for substantive institutional politics. He even condemns certain proponents of discursive wars as concealing their political inaction and impotence. We believe that there are real limits to how far the protesting voice of the weak can go without the backing of an institutional framework. As a sad reminder of this point, the Third World and nonaligned nations made some headway in their attempt to restructure the New World Information and Communication Order (NWICO) issue agendas in the 1970s (MacBride, 1980) only insofar as the United States was still tolerating conference diplomacy in the United Nations-related agencies, where national sovereignty was assumed to be equal. But irked by the voting majority, the predatory hegemonic regimes of Reagan-Thatcher abruptly decided to withdraw from the UNESCO in the early 1980s, and since then these poor and weak nations have been deprived of an international forum and hearing, making their discursive contest totally ineffective, if not irrelevant, in the gallery of international power (Lee, 1989). Their feeble voices have fallen to the deaf ear. Discursive contestation, in this case, may be reduced to unfocused media grumbling.

6. We argue that even so, internationally, discursive contestation may be an essential but insufficient (and not necessarily effective) "weapon of the weak" (Scott, 1988), the very people who lack requisite resources and power to foster a common front for institutional struggle. In the case of the Hong Kong handover, what we have witnessed is almost a unilateral, yet parallel, declaration of national positions, preferences, and biases in the anarchic global news order, without really joining the battle with one another. It is almost a (mis)match between distant shouters. However, for Hong Kong, if major human rights abuses should occur, the world media can be expected to send out the first warning. In the worst-case scenario, Marcus Eliason of the Associated Press explains, the media are likely to raise issues with the U.S. president in regard to invoking the United States-Hong Kong Policy Act that mandates sanctions against Beijing. In the case of incremental deterioration, he notes, only the media will notice it and ask questions in press conferences that would

oblige the president to respond. The president's policy response will undoubtedly hinge on an overall assessment of U.S. national interest in regard to China; considerations of China will take precedence over those for Hong Kong. After all is said and done, however, Hong Kong would be worse off without the close watch of world media.

7. We argue that the effectiveness of discursive constestation hinges on who wages the fight, for whose interest. To the extent that the fight (such as the NWICO debate) is hostile to the interests of western nations and their media, it is likely to be marginalized and dismissed. In the 1970s and its aftermath, the western media treated Third World countries' struggles for fairer media voices and representations as nothing but a "cry of pain" by dictators who attempted to muffle the free flow of information. They refused to acknowledge that such struggles were at least partially a legitimate challenge to western privileges and domination, and were broadly compatible with the avowed liberal ideals of equality of which they themselves profess to be ardent subscribers. Worse, the conservative (some say reactionary) administrations in the United States and Britain took deliberate, imperialistic measures to incapacitate the international institutional framework in which a modicum of grievances could be aired. On the other hand, if the fight is perceived to be in line with the enduring interests of western nations—such as protecting Hong Kong from Communist mistreatment—there might be a likelihood for discursive contestation to yield substantive results. The seeming contradictions between these two cases actually underscore the enduring continuity between national interest and media performance.

Coda

We have tried to argue that media events provide a site and moment for the media to engage in international discursive contestation, which is ultimately grounded in the unequal power inherent in the international political economy Based on our comparative perspectives, where do we stand in regard to the role of the media in the authority structure?

We have little sympathy for the traditional naïve liberal myth that professional journalists report from "nobody's point of view" because they just let objective facts speak the truth. We don't believe that international media *objectively* report events without bias. "How do you deal with the 'half-glass full' or 'half-glass empty' question?" Dorinda Elliot of *Newsweek* reflects, "That's why journalism is subjective." To the extent that journalists report from somebody's point of view, this subjectivity is not only caused by personal predispositions but, more important, by their role as unwitting carriers of larger organizational, national, and cultural imprints. National journalists may select and repackage information to best suit their conceptions of domestic (national) needs. They do so not self-consciously because these imprints have been naturalized as part of their taken-for-granted worldviews. The extent to which resident correspondents can develop an empathetic "other" view should be acknowledged but not exaggerated.

Nor do we ally with unvarying and homogeneous grand narratives that treat the media as a subservient lapdog of the power structure. It would be analytically unproductive and morally fatal of the "propaganda model" (Herman and Chomsky, 1988) and its variants to dismiss relative autonomy of the liberal media to the point of blunting the real and substantial differences in the role and function between, say, the *New York Times* and the *People's Daily*. To the extent that the liberal media collaborate with the authority structure in the hegemonic coverage of international affairs, this process is conducted not through forced coercion, but through shared consent about what the best interest is for the nation abroad. Since the liberal media index the range and dynamics of elite consensus (Bennett, 1990), their relative autonomy becomes crucial in enlarging the wedge of "legitimated controversy" (Hallin, 1986). The British media have reported the PRC's virulent attacks on the British nation (albeit dismissively) and the internal policy conflict toward China within the British foreign policy establishment. Even if falling short of their own rhetoric and ideals, let alone radical expectancies, the liberal media's *hegemonic* role is vitally different from—and in our view, (if the choices have to be between these two) far superior to—the *instrumental* mouthpiece role of the authoritarian media, as in China (Kellner, 1990).

The liberal media also differ from the authoritarian media in their definition of news that results from their different institutional distances to the power structure and the market forces. The authoritarian mouthpieces are cheerleaders of the regime; good news is good news. The Australian television reporter Jane Hutcheon attributes China's getting a lot of bad press to the gulf China puts up between foreign journalists and the Chinese people and to the restrictions placed on journalists to see certain statistics or visit certain institutions. She adds, "If you allow people to see what you have, good and bad, at first there is going to be a lot of negative stories, but eventually it will die down." On the other hand, the western liberal media generally take a skeptical view about the morality of politicians and corporate leaders; they are critical of the office holders, while supporting the system itself. For them, bad news, which sells, is good news. Jonathan Mirsky of the *Times* of London quotes Ernest Hemingway, a reporter-turned-writer, to say, "When interview-ing someone, I need to constantly remind myself why this son-of-a-bitch is lying to me." Western journalists, in their interviews with us, often caricature their detractors as not knowing that negativity, rather than cheerleading, is the basic function of news. Western journalists complain about how hostile the PRC is to them and compliment Governor Patten and the democratic activist Martin Lee for being accessible and eloquent—which means that the latter's "spin" strategies have worked magically. As we have shown, the western media may be scathingly critical of national leaders, especially in the way cer-tain policies are implemented (remember how the *Washington Post* criticizes President Clinton's policy of engagement with China), but in the end they still sing their national anthems. None of the western media systems question the legitimacy of their national interests in Hong Kong and China; they simply concentrate on how to realize such goals.

In sum, the age of media globalization is an age of contending national ideologies. Global media events inspire and reify international discursive con-testation. So, what will happen to Hong Kong? Time will be the best judge. But even in the unlikely event of unequivocal evidence, media struggle will con-tinue to refract different ideological lights. Under the glare of global media spectacle, ideological fights will go on. The story of Hong Kong reveals the wonder—dynamics, puzzles, hopes, despairs, achievements, and failure—of world journalism.

Epilogue

After the Handover

Hong Kong is a graveyard for political prognosticators. Everybody predicted we'd have a bumpy ride politically but the economy would take care of itself. Exactly the opposite has happened.
> —Daniel R. Fung, Solicitor General of Hong Kong

The real transition is about identity and not sovereignty.
> —Anson Chan, Chief Secretary of Hong Kong
> Special Administrative Region (SAR)

The economy, not Beijing, is Hong Kong's biggest headache.
> —The *Los Angeles Times*, July 1, 1998

Recent events suggest that the one country is rapidly subsuming the two systems.
> —The *New York Times*, July 1, 1999

Now Hong Kong is China's, not Britain's. "Hong Kong loses its uniqueness (after the handover) and will be treated as part of the larger China story," as Dorinda Elliot of *Newsweek* prognosticated several days after the fatigue of the "handover hysteria" in 1997. "It will be difficult to keep Hong Kong news alive." The fact, after one year of power transition, is that news has declined but not disappeared. However, since the anniversary, Hong Kong appears to be fading away rapidly from the world's news radar, with the *Guardian* being the only one among the sampled American and British newspapers carrying an anniversary article in the year 2000. Hong Kong turns out to have partly contradicted world journalists in their political and economic predictions, and partly confirmed their perception of the impotence of the new government. In 1997 most media, except those in the People's Republic of China, were pessimistic about Hong Kong's political prospects under Chinese rule but confident about its economic prosperity. Since the first anniversary, they have found just the

opposite: politically Hong Kong is not as bad as previously envisaged; economically, it has been engulfed in a major financial crisis that sweeps across
almost the whole of Asia and almost wrecks world economy. Is this enough
to revamp the news paradigms of the world media? (The PRC media must reconcile the reality of economic hardship and declining public confidence in the
SAR government with the rhetoric of a more "splendid" Hong Kong in the
arms of the motherland.) As the sampled American and British media outlets
carry only a few articles on Hong Kong during the second and third anniversary of sovereignty transfer, we shall base the current analysis mainly on the
coverage of the first anniversary in 1998.

Explaining "the Surprise"

The world media find Hong Kong no longer "the Pearl of the Orient," but
a "subdued" place in the midst of an Asian economic meltdown. People are in
"no mood to celebrate" the first anniversary of handover; official celebration,
BBC News (July 1, 1998) observes, is "gloomy."[1] Even the Chinese official
organ, the *People's Daily* (July 1, 1998), admits to the "unusualness" of the situation that tests how "Hong Kong people run Hong Kong." Surprise is a common theme.

Table 10.1 summarizes the main stories or features about the handover
carried by selected media from the United States, Britain, China, Taiwan, and
Hong Kong from June 30 to July 2, 1998.[2] U.S. and British newspapers find
that politically Hong Kong "has changed little from colonial days." Hong Kong
is "a less prosperous and confident metropolis than it once was" (*Wall Street
Journal*, July 1), but few of its "worst problems are the fault of Beijing" (*Los
Angeles Times*, July 1). "Defying predictions by experts here and in the West,"
the *New York Times* (July 1, 1998) reports, "Beijing has left Hong Kong largely
untouched." The *Los Angeles Times* even credits China for acting as "a stabi-
lizing force for Hong Kong's economy."

Although the western media seem to have rehabilitated Beijing's credibility in some way, their journalistic paradigms—framing the reality through the
lenses of western ideology and systems—remain largely intact. In the international "ideological repair shop" (van Ginneken, 1998: 32), foreign journalists
appear to have taken three approaches to repair their news paradigms: (a) by
limiting the scope of discrepancies between facts and expectations; (b) by explaining away the troubled facts; and (c) by introducing new criteria.

LIMITING THE SCOPE OF DISCREPANCIES. Hong Kong is only "better than
expected" (BBC News, July 1), but only "the causal observer" will be fooled by
the surface impression. Maggie Farley of the *Los Angeles Times* acknowledges
little change in Hong Kong before turning around to say that people on the

Table 10.1

Headlines of Hong Kong Anniversary Stories in the World Media

Country	Media	Date	Headline
U.S.A.	*New York Times*	July 1, 1998	Hong Kong surprise: Politics steady but economy falters
	Los Angeles Times	July 1, 1998	The economy, not Beijing, is Hong Kong's biggest headache
	Washington Post	July 1, 1998	Competing visions for Hong Kong's future point up China's challenge
	Wall Street Journal	July 2, 1998	Hong Kong's anniversary is subdued; After one year, recession, not repression, is feared
		July 1, 1998	No ordinary ex-economy.
U.K.	*Times*	July 1, 1998	Hong Kong ends first year under China scarred by Asian crisis
	Independent	June 30, 1998	Patten's anniversary address stirs passion in Hong Kong
		July 2, 1998	Hong Kong's capitalists fly the red flag for Chinese VIP
	Guardian	July 1, 1998	Clinton in China, Hong Kong relaxed one year on
	Financial Times	June 30, 1998	One year passes in Hong Kong
		July 2, 1998	Jiang pledges to reassure Hong Kong currency "will not devalue"
China	*People's Daily*	July 1, 1998	Aura remains, grace remains—The successful practice of "one country and two systems" in Hong Kong
		July 2, 1998	Hong Kong SAR government holds a massive meeting celebrating one year anniversary of Hong Kong's return to the motherland
Hong Kong	*South China Morning Post*	July 2, 1998	"Hong Kong, China's pearl in the lap of South China Sea, will shine even brighter," We'll *win through*, says Jiang
	Ming Pao	July 2, 1998	Jiang proposes six measures to support Hong Kong
	Apple Daily	July 2, 1998	Jiang supports keeping the tie of Hong Kong and U.S. currencies
Taiwan	*China Times*	July 1, 1998	Freedom of expression, surprisingly not repressed
		July 1, 1998	Human rights and rule of law are OK: Beijing did not interfere in SAR government operation
		July 2, 1998	Jiang: One country and two systems exemplar to Taiwan

street may hardly notice "a quiet, incremental adjustment of Hong Kong's political and legal infrastructure"—including "the appearance of favoritism for those with close China connections." Mark Landler of the *New York Times* (July 1, 1998) reports, "Chinese officials are seeking to influence Hong Kong's leaders through hints delivered in back-channel conversations," noting public fears about the integrity of Hong Kong's legal system. Keith Richburg of the *Washington Post* (July 2, 1998) quotes Martin Lee as saying, "It could have been worse." Local democrats—Martin Lee, Emily Lau, Christine Loh, and Margaret Ng—continue to be favored sources.

While sharing this basic framework, the media have their own specific national concerns. The British media privilege their own authoritative figures, while the U.S. media peg their anniversary coverage to President Clinton's trip to China. Stephen Vines (July 2, 1998) of the *Independent* thus starts his report: "Celebrations marking Hong Kong's first year under Chinese rule have given the people of the former British colony an opportunity to feast their eyes on a full scale wax model of Margaret Thatcher." He notes that the celebration started with "dull speeches" by China's President Jiang and Chief Executive Tung. Tung's speech "appeared to have been drafted on a Chinese Communist Party word processor," and the meeting of Jiang and Tung with the performers "was conducted much in the style of the royal variety performances held in a bygone era." Vines's impression (June 30, 1998) that most of the signs of the former colonial administration have been expunged" contrasts that of Richburg in the *Washington Post* that China's hands-off policy has left "them 'untouched.'" Vines claims that "Hong Kong has become a colony of China": Tung's autocratic governing style mimics that of "the great imperial Governors" in the old days, but now he is only one telephone call away from Beijing, "whereas London was a clipper's journey away." Vines continues to iconize Patten as a hero. Taking the home orientation, the *China Times* (June 30, 1998) insists that even if Beijing has behaved well in Hong Kong, the "one country and two systems" framework does not apply to Taiwan. Hong Kong media primarily report about the activities of celebration and Beijing's pledge to help solve the economic crisis.

EXPLAINING AWAY THE TROUBLING FACTS. The *Wall Street Journal* (July 1, 1998) thinks it uncharacteristic of Communist China to leave Hong Kong alone; this restraint stems from "the sophistication of Hong Kong people" who "have segued into a new reality with their standards and expectations intact." The *Washington Post* (July 2, 1998) credits the vocal democrats in Hong Kong and "the vigilance of the international community and the foreign press" for helping to "thwart some of Beijing's most regressive designs for Hong Kong." Despite Beijing's restraint, the *New York Times* (July 2, 1998) uses the "vox populi" technique (van Ginneken, 1998: 100) by quoting an unnamed local resident to say that China has "muted Hong Kong's freewheeling atmosphere."[3]

The *Washington Post* (July 1, 1998) argues that Hong Kong continues to reflect the fundamental incompatibility between western capitalism and Communist authoritarianism. Failing to see the conflict, the *Financial Times* (June 30, 1998) warns, would run the "risk of complacency." China's low profile in Hong Kong, according to the *New York Times* (July 1, 1998), only shows Beijing's "masterly public relations," because "even staunchly pro-Beijing people are not ready to predict that Hong Kong will never clash with China." On the same day, BBC News reports that Beijing's hands-off is "to persuade Taiwan to accept the same formula for reunification" and to attract hard currency investment through Hong Kong. When the PRC-installed provisional legislature expires, a record high 53 percent of the population turns up to cast their votes in the election for the regular legislature. The *People's Daily* (June 30, 1998) interprets the high voter turnout as a "full proof that people support and trust the Special Administrative Region (SAR) government." Western and Taiwan media view it as a sign of the public desire for more democracy.

INTRODUCING NEW CRITERIA. Having found no overt suppression of liberty in Hong Kong, the foreign media develop new hypotheses from their old news paradigms by introducing new and potentially more stringent criteria to assess China's performance in Hong Kong. The criteria are no longer whether China will keep its hands off, but if Hong Kong tomorrow will "look like Hong Kong today" (as U.S. Secretary of State Albright states upon arriving in Hong Kong to attend the ceremony). The new criteria point to a full democracy and the formation of a Chinese identity among Hong Kong people.

While the PRC press rushes to celebrate the successful "one country, two systems" policy, other media scream: "Not yet!" The devil, according to the latter, lies ahead in the implementation of the Basic Law. The *Financial Times* (June 30, 1998) says that although Beijing has "so far" kept its promise of local autonomy, "democracy (in Hong Kong) faces tests." It quotes Martin Lee and Michael DeGolyer, an American teaching at a local university, to say that the SAR government has been ignoring public demand for more democracy and may build up resentment. Recapitulating its position expressed a year ago (see chapter 6), the *Wall Street Journal* (June 30, 1998) editorially urges that President Clinton, who is scheduled to be in Hong Kong after his visit to China, make a "more explicit defense of political freedom in Chinese history and culture." All western and Taiwan media prominently cover the president's meeting with Martin Lee and his calls for democracy.

New facts must be culled to "prove" new hypotheses. A *Financial Times* story (June 30, 1998) reports that one year after living under the Chinese rule, Hong Kong people have "no backlash against all things British" but remain "contemptuous" of the mainlanders and recent mainland immigrants. The contention is not new, but the formation of a Chinese identity has become a new benchmark for measuring the success of the handover. The *Washington Post*

(July 1, 1998) characterizes Hong Kong as a "schizophrenic city" locked in a fierce contest between two visions:

> The final outcome of these competing visions will have a great deal of influence on the future of Hong Kong as this outcropping of skyscrapers and trading houses seeks to navigate between its ambiguously Westernized shell and its ambivalent Chinese heart. At root, the fight is simple: Will Hong Kong be able to foster and maintain an identity that is fundamentally separate from that of China? Or will it shed the things that have made it less Chinese, slowly bonding with the ancient motherland, except with a better airport, more efficient port, and a telephone system that works?

In another story, the same paper (June 30, 1998) reports, "For many, love of the motherland is a forced one they do not really feel." The Chief Secretary, Anson Chan, is widely quoted as saying that "the real transition is about identity and not sovereignty," but she is also chided for expressing patriotic feelings when she sees the national flag on the National Day (see, for example, the *Daily Telegraph*, June 30, 1998).

The western media tend to interpret occurrences in view of their original news paradigms. Based on Beijing's overruling a Hong Kong court on a landmark immigration case and the U.S. Senate's decision to treat Hong Kong like the rest of China in exporting American technology with military applications, the *New York Times* (July 1, 1999) concludes that these events suggest that "the one country is rapidly subsuming the two systems," with Hong Kong taking on a "disquieting resemblance to its motherland." Similar concerns are echoed by some British newspapers. For instance, the *Financial Times* (July 1, 1999) sounds alarm over the deterioration of the rule of law, as reflected by the drop of public confidence in the Hong Kong government. Quoting Martin Lee, leader of Hong Kong's Democratic Party, the *Daily Telegraph* (June 28, 1999) says Beijing's ruling marked the "beginning of the rule of law in Hong Kong."

Repairing the News Paradigms

Compared with newspapers, TV coverage of Hong Kong during the year of the first anniversary is limited. CBS Evening News devotes no single item to Hong Kong's anniversary even though at that time the network is following President Clinton, who would be in Hong Kong after his visit to China. The network finally files a story about the president leaving Hong Kong for home, but makes no mention of the anniversary. Again, on July 5, 1998, CBS has another item about Hong Kong's new airport (which is inaugurated to mark the anniversary), again without saying a word about the occasion. We run a search of Lexis-Nexis database for TV news transcripts, yielding two CNN stories on the anniversary (aired in CNN Today on July 1, 1998). They do not deviate from the U.S. print stories. Later that day, CNN Worldview airs a report by Andrea Koppel on Clinton's scheduled visit to Hong Kong and his scheduled meeting with Martin Lee and other democratic legislators. Both American networks' systematic, if not deliberate, inattention to the anniversary completely reverses the hyped TV hoopla presented a year ago.

In contrast, BBC News has continued to give extensive coverage to Hong Kong during the first year and to the anniversary itself. We search the BBC News archive online, yielding three long stories on the first anniversary on July 1, 1998. One of them depicts the change of Hong Kong's economy from "the biggest boom in history" to being "mired in recession." Another describes Hong Kong's "gloomy celebration." And the third explains why the previous expectations of Hong Kong all turn out to be wrong.

Hong Kong has gone through its first year after handover in what the finance secretary describes as "a roller-coaster ride" (quoted by the *Financial Times*, July 2, 1998). Locally, the *Ming Pao Daily News* (July 1, 1998) says that the year is filled with "nightmares and public resentment." Disputing the PRC's claims of "more prosperity," the populist *Apple Daily* (June 30, 1998) observes that the year has seen Hong Kong's wealth "evaporated." The SAR government seems also to have mismanaged a series of accidents: the bird flu, the poisonous red tide that seriously hurts the local fishing industry, the right to abode by mainland children born of a Hong Kong parent, the controversial rules for the first legislative election, and the chaos in the new airport. In some way, the tough year for Hong Kong might have helped to prevent Hong Kong from disappearing from the world media.

How does the foreign media cover the entire year in the wake of the handover? A search of Lexis-Nexis from July 6, 1997 to July 5, 1998 shows that Hong Kong continues to receive a fair amount of coverage by top U.S. and British newspapers[4] (Table 10.2). As part of the legacy of the previously staged "handover spectacle," they probably feel obliged to keep Hong Kong under constant surveillance. The *New York Times* (March 22, 1998), for example, quotes Martin Lee as saying that if nobody paid attention to Hong Kong, its freedoms would "erode away." In contrast to the print media's vigilance, TV shows little enthusiasm for Hong Kong. For the whole year, CBS News has only twenty-one stories about Hong Kong; all three political items are nothing but brief announcements read by Dan Rather.[5] Most prominently covered are the health scare caused by the bird's flu (nine stories) and the plunge of the stock market amidst the Asian financial crisis (eight stories).[6] Reliance on domestic authorities is obvious: four of the nine "health" stories refer to health officials from the United States or world health organizations, and two other stories quote domestic "health experts." Clearly, for reasons of high cost and

Table 10.2
Topical Distribution of U.S. and British Media Coverage of Hong Kong[1]
(July 6, 1997–July 5, 1998)

	Topical Categories				
Media	Politics (%)	Economy (%)	Health (%)	Other (%)	Total (n)
CBS Evening News	14	38	43	4	21
New York Times	47	35	15	4	101
Washington Post	36	30	30	4	92
Los Angeles Times	45	16	24	14	49
The Times	48	13	16	23	62
Daily Telegraph	47	16	19	18	79
Guardian	58	7	16	18	55

1. The figures are based on a Lexis-Nexis database search. The percentages do not add up to 100% due to round-ing error. "Politics" includes stories about court rulings, protests, changing election rules, the Provisional Legis-lation, individual rights, political structure, the right to abode, legislative elections, the Chief Executive's statements and policy address. "Economy" includes stories about the stock market, the property market, the changing economic structure and policies, various aspects of the economic activities. "Health" includes stories about the "bird's flu" and the "red tide."

obsession with good visuals, CBS has done a poor job at taking the undercur-rent's pulse of *subtle, incremental,* and thus *less visible* structural changes in Hong Kong. For American television, catching the graphically eye-catching bad news is the name of the game. (Throughout the year, BBC News is much more attentive to Hong Kong, consistent with the British vow to monitor the former colony. From July 4 to July 9, 1998, it reports eight stories about the new airport, thanks partly to the attendance of Prime Minister Blair and Foreign Secretary Cook at the anniversary ceremony.)

In contrast to CBS's almost exclusive emphasis on Hong Kong's bad economy and health scare, top U.S. and British newspapers devote nearly a half of their coverage to its political development. Television turns away from the "nitty-gritty" items, such as those reported by the *Los Angeles Times*: a ruling by the Hong Kong Court of Appeals that dismisses the challenge to the Provi-sional Legislature (July 30, 1997), the passage of election law in the Provi-sional Legislature (September 13, 28, 30, 1997), the Chief Executive's policy address to the legislature (October 9, 1997), the controversy over "mother-tongue education" (March 9, 15, 1998), the first legislative election (May 23–29, 1998). U.S. television networks seem to have no memory of their man-ufactured hysteria just a year back. CBS has no bureau in Hong Kong; with its local bureau and more generous airtime, CNN fares only slightly better.

In Taiwan, the *China Times* gives Hong Kong comprehensive coverage throughout the year; it asks its correspondents and invited scholars and former officials to write about the implications of the "one country, two systems" scheme to Taiwan. Even though Hong Kong seems to experience "little change" politically after the handover, according to the paper (January 1 and 18), it has received "the heaven's curse" and run into so many bad situations. The paper covers Taiwan-related issues extensively: for example, a Taiwan delegate to the APEC summit rebuffed Chief Executive Tung who suggests that "one country, two systems" is applicable to Taiwan (November 24, 1997); and Hong Kong's ban on the display of Taiwan's flag on its National Day. Hong Kong media also pick up these stories but frame them on the basis of "the right to free expression." Before and after the first anniversary, the *China Times* publishes many column articles expressing concern that Taiwan may see its international space further shrunk by the Hong Kong example. It urges President Clinton not to praise the "one country, two systems" policy while in Hong Kong, for it is both "unnecessary and hurtful to Taiwan."

As expected, the PRC media cover Hong Kong prominently throughout the whole year. The *Guangzhou Daily*, a local paper in the capital of Guangdong province adjacent to Hong Kong, covers topics ranging from street crimes to Mr. and Mrs. Tung's celebration of the Chinese New Year with children. The paper reports that the Hong Kong SAR government is taking strong measures to boost its faltering economy, while completely ignoring local democrats in Hong Kong. In contrast, Hong Kong papers are highly critical of the SAR government's incompetence and declining credibility, while covering local democrats extensively.

As with their anniversary reports, the western press throughout the year also seeks to repair their news paradigms by resorting to the three approaches we have identified earlier. The *Los Angeles Times* (October 8, 1997) accuses the SAR government of "strip(ping) away the fledgling rights and democratic reforms enacted during the last days of British rule" even though there are "few signs of the market chaos, political repression or economic interference from Beijing." Edward Gargan of the *New York Times*, in summing up the first 100 days after handover on October 9, 1997, reports that even a pro-Beijing real estate tycoon "after some prodding, admitted that at least politically, the territory had regressed under Beijing's hand." On the same day, Keith Richburg of the *Washington Post* stresses the fact that Tung's first policy address "was almost devoid of any discussion of politics or civil liberties." On May 9, 1998, Farley of the *Los Angeles Times* reiterates her view: "Piece by piece, law by law, the elements that made Hong Kong independent and unique before its restoration to Chinese rule last July are being eroded." The embedded ideological framework enables the western press to see the first anniversary in the same vein.

In sum, we have been impressed with (a) the persistence of national prisms; (b) the continuing ideological contestation between the PRC media and all other media systems in the U.S.-led camp; (c) the media's reliance on domestic authorities to "repair" their news paradigms; and (d) U.S. television networks' retreat from Hong Kong compared with the relative vigilance of the U.S. and British newspapers. Surprise and bad news combined have managed to keep Hong Kong in the news. The media acknowledge the surprises before they quickly return to old paradigms to dismiss the significance of these surprises. The news paradigms, in the face of (un)comfortable evidence, are thus "repaired."

U.S. Secretary of State Madeleine Albright comes to Hong Kong handover as a guardian of democracy.

Inside the Press and Broadcast Center thousands of reporters from around the world make use of the communication facilities.

Hong Kong citizens watch live broadcasts of the handover events on June 30, 1997.

Chris Patten leaves the Government House as hundreds of Hong Kong citizens bid farewell along the street.

Visitors take the opportunity to have a shot of things British.

Protesters take to the street and show their defiance against the Chinese leaders.

Things British are on the way out of Hong Kong and quickly become hot collectors' items.

CNN's Asian anchor reports live in Hong Kong during the handover.

The wife of late patriarch leader Deng Xiaoping attends the handover in Hong Kong.

Appendix I

Sampled Media Organizations[1]

Apple Daily: Hong Kong's mass-circulated newspaper, populist, critical of the PRC, sensational, founded in 1995. Readership (1999): 1,780,000.

Asahi Shimbun: Founded in 1979, Japan's quality national paper. Circulation (1999): 8,321,138 (morning edition), 4,239,094 (evening edition).

Asahi TV: Founded in 1957, located in Tokyo, currently with 26 local affiliated stations, one of the biggest national broadcasting corporations in Japan.

Associated Press (AP): Global newsgathering organization, a nonprofit cooperative established in 1948. Based in New York, sending more than 20 million words per day to more than 15,000 news organizations in 112 countries.

Australian: Australia's national quality newspaper. Founded in 1824, acquired by Rupert Murdoch's News Corporation in 1964. Estimated circulation: 129,000.

Australian Broadcasting Cooperation (ABC): Founded in 1932, Australia's only national public broadcaster. Weekly reach of ABC Television averages 8.9 million people in the five metropolitan cities and 4.2 million people in regional areas.

British Broadcasting Corporation (BBC): Founded in 1927 as Britain's public service broadcaster, with far-reaching global influence and prestige. Funded by the license fee. Survived Prime Minister Margaret Thatcher's attempts to make the BBC carry advertising (1979–1990). BBC1 caters to the majority interest, and BBC2 serves the minority interest. BBC World (TV) is influential overseas; BBC Radio broadcasts in English and 40 other languages.

Cable News Network (CNN): Launched in 1980 by Ted Turner as an all-news network. Now owned by AOL Time-Warner. Atlanta-based, specializing in international news

---

[1]Partial sources: Tunstall and Machin (1999); Chan and Lee (1991); Lee (2000a, 2000c).

reporting. Feeding its service to foreign broadcasters and "international" hotel rooms. Built up its European audiences during the 1990s and became one of the only three profitable pan-European networks. CNN International (CNNI) was launched in 1985 as a separate entity.

Cable Television (CTV): Founded in 1993, Hong Kong's pay cable television. Subscribers (1999): 450,000.

Canadian Broadcasting Cooperation (CBC): Founded in 1932, Canada's national public broadcasting network of ninety-five owned stations and other affiliates. Public funding with supplemental advertising revenues.

Central Daily News: Founded in 1927, official organ of the Nationalist Party (Guomindang) in Taiwan with declining influence. Estimated circulation: 87,000.

Central News Agency (CNA): Founded in 1924 as an organ of the Nationalist Party (Guomindang), turned into Taiwan's national news agency in 1996.

Chicago Tribune: Founded in 1847, Chicago-based daily, with regional influence. Conservative editorial position. Weekday circulation (2000): 674,603. The parent Tribune Company now also owns the *Los Angeles Times*.

China Central Television (CCTV): Launched in 1958, China's state-owned flagship national TV network, currently with 8 channels and a regular staff of 3,698, broadcasting 138 hours of programs daily, covering 87.4 percent of national audience.

China Times: First established in 1950, one of the two major press conglomerates in Taiwan. Centrist editorial policy. Estimated circulation: 900,000.

Chinese Television Network (CTN): Hong Kong-based satellite TV news channel. Originally owned by *Ming Pao*, now acquired by Taiwan interests.

Columbia Broadcasting System (CBS): One of the New York-based broadcasting networks with international influence. Founded in 1927, the second oldest broadcasting network (after NBC) in the United States. Currently owned by Viacom.

Daily Telegraph: Founded in 1855, major national quality newspaper in Britain. Acquired by the Hollinger Company and its chairman, Conrad Black, a Canadian, in 1986. Supporter of the Conservative Party (pro-Thatcher, anti-Major, pro-USA, anti-Europe). Circulation (2000): 1,033,680.

Des Moines Register: A respected local newspaper in the state of Iowa, the "heartland" of America. Weekday circulation (2000): 157,705.

Economic Daily: Founded in 1983, nationally circulated organ paper of the PRC's State Council. Circulation (1998): 578,411.

Far Eastern Economic Review: Launched in 1946, Hong Kong-based, premier regional English-language economic and political weekly journal. Published by Review Publishing, a wholly owned subsidiary of Dow Jones. Circulation (2000): 95,000.

Financial Times: Founded in 1888, Britain's leading financial paper with international influence (outselling the *Wall Street Journal* on the continent of Europe). Grew rapidly after 1950s with the expansion of the London financial market. Pearson-owned. Has now the largest British newspaper team of foreign correspondents. Owns leading financial dailies in Paris, Madrid, and Hamburg (with Bertelsmann). Now prints each day in five European locations outside Britain, in two Asian locations, and in three U.S. locations. Circulation (2000): 457,653.

Globe and Mail: Founded in 1844, Canada's Toronto-based national quality newspaper, with strength in national and international news coverage. Weekday circulation (1998): 330,679.

Government Information Services (GIS): Hong Kong government's information arm. During the handover, it hosted local and international media, issued press credentials, organized field trips, provided background information and daily briefing.

Guangming Daily: Founded in 1949, Beijing-based national newspaper targeting the PRC's intellectual readers. Circulation (1998): 303,802.

Guangzhou Daily: Founded in 1952, Communist Party organ of the Guangzhou municipality in Guangdong province. China's first officially approved "newspaper group" and top advertising revenue earner (US$1,171 million in 1999). Circulation (1999): 1,200,000.

Guangzhou TV: Metropolitan official broadcaster operating under the jurisdiction of the Guangzhou municipal government, with regional influence in Guangdong province.

Guardian: Founded in 1821, major British national quality newspaper, read by affluent Labor supporters. Circulation (2000): 396,534.

Independent: Founded in 1986, based in London, major British national quality newspaper. Since 1998, wholly owned by the Irish Independent Group and its chairman, Tony O'Reilly. Circulation (2000): 224,224.

Independent Television (ITV): Britain's commercial broadcaster, a federation formed by fifteen independent regional contractors, each with a franchise for a set period, broadcasting in fourteen regional areas. Average peak-time audience share: 38.8 percent (1999).

Japanese Broadcasting Corporation (NHK): Founded in 1925, Japan's influential public-service broadcaster, financially independent of government, all funded by the receiver fee.

Kyodo News Agency: Japan's leading national news agency. Established in 1945 as a not-for-profit cooperative. Serving 47 million people (1999) through newspaper subscriptions.

Liberty Times: A proindependence mainstream newspaper, with a fast-growing reader-ship in Taiwan.

Los Angeles Times: Founded in 1881, one of the elite newspapers in the United States and most influential on the West Coast. Coowns a syndicated news service with the *Washington Post*. Now bought by the Tribune Company, which also owns the *Chicago Tribune*. Weekday circulation (2000): 1,153,706.

Maclean's: Canada's most influential weekly newsmagazine. Paid circulation (1999): 503,369.

Ming Pao: Founded in 1959, Hong Kong's major elite Chinese-language paper. Founded by Louis Cha. Now owned by a Malaysian-Chinese tycoon with considerable investment interests in China. Readership (1999): 285,000.

Minzhong Daily: A small proindependence newspaper in southern Taiwan.

New York Times: Founded in 1851, "a newspaper of record," one of the most influential newspapers in the world. The parent company owns the *Boston Globe* and coowns the Paris-based *International Herald-Tribune*. Its syndicated news service has global influence. Weekday circulation (2000): 1,149,576.

Newsweek: Founded in 1933 and bought by the Washington Post Company in 1961. America's most influential news magazine, along with *Time* (owned by AOL Time-Warner). Newsweek International publishes in four English-language editions. Circulation (1999): 4,443,261 (U.S. edition); 752,000 (Newsweek International, in four English-language editions).

Nihon Keizai Shimbun: Founded in 1876, Japan's leading business and financial newspaper. Circulation (1998): 3,007,792 (morning edition), 1,656,341 (afternoon edition), 52,835 (international edition).

Oriental Daily News: Major mass-circulated newspaper in Hong Kong, sensational, founded in 1969. Readership (1999): 2,551,000.

People's Daily: Founded in 1948, official organ of the Chinese Communist Party. Politically most important in China. Circulation (1998): 2,001,058.

People's Liberation Army Daily: Founded in 1956, official organ of the People's Liberation Army in China. Circulation (1998): 470,000.

Reuters: Founded in 1850, Britain-based global news and television agency, with 2,101 journalists in 184 bureaus in 109 countries, reaching 521,000 users in 52,800 locations and providing news and information to over 900 Internet sites.

San Jose Mercury News: A newspaper in Silicon Valley, California. Weekday circulation (2000): 289,462.

Sankei Shimbun: A leading national financial daily in Japan, with mainstream conservative editorial policy. First established as *Japan Industry News* in 1933; renamed as *Sankei Shimbun* in 1958. Circulation (1999): 1,951,546.

South China Morning Post: Founded in 1903, Hong Kong's most influential English-language newspaper. Readership (1999): 206,000.

Taiwan Television Company (TTV): Founded in 1962, Taiwan's first commercial television, broadcasting thirty-seven hours of news programs per week in 1999.

Television Broadcasts Limited (TVB): Founded in 1967, Hong Kong's dominant television station. Owns TVBS, a satellite TV channel, in Taiwan. Average primetime audience share (1999): 71 percent (Chinese Jade Channel), 76 percent (English Pearl Channel).

The Times: Founded in 1785, Britain's flagship newspaper targeted at intellectuals and officials. Acquired by the News Corporation and Rupert Murdoch (an Australian-turned-American citizen) in 1981. Supports the Conservative Party (pro-Thatcher, pro-U.S.A., anti-Major, anti-Europe). Waged a price war against the better-selling *Daily Telegraph*. Circulation (2000): 722,642. (Murdoch owns the Fox Channel in the United Sates, the Sky Channel in Britain, the *Australian* in Australia, and the Star television in Hong Kong. A supporter of Margaret Thatcher and Ronald Reagan, he has recently befriended Beijing leaders.)

United Daily News: Founded in 1951, one of the two major press conglomerates in Taiwan. Somewhat conservative editorial policy. Estimated circulation: 800,000.

Wall Street Journal: Founded in 1889, the world's leading financial daily. Based in New York. Takes a conservative editorial policy. Grew rapidly after 1950s with the expansion of the New York financial market. Now prints each day in four European locations and four Asian locations. Weekday circulation (2000): 1,812,590. The parent company, Dow Jones, also owns the *Asian Wall Street Journal* and *Far Eastern Economic Review*, both based in Hong Kong.

Washington Post: Founded in 1877, one of the most influential newspapers in the United States. The parent company owns *Newsweek* and coowns the Paris-based *International Herald Tribune* with the *New York Times*, as well as coowning a syndicated news service with the *Los Angeles Times*. Weekday circulation (2000): 812,559.

Xinhua (New China) News Agency: Founded in 1931 as an official organ of the Chinese Communist Party, now state-owned and official national news agency. Number of customers (1998): 5,298.

Yazhou Zhoukan (Asia Weekly): Hong Kong-based Chinese-language news weekly magazine, owned by *Ming Pao*.

Yomiuri Shimbun: Founded in 1874, national mass newspaper with highest circulation in Japan. Circulation (1999): 10,223,923 (morning edition), 4,252,200 (evening edition).

Appendix II

Interviewees

Fiona ANDERSEN	Hong Kong Bureau Chief, BBC (UK)
CHAN Chung-kwan	Chief Assignment Editor, *Oriental Daily News* (Hong Kong)
CHAN Wai-yee	Political Editor, *Apple Daily* (Hong Kong)
Raymond CHAU	Reporter, Associated Press (USA)
CHIA Kuan-ching	Deputy Chief, Domestic News Division, China Television Service (Taiwan)
Mike CHINOY	Hong Kong Bureau Chief, CNN (USA)
John COLMEY	Hong Kong Correspondent, *Time Magazine* (Asian Edition) (USA)
DAI Zhong-ren	Deputy Head and Anchor, News Department, Taiwan Television (Taiwan)
Marcus ELIASON	Hong Kong Bureau Chief, Associated Press (USA)
Dorinda ELLIOT	Hong Kong Bureau Chief, *Newsweek* (USA)
FUNG Tak-hung	Head of Assignment Desk, Cable TV (Hong Kong)
Susanne GANZ	Staff Correspondent, Kyodo News Agency (Japan)
Edward GARGAN	Hong Kong Bureau Chief, *New York Times* (USA)
GU Yuan*	Correspondent, Hong Kong Bureau, *People's Daily* (China)

---

*Pseudonym is used for PRC journalists to protect identity. For most Chinese journalists, the surname precedes the given name.

Andrew HIGGINS	East Asia Correspondent, *The Guardian* (UK)
HUANG Yili*	Director, News Department, Guangdong TV (China)
HUANG Zhao-song	President, *China Times* (Taiwan)
Jane HUTCHEON	China Correspondent, Australian Broadcasting Corporation (Australia)
Graham HUTCHINGS	China Correspondent, *Daily Telegraph* (UK)
Hamayi ICHIKAWA	Correspondent, *Asahi Shimbun* (Japan)
Akira IWASE	Staff Correspondent, Kyodo News Agency (Japan)
Joseph KAHN	China Correspondent, *Wall Street Journal* (USA)
Antonio A. KAMIYA	Deputy Editor, World Service Section, Kyodo News Agency (Japan)
Kristi KHOCKSHORN	Correspondent, *San Jose Mercury News* (USA)
Miki KOGAI	Producer, Asahi TV Production House
V. G. KULKARNI	Regional Editor, *Far Eastern Economic Review* (Hong Kong)
LAN Xuan	Reporter and News Anchor, TVBS (Taiwan)
Frank LANGFITT	Correspondent, *Baltimore Sun* (USA)
LI Yuet-wah Daisy	Assistant Chief Editor, *Ming Pao Daily News* (Hong Kong)
LIN Shan*	Correspondent, Xinhua News Agency (China)
LIN Tian-gui	Deputy Managing Editor, *Liberty Times* (Taiwan)
LIU Kun-yuan	Hong Kong Bureau Chief, Central News Agency (Taiwan)
Paul LOONG	World Editor, Canadian Press (Canada)
Carmen LUK	News Manager, TVB News (Hong Kong)
LUO Can*	Director, General Editorial Office, CCTV (China)
LUO Ding-wei	Hong Kong reporter, *Minzhong Daily* (Taiwan)
Charles MAK	Assistant News Director, Fairchild Television (Canada)
MAK Yiu-on	Assistant Managing Editor, Chinese Television Network (Hong Kong and Taiwan)
Richard McGREGOR	Correspondent, *The Australian* (Australia)
Jonathan MANTHORPE	Asian Correspondent, Southam News (Canada)

Risa MARTYN	Business Consultant, National Newspaper Association (USA)
MENG Rong-hua	Head, Political News, *Central Daily News* (Taiwan)
James MILES	Correspondent, BBC (UK)
Jonathan MIRSKY	Hong Kong Bureau Chief, *The Times* (UK)
Ryuichiro NAKABURA	Hong Kong Bureau Chief, NHK (Japan)
Maynard PARKER	Editor-in-chief, *Newsweek* (USA)
PENG Chun-bi	Reporter, Broadcasting Corporation of China (Taiwan)
PENG Wen-zheng	Reporter, TVBS (Taiwan)
Pilar PEREYRA	Reporter, Hong Kong Bureau, Kyodo News Agency (Japan)
Eric RANKIN	Producer, Pacific Rim Report, Canadian Broadcasting Corporation (Canada)
Joseph RIDDING	Hong Kong Correspondent, *Financial Times* (UK)
Satoshi SAEKI	Correspondent, *Yomiuri Shimbun* (Japan)
SHUI Lo-sin	Assistant Director, Radio Television Hong Kong (Hong Kong)
Angela SO	Reporter, UBT (Feifan Satellite Television) (Taiwan)
Lillian SO	Senior Editor, Chinese Edition, *Maclean's Magazine* (Canada)
Akihio SUZUKI	Correspondent, *Asahi Shimbun* (Japan)
SZE Mei-ling	Assistant News Director, Managing Editor and Anchor, KTSF Lincoln Broadcasting Co. (USA)
Mr. TAMI	Correspondent, Asahi Broadcasting Corporation (Japan)
Hideo TAMURA	Hong Kong Bureau Chief, *Nihon Keizai Shimbun* (Japan)
TAN Zhi-qiang	Reporter, Hong Kong Bureau, *China Times* (Taiwan)
TSANG Yui-sang	Consultant, BBC TV (UK)
Steve VINES	Correspondent, *Independent* (UK)
Nora WANG	Reporter, Broadcasting Corporation of China (Taiwan)
Ian WILLIAMS	Correspondent, ITV (UK)
Jan WONG	Reporter, *The Globe and Mail* (Canada)

Chris WOOD	Vancouver Bureau Chief/Senior Editor, Chinese Edition, *Maclean's Magazine* (Canada)
WU Ge-qing	News Manager, TVBS (Taiwan)
WU Xian-shen	Correspondent, Hong Kong bureau, Central News Agency (Taiwan)
XU Fang*	Associate Director, Guangdong TV (China)
L. P. YAU	Editor-in-Chief, *Yazhou Zhoukan* (Hong Kong)
YAU Shing-mu	Chief Reporter, *Hong Kong Financial Times* (Hong Kong)
Chris YEUNG	Political Editor, *South China Morning Post* (Hong Kong)
ZHANG Qiaoling*	Correspondent, Hong Kong Bureau, Radio Beijing (China)
ZHENG Han-liang	Hong Kong Bureau Chief, *China Times* (Taiwan)
ZHENG Qiang*	Chief, Hong Kong Bureau, *People's Daily* (China)
ZHOU Chuan-zou	Reporter, Taiwan Television (TTV) (Taiwan)

Appendix III

Guideline for Interview

I. Organizations

1. Do you have a regular correspondent or stringer stationed in Hong Kong?

2. How important is news about Hong Kong to your media organization?

3. How important is the handover as a news topic? Why is it important?

4. How much newshole or airtime do you have regularly? How much will you have on July 1? Do you have to fight for it? In what format (special programs, regular news, etc.) are your stories about the handover being presented?

5. How do you coordinate your efforts with home editors? Have you encountered any obstacles with them? When you come up with an idea, do you have to seek their approval? When in disagreement, how do you resolve it?

6. How many journalists does your organization have for covering the Hong Kong handover? How many of them are regularly stationed in Hong Kong? How long have they been stationed here? How many of them are on temporary assignment? How long are they going to be here? What sort of backgrounds do they have? How do you divide the labor?

7. How many helpers do you hire? What do they do? Do you need help in translation or interpretation?

II. Self

A. General Characteristics

1. Gender, approximate age, years of journalistic experience in the field and in the present organization, job title.

2. Name of news organization, country of origin.

3. Reading and speaking proficiency in Chinese.

B. Personal Experience and Knowledge

1. How were you chosen to cover Hong Kong?

2. How often have you been to Hong Kong, China, or Asia? Have you covered any other Asian country? How transferable is that experience to covering Hong Kong?

3. For you, what are the most frequently used or most useful sources of information about Hong Kong?

4. How do you prepare yourself for covering the handover? How long have you been following Hong Kong and China?

5. What is your impression of Hong Kong? How different is it from what you thought it would be like?

C. Political and Journalistic Attitudes

1. In your opinion, where will Hong Kong be ten years from now? Will the "one country, two systems" model work? How will Hong Kong fare in terms of its political democracy, economic development, and press freedom? What kind of a relationship will Hong Kong have with China?

2. What kind of things do you do to help your home readers understand what is happening in Hong Kong?

D. Perception of Readers or Audiences

1. Please describe for me a profile of your average readers or viewers. How much do you think they know about Hong Kong? Do you think they really care about Hong Kong?

2. How do you find out their interests?

III. News Net

1. How do you develop and process news tips while in Hong Kong? To what extent do you rely on the local media as sources? How good are they?

2. To what extent do you interact with local journalists and academics? Do you seek their help? How helpful are they?

3. Do you seek help from the Government Information Services (GIS)? Do you seek help from the Xinhua News Agency? How helpful are they?

4. How have you built up contacts in Hong Kong within a relatively short period of time?

5. Has anyone approached you to give you an interview?

6. Have you approached the following individuals for interviews: Chris Patten, Tung Chee-hwa, Anson Chan, Lu Ping, Martin Lee? Have you approached any other important individuals for interview? What are your major impressions of these people?

IV. Working Conditions

1. With whom are you competing? How keen is this competition? What do you do to be different from your competitors?

2. How much do you consult the wire services? How much do you consult the work of your competitors? Do you compare notes with your colleagues from other media or with the leading media? Do you think they do a good job? How different is your work from their work?

3. Would you be feeling uncomfortable if you find your interpretation of a story different from that of other leading media? In that situation, what would you do?

4. Do top international journalists get special treatment from the GIS or from the sources?

V. Framing

A. Agenda-setting

1. What do you think are the most important problems facing Hong Kong?

2. What are the most important issues that you have covered or planned to cover? What topics would you hate to miss the most?

3. What are the issues or topics that you think should be covered but were not covered? Why?

B. Themes

1. What are the primary themes of your media organization with respect to the handover of Hong Kong? What are the secondary themes? Why are these themes important?

2. Do you see different themes that different media from different countries emphasize? What are these themes?

C. Processes

1. How do you decide on which topics and themes to cover? Do you discuss these topics with your editors—or your colleagues, or people from other media organizations—beforehand? What do you talk about?

2. When your views differ from your editors' views, what do you do? Do you incorporate their views and adjust your own perceptions?

3. Overall speaking, what topics do you think have been well covered by foreign journalists? What topics have not been well covered? Are there any topics you think should be covered but are not?

4. Among all of the journalists, who do you think has done the best job? Is a particular national group doing a better job than others? What makes them stand out?

5. What role do you see international media playing in Hong Kong? What impact do you think they will have on the future development of Hong Kong?

6. What role do you see western nations playing in Hong Kong? What impact will they have on the future development of Hong Kong?

D. Cases

(a) The Story That Best Captures Hong Kong

1. Please show me a story that you think would capture the essence of Hong Kong.

2. How do you get the idea? How do you develop it? What angle do you take? What other angles have you considered? Why do you take this angle?

3. Who else are involved in developing this story? Do you discuss it with your editors while developing this story? Do they give you specific instructions? Do you agree with them? If not, what do you do?

4. Who are your major sources for this story? How do you identify them? How do you contact them? Are there instances where sources try to influence you and push their points of view really hard? In those cases, what do you do?

5. When your sources have different views, how do you assess their credibility? Do you consult with your editors?

6. Do your editors change the story you file? What do you think of these changes they make? Do you ever argue with your editors over the story? If yes, what do you argue about? How does it turn out?

7. While developing this story, do you talk to reporters from your country, local reporters in Hong Kong, or reporters from other nations?

(b) July 1 Ceremonies
1. What kind of a story would you write about the handover ceremony?

2. There will be many activities going on simultaneously. How would you divide the labor among your colleagues? Where are they going to be posted? Whom are you and your colleagues going to interview?

3. Do you talk to your editors about the field situation? What do you talk about?

4. Would you prepare a background piece to go along with the ceremony? What will the main takes of this background piece be?

5. What do you have to do to make the story about the handover of Hong Kong appealing to your readers or viewers?

6. What kinds of pictures will you take?

7. Do you run into any obstacles in taking photos and getting your people stationed at the right places? What obstacles do you expect in carrying out the "game plan" of coverage on July 1?

Appendix IV

Content Analysis

We perform a content analysis of 26 media outlets from 7 national media systems, totaling 3,883 stories (Table 1.1). For television, we only code the main regular newscasts, but not special programs. We decide not to do a full-scale content analysis of all the data collected due to (a) resource constraints; (b) sampling efficiency; and (c) methodological limitations. From the sampling perspective, a complete sample may not yield additional insights that justify the tremendous additional effort. Moreover, we feel that the current status of the arts in content analysis is inadequate for revealing the thematic, rhetoric, and syntagmatic features of media discourses (Pan and Kosicki, 1993). We use the content analysis as a supplement to the discourse analysis, in setting the parameter and in providing some, albeit limited, basis for generalizing our inferences.

This content analysis does not include Japan. None of us reads or speaks Japanese. We hire a Japan-educated media scholar to read the sampled newspaper issues and watch taped television newscasts; he translates each story title and writes down a thematic summary of the story. We hold frequent communication with him to get an overall perspective.

Having defined the coding variables, we proceed to develop a coding scheme. The research assistant assembles an assortment of newspaper articles and television newscasts for us to do a trial round of coding. We study the intercoder reliability coefficient with a view to revising the coding scheme and refining the operational definition of each variable. After three trial runs we finalize the coding scheme (Appendix V). The level of agreement among the four coders on the "factual" variables (such as the size and time of a story) reaches above 90 percent. They agree around 80 percent on the more "subjective" variables (such as the "tone").

Table IV-1 summarizes the amount of media coverage. In terms of the size of newspaper coverage (in squared centimeters), Hong Kong and the PRC rank highest, followed by Taiwan, Britain, and Australia. The United States ranks low because the *Wall Street Journal* and two "local" papers (the *Chicago Tribune* and the *Des Moines Register*) devote a smaller space to the handover, but the three elite papers (the *New York Times*, the *Washington Post*, and the *Los Angeles Times*) all produce large amounts of stories. The amount of television coverage (in seconds) differs only slightly. CCTV (China) ranks first, followed by TVB (Hong Kong) and TTV (Taiwan), and Australian, British, and US networks.

Table IV-1
Amount of Media Coverage[1]

	Number of outlets coded	Number of Items	Total newspaper Space (cm²)	Total TV Airtime (seconds)	space per paper (cm²)	Time per channel (seconds)
PRC	3	717	213,015	24,134	106,508	24,134
USA	8	335	143,398	13,742	23,900	6,871
Britain	5	503	140,538	11,820	46,846	5,910
Hong Kong	4	1,607	428,130	13,554	142,710	13,554
Taiwan	2	500	79,250	11,791	79,250	11,791
Australia	2	84	44,836	7,018	44,836	7,018
Canada	2	137	39,926	2,100	39,926	2,100
Total	26	3,883	975,379	84,159	—	—

1. The figures include only the items (news, editorials, column articles, photos, and tidbits) from 26 media outlets that are directly relevant to the handover. For television, only main newscasts are coded.

The handover, as a prescheduled calendar event, has a clear life cycle. Media coverage peaks on June 30 and July 1. Table IV-2 shows the standardized size of daily media coverage by country in three phrases of the study period. The score is generated by dividing the size of an item (in newspaper squared centimeters or in TV seconds) by the range of story size (maximum minus minimum) of a particular media outlet. During the prehandover preparatory period (June 16–29), daily media coverage is only 11 percent to 33 percent of the amount produced in the peak period. The posthandover coverage (July 2–5) tails off to range from 7 percent to 39 percent of the amount produced in the peak period.

We construct a summary measure of source diversity based on the content data. We coded the top ten sources quoted (Table 3.5). Where there were multiple sources in a story, we coded only the first ten sources. Based on the data, we classified the sources in terms of (a) their national affiliation; (b) social position (officials, political opinion leaders, business elite, media and journalists, academics and think thanks, other kinds of opinion leaders, and ordinary people.) For each of the two dimensions, we calculated an H-statistic, or the entropy measure in the information theory (Shannon and Weaver, 1964). The statistic is calculated in the following formula:

$$H = -\Sigma\, p_i \ln p_i$$

where, p_i = the percentage of cases falling into category i;
        i = 1 to I, with I equals to the total number of categories involved;
        $\ln p_i$ = the natural logarithm of p_i.

The resulting H statistic has a minimum of 0 (least diverse), if all the cases fall into a single category. The maximum value (most diverse) is the natural logarithm of the

Table IV-2
Daily Volume of Media Handover Coverage[1]

	Preparatory Phase (June 16–29)	Peak Phase (June 30–July 1)	Tail-off Phase (July 2–5)	Prep./Peak Ratio (%)	Tail./Peak Ratio (%)
PRC	229.38	2180.94	419.07	10.5	19.2
USA	514.88	1787.18	361.63	28.8	20.2
Britain	412.41	1418.46	345.72	29.1	24.4
Hong Kong	753.37	2715.38	730.61	27.7	26.9
Taiwan	248.65	1192.97	223.64	20.8	18.7
Australia	152.11	456.32	180.28	33.3	39.5
Canada	74.91	459.84	31.77	16.3	6.9

1. The cell entries are standardized daily volume. The standardized scores are calculated by using the following formula: standardized score = size of an item in the original metric (cm^2 or second) = (maximum − minimum) of story size of a media outlet.

number of categories, with equal cases in every category. This statistic has a theoretical rectangular distribution, unsuitable for parametric tests. We standardize the H-statistic within each country—by multiplying it by $100/\ln I^2$—into a scale ranging from 0 to 100, to facilitate comparison across variables and samples.

Table IV-3 shows both the raw and standardized H scores. The "diversity in country of origin" measures the extent to which a national media system gives voice to sources in a multiplicity of countries. Australia and Taiwan media score high. The PRC media rely primarily on domestic sources; Hong Kong and Canadian media are low too, for they treat the handover as a domestic story.

The other set of H statistic measures the diversity of the news sources in terms of their social positions. This H statistic is even lower than "country diversity." Most media rely on officials and members of the political and economic elite to make news. The PRC media score high because they spread their sources across different social categories to create the spectacle of national celebration; very often, they show many people on the street who utter the same thing. Hong Kong media also score high in their effort to "record the history" and to "reflect how people feel." Australian and Taiwan media may quote sources from a wide range of countries, but these sources are likely to be officials, elite members, and other media.

		Diversity in Country	
		Low	High
Diversity in Social Position	Low	—	Australia, Taiwan
	High	PRC, Hong Kong, Canada	USA, Britain

Table IV-3
Diversity of News Sources (H-Statistic)[1]

	Diversity in Country of Origin		Diversity in Social Position	
	Raw	Standardized	Raw	Standardized
PRC	1.36	69.89	.96	49.33
USA	1.48	76.06	.90	46.25
Britain	1.40	71.95	.77	39.57
Hong Kong	1.25	64.24	.87	44.71
Taiwan	1.60	82.22	.55	28.26
Australia	1.65	84.79	.57	29.29
Canada	1.17	60.13	.84	43.17
Overall	1.49	76.57	.86	44.20

1. The H statistic is computed as $-\Sigma\, p_i \ln p_i$ and it is then standardized by multiplying the raw score by $100/\ln I^2$, where p_i = percentage of cases falling into the ith category and I = total number of categories.

Table IV-4
Rank Order Correlations (Spearman Rho) of the
10 Most Frequently Cited Sources by Country

	China	UK	Hong Kong	Taiwan	US	Canada
UK	.09					
Hong Kong	.10	.60**				
Taiwan	−.20	.08	.08			
US	.24	.57**	.56*	.05		
Canada	.18	.74**	.72**	.11	.75**	
Australia	−.01	.69**	.56*	.15	.47*	.74**

*p < .01; ** < p.001

Three patterns of media system are revealing:

1. The resource-rich pluralistic system: The U.S. (a global power) and the British (an outgoing sovereign) have media resources that enjoy an easy access to news sources from various countries and from various walks of life. To them, the handover is a global event.

2. The resource-restricted pluralistic system (Australia, Canada, and Taiwan) that regards the handover as a globalized regional event.

3. The resource-rich system, including Hong Kong and its diaspora, Canada, that regards the handover as a "local" event with global implications. The PRC media treat the event as a national celebration.

To further assess the extent to which the news sources overlap across nations, we calculate the rank-order correlation coefficients (Spearman's Rho) of the ten most frequently cited sources in seven national media systems (Table IV-4). China and Taiwan differ from one anther significantly. Both are also distinct from all other systems. The remainder—Hong Kong, U.S., UK, Canada, and Australia—seem to share a highly overlapping pool of top ten news sources. Although operating in a marketized and democratized environment, Taiwan media have a local lens so strong as to differ markedly from Hong Kong and western media.

Appendix V

Coding Scheme

Name of coder: _____ Analysis date: _____ Time needed: _____

Note: 1. Remember to photocopy the newspaper, but do not enlarge or reduce it.
2. Use a ruler to map the perimeter of the photocopied article.
3. Use felt pen to highlight the people mentioned and information source in the article.

Name of newspaper: _____ Date of newspaper: _____
Name of Page: _____ Page number: _____

Type of article:
    (1) pure news   (2) interview   (3) feature (soft) (4) editorial
    (5) news analysis (6) commentary (7) others: _____

Source of article:
    (1) from own reporter/editor   (2) from local news organizations
    (3) from international news agencies (4) from various sources
    (5) submission by author   (6) others: _____

Prominence of article position:
    (1) front page, headline   (2) front page, but not headline
    (3) nonfront page, headline   (4) nonfront page, not headline

Accompanied by photograph(s):   (1) yes   (2) no

Area of article (excluding article title):
    (excluding photo) _____ cm^2
    (including photo) _____ cm^2

Area of article title: _____ cm^2
Number of words: _____ (in case the areas cannot be ascertained)

Article's tone 1 (prediction about Hong Kong's situation after handover):
  • Will Hong Kong change?
        (1) yes   (2) no   (3) not mentioned
  • If Hong Kong will change, the direction is:
        (1) better   (2) both better and worse   (3) worse   (4) not certain

Article's tone 2 (attitude/stand towards mainland Chinese government):
        (1) friendly, positive   (2) neutral, balanced
        (3) hostile, negative   (4) not certain   (5) not mentioned

Thematic categories:
        (1) British colonialism
        (2) British legacy, influence, promises
        (3) China's observance of "one country, two systems"
        (4) People's Liberation Army (PLA)
        (5) China market for Hong Kong
        (6) Hong Kong economy, economic prosperity
        (7) Hong Kong's influence on China
        (8) Democracy, human rights, press freedom
        (9) Profiles of Hong Kong: social reaction, daily life
        (10) Handover ceremonies, hoopla, fun, pomp
        (11) New chief executive and SAR government
        (12) U.S. policy, U.S.–China or U.S.–HK relations
        (13) Reactions: China
        (14) Reactions: Taiwan
        (15) Reactions: Chinatowns, overseas Chinese communities

Specific mentioning of the following in the article:
        (1) June 4, 1989, or the Tiananmen Square crackdown
        (2) Taiwan
        (3) Singapore
        (4) One country, two systems

Notes

Chapter 1

1. We use "journalists" in a broad and generic sense. The majority of them are undoubtedly technical staff of television, including engineers, camera people, electricians, and producers. This total figure is based on applications made to the Government Information Services (GIS) of the Hong Kong government for media accreditation. How many of them did actually come is unknown, but even half of the 8,000 people would be considered very formidable.

2. The *New York Times* editorials had given Hong Kong sustained attention before 1997, but rarely commented on Hong Kong after the handover. In contrast, it has given substantially more prominent coverage to China in the late 1990s.

3. As the subject matters and themes call for, not all chapters involve the analysis of all national media systems. Chapter 5 is exclusively an analysis of the U.S. media, chapter 6 is primarily an analysis of the British media in comparison with the PRC media, while chapter 7 is an analysis of the media systems in three contending Chinese societies. Chapter 4 does not include Japan, but the general theoretical points still hold.

Chapter 2

1. In fact, eight years before 1997, some media in Europe already contacted Hongkong Telecom about renting satellites during the handover period. The Japanese media have also started to book satellite time a few years ago. As a result, Hongkong Telecom has spent U.S.$6.5 million to upgrade its facilities. Between June 15 and July 10, Hongkong Telecom rented out 5,000 hours of satellite time, which is about double the normal demand. It has a team of 300 people to serve the eight huge satellite dishes in its Stanley transmission station (*Apple Daily*, July 1).

Chapter 5

1. However, human rights abuses of similar magnitude committed by U.S. allies have been played down (Mahlasela, 1990; Herman and Chomsky, 1988). The reductive

themes of anti-Communism in the Tiananmen reports also missed many historical and sociological dimensions (Wasserstrom and Perry, 1994).

2. They are Edward Gargan (Hong Kong bureau chief and formerly, Beijing bureau chief), Seith Faison (Shanghai bureau chief), aided by Patrick Tyler (Beijing bureau chief), Nicholas Kristof (former Beijing and, in 1997, Tokyo bureau chief) and his wife, Sheryl WuDunn. Kristof and WuDunn won a Pulitzer Prize for their reports of the Tiananmen movement.

3. For the ten days before Rather arrived in Hong Kong, from June 15 to 24, CBS offered ten brief stories about the handover, all measured in seconds, including an announcement of his trip to Hong Kong. The 25 longer stories, from June 25 to June 1, were all measured in minutes. He also anchors a one-hour live special on the handover ceremony (June 30).

4. During the eight-day interval before Shaw's arrival (from June 15 to June 22), CNN's daily one-hour Worldview news program broadcasts only five stories related to Hong Kong's handover, but after his arrival it offered a total of 45 such stories (from June 23 to July 1).

5. Lee (2000a) argues, contrary to writers such as Tuchman (1978), that the media in Hong Kong use "strategic rituals" not so much to reify the established order, but to create journalistic space in a politically turbulent environment.

6. On July 6, 1997, CBS News analyst Laura Ingraham muses on the significance of Independence Day:

> This past week two countries celebrated their independence from British rule, but for two very different reasons. Where America honors liberty, China crushes it. Hong Kong, once one of Asia's freest cities, is now under the control of the one of the world's most repressive regimes. So many of the images of the transfer last week were of smiles and dancing and parties . . . The mobs celebrating in Tiananmen Square might lull us into believing that the clampdown of '89 was an aberration. China should serve as a constant, haunting reminder to us that the cause of liberty has not yet triumphed.

She continues to argue that while big business is making big money in China, American foreign policy makers should not be blind to "all that China has done to its own people, and maybe later to the people of Hong Kong."

Chapter 6

1. In the 1964 World Youth Forum, Moscow deliberately included Hong Kong and Macau in a resolution on the elimination of colonies in Asia. China accused the Soviets of "interfering in the internal affairs" and reiterated its intention of recovering Hong Kong and Macau "at an appropriate time." To a similar charge made in early 1963 by the U.S. Communist Party, the *People's Daily* claimed in a sharply worded editorial that the PRC could not be held accountable for an issue left over by unequal treaties signed between the Qing dynasty and the British imperialists (Lane, 1990).

Chapter 7

1. Jinghai Temple is where the negotiation for the Nanjing Treaty took place in the summer of 1842. In 1989, on the site of the old temple, a museum was built to display the historical archives related to the first Opium War and the Nanjing Treaty.

2. Among these cities are Shanghai (the CCP's birthplace), Nanjing (where the treaty of ceding Hong Kong was signed), Guangzhou (the capital of Guangdong province adjacent to Hong Kong), Shenzhen (a special economic zone next to Hong Kong), and Dongguan (a small city along the Hong Kong border where burning of British opium triggered a war that lost Hong Kong).

3. The *Oriental Daily News* has bought eight time-sharing digital cameras particularly for the occasion, each costing over US$26,000. Other local newspapers also invest heavily to buy professional-grade digital cameras and portable computers so that their reporters can send pictures back to the organizations as soon as possible. The Kodak Company in Hong Kong reveals that in May sales figures of digital cameras jump five times compared with the same time period in previous year.

4. Just before July 1, TVB airs 90 hours of nonstop handover programs via microwave channels and the outside broadcast (OB) facilities. The fiber optics alone cost more than US$100,000 for two days' use.

5 The Hong Kong branch of Xinhua News Agency has, until 1999, been China's command post; its news function was only of secondary importance. See Chan and Lee (1991) for an analysis of its role in media management. The political arm of Xinhua News Agency has been renamed the Liaison Office of the Central Government in Hong Kong. Xinhua is a news operater now.

Chapter 8

1. The biggest newspaper chain in Canada has bought *Sing Tao's* Canadian editions. Each year Hong Kong's TVB hosts a major charity in Toronto or Vancouver and broadcasts the program for Hong Kong audiences. In the past few years, the winners of Miss Hong Kong are residents from Vancouver.

2. The Canadian Commission (renamed Canadian Consulate after 1997) is one of the largest federal government offices abroad, headed by a commissioner with an ambassadorial rank. Many provinces have established their own offices in Hong Kong to handle immigration, trade, and tourism. The Canadian Chamber of Commerce in Hong Kong— the largest branch outside of China—has published a bimonthly magazine *Canada Hong Kong Business* since 1988. The nonprofit Canada China Business Council launched another bimonthly business magazine, the *Canada China Business Forum*, in 1992.

3. Many Hong Kong celebrities and billionaires are citizens of Canada, where Li Ka-shing, Hong Kong's richest man, has major business investments (Husky Oil and others). Ethnic Chinese have gained increasing visibility in Canada's political life,

counting the Governor-General of Canada (Adrienne Clarkson), the former Lieutenant Governor of British Columbia (David Lam), and a current Secretary for Asia-Pacific Affairs (Raymond Chan) among them. The Hong Kong Bank of Canada, wholly owned by HSBC Holdings in Hong Kong, is the largest foreign bank in Canada with over 100 branches from coast to coast.

4. He does not forget to remind the readers of Hong Kong's success as measured by its being the world's seventh-largest trading economy, fourth-largest stock market, largest exporter of clocks, calculators, imitation jewelry, and radios. Hong Kong also has the world's tallest outdoor seated bronze statue of Buddha, the world's largest road and rail suspension bridge, the world's highest rate of horse-race betting, the world's highest consumption of Cognac, and five of the world's busiest McDonald's restaurants. (Marcus Gee, "Brash, Booming Hong Kong," The *Globe and Mail*, June 25, p. A23)

5. Australia reversed its notorious "White Australia" policy in the 1960s. By 1991, 51% of the migration intake was drawn from Asian nations, and 4.1% of the Australian population had been born in Asia. Multiculturalism has replaced assimilation and integration as a keystone of ethnic policy. The policy of enmeshment with Asia has gradually reduced the influence of European stereotypes.

6. In 1997, about 350 Australian companies maintain offices in Hong Kong and a further 1,000 companies are estimated to have regional offices in the territory. The Australian Chamber of Commerce in Hong Kong, established in 1986, is the second largest of its kind in Hong Kong and is Australia's largest business association overseas, with 1,200 members. For many years, Australia has enjoyed a significant trade surplus with Hong Kong. The Hong Kong immigrants in Australia bring investments that benefit the real estate market and finance sector (Taneja, 1994). Hong Kong has been Australia's largest education market in terms of financial return. In 1996, more than 12,000 Hong Kong students were enrolled in Australian schools, which amounted to about 10 percent of all students studying in Australia. While Hong Kong was Australia's ninth largest source of visitors in 1995, Australia was Hong Kong's sixth largest sources of visitors in the same year. Also, Hong Kong was the sixth largest destination for Australian overseas investment, while Hong Kong was the fourth largest source of foreign investment in Australia (Joint Standing Committee on Foreign Affairs, Defense and Trade, 1997).

7. A survey conducted by the Australian Chamber of Commerce in Hong Kong in 1994 indicated that 82% of the Australian business people intended to remain in Hong Kong after the handover. Another survey by the AustCham also found that over 90% of respondents said they were confident that they would be active in Hong Kong after 2000 (Joint Standing Committee on Foreign Affairs, Defense and Trade, 1997).

8. Hong Kong people rank second in having taken advantage of Australia's more lax immigration laws since 1982. Canada requires immigrants to have at least three years of continuous residency to develop commitment and loyalty before they can apply for citizenship. Australia only requires two years of cumulative (not necessarily continuous) stay; hence many return to live in Hong Kong. Political representation of Chinese in Australia is insignificant, as is Hong Kong's media involvement there.

9. Japan's investment in Hong Kong in 1999 increased by 40.5% over the previous year.

Chapter 9

1. Some writers have pointed out that these three categories of "ceremonial politics" may not be inclusive of "disaster marathons" (Liebes, 1998) or "political rituals of shame, degradation, and excommunication" (Carey, 1998). Thompson (1995) distinguishes "media events" from the media genre of "receipt address," mediated everyday activity, and fictionalized action. Scannell (1995), in a generally sympathetic view, criticizes Dayan and Katz for a lack of historical depth in their analysis. He also questions whether different events—ranging from the moon landings and the British royal wedding to President Sadat's journey to Jerusalem and President Kennedy's assassination—are of the same order.

2. Scannell (1995) notes that historically television has been associated with the slow erosion of autocratic authority and the decay of charisma.

Epilogue

1. Unless otherwise noted, all the dates in this epilogue refer to 1998.

2. For the media outlets that have multiple anniversary pieces, only the most important piece, based on the location and the size of headline, is included in the table.

3. "Communist Hong Kong has its first birthday."

4. On the U.S. side, there are 101 items on the *New York Times* (Foreign and Editorial Desks), 49 items on the *Los Angeles Times* (Foreign and Editorial Desks), 92 items on the *Washington Post* (A Section and Op-Ed Sections). On the British side, there are also 62 items on the *Times* of London (Overseas News Section), 55 items on the *Guardian* (Foreign and Editor Pages), and 79 items on the *Daily Telegraph* (International Section). This search does not include stories published in the financial, fashion, style, and entertainment pages.

5. These three stories report that Hong Kong police allow a peaceful demonstration (July 22, 1997), Hong Kong celebrates the first Chinese National Day after the handover (October 1, 1997), and Hong Kong is holding its first legislative election (May 24, 1998).

6. The series on the bird's flu starts with the first death attributed to "influenza A" and ends with the slaughter of all chickens in Hong Kong. In between, there are officials from the World Health Organization explaining how "the Hong Kong flu" might be transmitted, and U.S. experts from the Center for Disease Control "rushing to create a vaccine for the Hong Kong flu virus."

Bibliography

Abercrombie, Nicholas, and Brian Longhurst (1998), *Audiences: A Sociological Theory of Performance and Imagination*. London: Sage.

Alexander, Jeffrey C., and Ronald N. Jacobs (1998), "Mass Communication, Ritual and Civil Society," in Tamar Liebes and James Curran (eds.), *Media, Ritual and Identity*. London: Routledge.

Altheide, David L., and Robert P. Snow (1979), *Media Logic*. Beverly Hills, Calif.: Sage.

Altheide, David L., and Robert P. Snow (1991), *Media Worlds in the Postjournalism Era*. New York: Aldine de Gruyter.

Althusser, Louis (1971), *Lenin and Philosophy and Other Essays*. London: New Left.

Anderson, Benedict (1983), *Imagined Communities*. London: Verso.

Appadurai, Arjun (1996), *Modernity at Large: Cultural Dimensions of Globalization*. Minneapolis, Minn.: University of Minnesota Press.

Aronson, Steven M. L. (1983), *Hype*. New York: Morrow.

Attallah, Paul (2000), "Public Broadcasting in Canada: Legitimation Crisis and the Loss of Audience," *Gazette*, 62: 177–204.

Bagdikian, Ben H. (1971), *The Information Machine*. New York: Harper and Row.

Barnet, Suzanne W., and John K. Fairbank (eds.) (1985), *Christianity in China: Early Protestant Missionary Writings*. Cambridge, Mass.: Harvard University Press.

Barthes, Roland (1982), "Myth Today," in Susan Sontag (ed.), *A Barthes Reader*. New York: Noonday Press.

Becker, Karin (1995), "Media and the Ritual Process," *Media, Culture & Society*, 17: 629–646.

Beckerman, Bernard (1990), "Theatre," in *The Encyclopedia Americana* (international edition, 26: 601–613). Danbury, Conn.: Grolier Inc.

Bell, Daniel (1962), *The End of Ideology*. New York: Free Press.

229

Bennett, W. Lance (1990), "Toward a Theory of Press-State Relations in the United States," *Journal of Communication*, 40, 2: 103–125.

Bennett, W. Lance (1996), *News: The Politics of Illusion*. New York: Longman.

Bennett, W. Lance, Lynn A. Gressett, and William Haltom (1985), "Repairing the News: A Case Study of the News Paradigm," *Journal of Communication*, 35, 2: 50–68.

Bennett, W. Lance, and Regina G. Lawrence (1995), "News Icons and the Mainstreaming of Social Change," *Journal of Communication*, 45, 3: 20–39.

Berger, Peter L., and Thomas Luckmann (1967), *The Social Construction of Reality: A Treatise in the Sociology of Knowledge*. Garden City, N.J.: Doubleday-Anchor.

Berkowitz, Dan (1992), "Non-routine News and Newswork: Exploring What-a-story," *Journal of Communication*, 42, 1: 82–94.

Billing, Michael (1995), *Banal Nationalism*. London: Sage.

Bird, S. Elizabeth, and Robert W. Dardenne (1988), "Myth, Chronicle and Story: Exploring the Narrative Qualities of News," in James W. Carey (ed.), *Media, Myths, and Narratives: Television and the Press*. Beverly Hills, Calif.: Sage.

Bockman, Harald (1998), "The Future of the Chinese Empire-state in a Historical Perspective," in Kjeld Erik Brodsgaard and David Strand (eds.), *Reconstructing Twentieth-Century China: State Control, Civil Society, and National Identity*. Oxford: Clarendon Press.

Boyd-Barrett, Oliver (1980), *The International News Agencies*. Beverly Hills, Calif.: Sage.

Braman, Sandra, and Annabelle Sreberny-Mohammadi (eds.). (1996), *Globalization, Communication and Transnational Civil Society*. Cresskill, N.J.: Hampton Press.

Breed, Warren (1955), "Social Control in the Newsroom: A Functional Analysis," *Social Forces*, 33: 326–335.

Bridgman, Joan (1999), "Diana's Country," *Contemporary Review*, 274:19–23.

Brody, Richard A. (1991), *Assessing the President: The Media, Elite Opinion, and Public Support*. Stanford, Calif.: Stanford University Press.

Buerk, Simon (1997), "Anchors Aweigh in the Great Ratings War," *South China Morning Post*, June 30, 1997, p. 23.

Burchill, Scott (1996), "Liberal Internationalism," in Scott Burchill and Andrew Linklater (eds.), *Theories of International Relations*. New York: St. Martin's Press.

Carey, James W. (1986), "The Dark Continent of American Journalism," in Robert Manoff and Michael Schudson (eds.), *Reading the News*. New York: Pantheon.

Carey, James, W. (1989), *Communication as Culture: Essays on Media and Society*. Boston, Mass.: Unwin Hyman.

Carey, James W. (1998), "Political Ritual on Television: Episodes in the History of Shame, Degradation and Excommunication," in Tamar Liebes and James Curran (eds.), *Media, Ritual and Identity*. London: Routledge.

Carrier, Rebecca (1997), "Global News and Domestic Needs: Reflections and Adaptations of World Information to Fit National Policies and Audience Needs," in Abbas Malek and Krita Wiegand (eds.), *News Media and Foreign Relations*. Norwood, N.J.: Ablex.

Chan, Joseph (2002), "Disneyfying and Globalizing the Chinese Legend Mulan: A Study of Transculturation," in Joseph Chan and Brycec McIntyre (eds.), *In Search of Boundaries: Communication, Nation-State and Cultural Identities*. Westport, Conn.: Ablex.

Chan, Joseph, and Chin-Chuan Lee (1991), *Mass Media and Political Transition: The Hong Kong Press in China's Orbit*. New York: Guilford Press.

Chan, Joseph, and Eric Ma (2002), "Transculturating Modernity: A Reinterpretation of Cultural Globalization," in Joseph Chan and Bryce McIntyre (eds.), *In Search of Boundaries: Communication, Nation-State and Cultural Identities*. Westport, Conn.: Ablex.

Chan, Ming K. (1997), "The Politics of Hong Kong's Imperfect Transition: Dimensions of the China Factor," in Ming K. Chan (ed.), *The Challenge of Hong Kong's Reintegration with China*. Hong Kong: Hong Kong University Press.

Chang, Tsan-kuo (1993), *The Press and China Policy: The Illusion of Sino-American Relations, 1950–1985*. Norwood, N.J.: Ablex.

Chen, Xiaomei (1993), "Occidentalism as Counterdiscourse: 'He Shang' in Post-Mao China," *Critical Inquiry*, 18: 686–712.

Chinoy, Mike (1999), *China Live*. Lanham, Md.: Rowman and Littlefield.

Chung, Pei-chi (2000), "The Cultural Other and National Identity in the Taiwanese and South Korean Media," *Gazette*, 62: 99–116.

Cleghorn, Reese (October 1997), "A Media Event to Top Them All," *American Journalism Review*, 19: 4.

Cohen, Akiba (2002), "Globalization, Ltd: Domestication at the Boundary of Television News," in Joseph Chan and Bryce McIntyre (eds.), *In Search of Boundaries: Communication, Nation-states and Cultural Identities*. Westport, Conn.: Ablex.

Cohen, Akiba A., Mark R. Levy, Itzhak Roeh, and Michael Gurevitch (eds.) (1996), *Global Newsrooms, Local Audiences*. London: J. Libbey.

Cohen, Bernard (1963), *The Press and Foreign Policy*. Princeton, N.J.: Princeton University Press.

Connell, Aldrich (1998), *The Lost Colonies*. London: Cambridge University Press.

Cook, Timothy E. (1998), *Governing with the News: The News Media as a Political Institution*. Chicago: University of Chicago Press.

Coser, Lewis (1957), *The Function of Social Conflict*. New York: Free Press.

Crouse, Timothy (1973), *The Boys on the Bus*. New York: Random House.

Curran, James, and Tamar Liebes (1998), "The Intellectual Legacy of Elihu Katz," in Tamar Liebes and James Curran (eds.), *Media, Ritual and Identity*. London: Routledge.

Darwin, John (1988), *Britain and Decolonization*. London: Macmillan.

Dayan, Daniel, and Elihu Katz (1992), *Media Events: The Live Broadcasting of History*. Cambridge, Mass.: Harvard University Press.

Debord, Guy (1987), *Society of Spectacle*. London: Rebel Press.

Debord, Guy (1990), *Comments on the Society of the Spectacle*. Translated by Malcolm Imrie. London: Verso.

Dimbleby, Jonathan (1997), *The Last Governor: Chris Patten and the Handover of Hong Kong*. London: Little, Brown.

Donohue, George, Phillip J. Tichenor, and Clarice Olien (1995), "A Guide Dog Perspective on the Role of Media," *Journal of Communication*, 45, 2: 115–132.

Douglas, Mary (1975), "The Meaning of Myths," in Mary Douglas (ed.), *Implicit Meanings: Essays in Anthropology*. London: Routledge & Kegan Paul.

Duara, Prasenjit (1995), *Rescuing History from the Nation: Questioning Narratives of Modern China*. Chicago, Ill.: University of Chicago Press.

Dunn, H. A. (1985), "Australian Interests in China," in H. A. Dunn and Edmund S. K. Fung (eds.), *Sino-Australian Relations: The Record 1972–1985*. Nathan, Australia: Centre for the Study of Australian-Asian Relations, Griffith University.

Edelman, Murray (1971), *The Politics of Symbolic Action*. New York: Academic Press.

Edelman, Murray (1988), *Constructing the Political Spectacle*. Chicago: University of Chicago Press.

Edgar, Andrew, and Peter Sedgwick (1999), *Key Concepts in Cultural Theory*. London: Routledge.

Elliot, Philip (1982), "Press Performance as Political Ritual," in D. Charles Whitney and Ellen Wartella (eds.), *Mass Communication Review Yearbook*. Vol. 3. Beverly Hills, Calif.: Sage.

Epstein, Edward (1973), *News from Nowhere: Television and the News*. New York: Random House.

Esherick, Joseph W., and Jeffrey N. Wasserstrom (1994), "Acting Out Democracy: Political Theater in Modern China," in Jeffrey N. Wasserstrom and Elizabeth J.

Perry (eds.), *Popular Protest and Political Culture in Modern China*. Boulder, Colo.: Westview Press.

Ettema, James S. (1990), "Press Rites and Race Relations: A Study of Mass-mediated Ritual," *Critical Studies in Mass Communication*, 7: 309–331.

Fanon, Franz (1968), *The Wretched of the Earth*. New York: Grove Press.

Featherstone, Mike (1995), *Undoing Culture*. London: Sage.

Featherstone, Mike, and Scott Lash (1995), "Globalization, Modernity and the Spatialization of Social Theory: An Introduction," in Mike Featherstone, Scott Lash, and Roland Robertson (eds.), *Global Identities*. London: Sage.

Fensterheim, Herbert, and Margaret Tresselt (1953), "The Influence of Value System on the Perception of People," *Journal of Abnormal and Social Psychology*, 48: 93–98.

Fieldhouse, David Kenneth (1966), *The Colonial Empires*. London: Weidenfeld and Nicolson.

Fish, Stanley E. (1980), *Is There a Text in This Class?: The Authority of Interpretive Communities*. Cambridge, Mass.: Harvard University Press.

Fisher, Walter R. (1984), "Narration as a Human Communication Paradigm," *Communication Monographs*, 51: 1–23.

Fishman, Mark (1980), *Manufacturing the News*. Austin, Tex.: University of Texas Press.

Fiske, John (1982), *Introduction to Communication Studies*. New York: Methuen.

Fitzgerald, John (1995), "The Nationless State: The Search for a Nation in Modern Chinese Journalism," *Australian Journal of Chinese Studies*, 33: 75–105.

Flournoy, Don (1992), *CNN World Report: Ted Turner's International News Coup*. London: Libbey.

Foucault, Michel (1972), *The Archaeology of Knowledge*. London: Tavistock.

Foucault, Michel (1986), "Of Other Spaces," *Diacritics*, 16: 22–27.

Franzosi, Roberto (1989), "From Words to Numbers: A Generalized and Linguistic-based Coding Procedure for Collecting Textual Data," in Clifford C. Clogg (ed.), *Sociological Methodology 1989*. Washington, D.C.: American Sociological Association.

Frederick, Howard H. (1993), *Global Communication and International Relations*. Belmont, Calif.: Wadsworth.

Freedom Forum (1993), *The Media and Foreign Policy in the Post-Cold War World*. New York: Freedom Forum Media Studies Center, Columbia University.

Fukuda, Kazuo John (1998), *Japan and China: The Meeting of Asia's Economic Giants*. New York: International Business Press.

Fukuyama, Francis (1992), *The End of History and the Last Man*. New York: Free Press.

Galtung, Johan (1971), "A Structural Theory of Imperialism," *Journal of Peace Research*, 2: 81–118.

Galtung, Johan, and Mari Ruge (1965), "The Structure of Foreign News," *Journal of International Peace Research*, 1: 64–90.

Galtung, Johan, and Richard Vincent (1992), *Global Glasnost: Toward a New World Information and Communication Order*. Cresskill, N.J.: Hampton.

Gamson, William A. (1988), "A Constructionist Approach to Mass Media and Public Opinion," *Symbolic Interactionism*, 11: 161–174.

Gamson, William A., and Kathryn E. Lasch (1983), "The Political Culture of Social Welfare Policy," in Shimon E. Spiro and Ephraim Yuchtman-Yaar (eds.), *Evaluating the Welfare State: Social and Political Perspectives*. New York: Academic Press.

Gamson, William A., and Andre Modigliani (1987), "The Changing Culture of Affirmative Action," in Richard G. Braungart and Margaret M. Braungart (eds.), *Research in Political Sociology*. Vol. 3. Greenwich, Conn.: JAI Press.

Gamson, William A., and Andre Modigliani (1989), "Media Discourse and Public Opinion on Nuclear Power: A Constructionist Approach," *American Journal of Sociology*, 95: 1–37.

Gamson, William A., David Croteau, William Hoynes, and Theodore Sasson (1992), "Media Images and the Social Construction of Reality," *Annual Review of Sociology*, 18: 373–393.

Gans, Herbert J. (1979), *Deciding What's News: A Study of CBS Evening News, NBC Nightly News, Newsweek and Time*. New York: Pantheon.

Garnett, J. C. (1994), "The National Interest Revisited," in Kenneth W. Thompson (ed.), *Community, Diversity, and a New World Order: Essays in Honor of Inis L. Claude, Jr*. Lanham, Md.: University Press of America.

Geertz, Clifford (1973), *The Interpretation of Culture*. New York: Basic.

Geertz, Clifford (1993), *Local Knowledge*. New York: Basic.

Gellner, Ernest (1997), *Nationalism*. New York: New York University Press.

Giddens, Anthony (1985), *The Nation-state and Violence*. Cambridge: Polity.

Giddens, Anthony (1991), *The Consequences of Modernity*. Stanford, Calif.: Stanford University Press.

Gilbert, Nigel, and Michael Mulkay (1984), *Opening Pandora's Box: A Sociological Analysis of Scientists' Discourse*. Cambridge: Cambridge University Press.

GIS (Government Information Services) (1992), *Bridge Across the Pacific*. Hong Kong: Government Information Services.

Gitlin, Todd (1980), *The Whole World is Watching*. Berkeley, Calif.: University of California Press.

Gitlin, Todd (1991), "The Politics of Communication and the Communication of Politics," in James Curran and Michael Gurevitch (eds.), *Mass Media and Society* (1st edition). London: Arnold.

Gitlin, Todd (1997), "The Anti-political Populism of Cultural Studies," in Marjorie Ferguson and Peter Golding (eds.), *Cultural Studies in Question*. London: Sage.

Goffman, Ervin (1973), *Frame Analysis*. New York: Harper Colophon.

Gratton, R. (1999), "The Media," in Richard Cashman and Anthony Hughes (eds.), *Staging the Olympics: The Event and its Impact*. Sydney, Australia: University of New South Wales Press.

Gronbeck, Bruce E. (1980), "Dramaturgical Theory and Criticism: The State of the Art (or Science?)," *Western Journal of Speech Communication*, 44: 315–330.

Hall, Stuart (1974), "Deviance, Politics and the Media," in Paul Rock and Mary McIntosh (eds.), *Deviance and Social Control*. London: Tavistock.

Hall, Stuart (1980), "Encoding/Decoding," in Stuart Hall, D. Hobson, A. Lowe, and P. Willis (eds.), *Culture, Media, Language*. London: Hutchinson.

Hall, Stuart (1996a), "Gramsci's Relevance for the Study of Race and Ethnicity," in David Morley and Kuan-Hsing Chen (eds.), *Stuart Hall: Critical Dialogues in Cultural Studies*. London: Routledge.

Hall, Stuart (1996b), "New Ethnicities," in David Morley and Kuan-Hsing Chen (eds.), *Stuart Hall: Critical Dialogues in Cultural Studies*. London: Routledge.

Hall, Stuart (1997), "The Spectacle of the Other," in Stuart Hall (ed.), *Representation: Cultural Representation and Signifying Practices*. London: Open University.

Hallin, Daniel C. (1986), *The "Uncensored" War*. New York: Oxford University Press.

Hallin, Daniel C. (1987), "Hegemony: The American News Media from Vietnam to El Salvador," in David L. Paletz (ed.), *Political Communication Research: Approaches, Studies, Assessments* (pp. 3–25). Norwood, N.J.: Ablex.

Hallin, Daniel C. (1994), *We Keep America on Top of the World*. New York: Routledge.

Hallin, Daniel C., and Todd Gitlin (1993), "Agon and Ritual: the Gulf War as Popular Culture and as Television Drama," *Political Communication*, 10: 411–424.

Hallin, Daniel C., and Gitlin, Todd (1994), "The Gulf War as Popular Culture and Television Drama," in W. Lance Bennett and David L. Paletz (eds.), *Taken by Storm: The Media, Public Opinion, and U.S. Foreign Policy in the Gulf War*. Chicago: University of Chicago Press.

Hallman, Eugene S. (1977), *Broadcasting in Canada*. Boston: Routledge & Kegan Paul.

Hamelink, Cees (1993), "Globalization and National Sovereignty," in Kaarle Nordenstreng and Herbert I. Schiller (eds.), *Beyond National Sovereignty*. Norwood, N.J.: Ablex.

Harris, Stuart (1996), "Australia-China Political Relations 1985-1995: Fear, Friendly Relations or What?" in Colin Mackerras (ed.), *Australia and China: Partners in Asia*. South Melbourne, Australia: MacMillan Education Australia.

Hartley, John (1992), *The Politics of Pictures: The Creation of the Public in the Age of Popular Media*. London: Routledge.

He, Zhou (2000), "Chinese Communist Party Press in a Tug-of-War: A Political-Economy Analysis of the Shenzhen Special Zone Daily," in Chin-Chuan Lee (ed.), *Power, Money, and Media: Communication Patterns and Bureaucratic Control in Cultural China*. Evanston, Ill.: Northwestern University Press.

Herman, Edward S., and Noam Chomsky (1988), *Manufacturing Consent: The Political Economy of the Mass Media*. New York: Pantheon.

Hilgartner, Stephen, and Charles L. Bosk (1988), "The Rise and Fall of Social Problems: A Public Arena Model," *American Journal of Sociology*, 94: 53–78.

Howard, Judith, and Jocelyn Hollander (1997), *Gendered Situations, Gendered Selves: A Gender Lens on Social Psychology*. Thousand Oaks, Calif.: Sage.

Huntington, Samuel (1993), "The Clash of Civilizations," *Foreign Affairs*, 71, 3: 22–49.

Jabri, Vivienne (1996), *Discourses on Violence: Conflict Analysis Reconsidered*. Manchester, U.K.: Manchester University Press.

Jacobs, Ronald N. (1996), "Producing the News, Producing the Crisis: Narrativity, Television and News Work," *Media, Culture & Society*, 18: 373–397.

Jin, Yaoru (1998), *A Confidential Account of the Chinese Communist Party's Hong Kong Policy*. Hong Kong: Tianyuan Press. (In Chinese)

Joint Standing Committee on Foreign Affairs, Defense and Trade, Australia (May 1997), *Hong Kong: The Transfer of Sovereignty*. Canberra, Australia: Parliament of the Commonwealth of Australia.

Katz, Elihu (1992), "The End of Journalism? Notes on Watching the Persian Gulf War," *Journal of Communication*, 42, 3: 5–13.

Kellner, Douglas (1990), *Television and the Crisis of Democracy*. Boulder, Colo.: Westview Press.

Kellner, Douglas (1992), *The Persian Gulf TV War*. Boulder, Colo.: Westview Press.

Kesavan, K. V. (1990), "Japan and the Tiananmen Square Incident: Aspects of the Bilateral Relationship," *Asian Survey*, 30: 669–681.

Knight, Alan, and Yoshiko Nakano (eds.) (1999), *Reporting Hong Kong: Foreign Media and the Handover*. London: Curzon.

Kuhn, Thomas S. (1962), *The Structure of Scientific Revolution*. Chicago: University of Chicago Press.

Lane, Kevin (1990), *Sovereignty and the Status Quo: the Historical Roots of China's Hong Kong* Policy. Boulder, Colo.: Westview Press.

Lang, Kurt, and Gladys Lang (1983), *The Battle for Public Opinion.* New York: Columbia University Press.

Lary, Diana (1992), "Canada in Hong Kong," in Joseph Y. S. Cheng and Paul C. K. Kwong (eds.), *The Other Hong Kong Report 1992.* Hong Kong: Chinese University Press.

Lazarsfeld, Paul F., and Robert K. Merton (1948), "Mass Communication, Popular Taste, and Organized Social Action," in Lyman Bryson (ed.), *The Communication of Ideas.* New York: Institute for Religious and Social Studies.

Lee, Alice Y. L. (1997), *Legitimating Media Education: From Social Movement to the Formation of a New Social Curriculum.* Unpublished doctoral dissertation, University of British Columbia.

Lee, Chin-Chuan (1989), "The Politics of International Communication: Changing the Rules of the Game," *Gazette,* 44: 75–91.

Lee, Chin-Chuan (1990), "Mass Media: Of China, About China," in Chin-Chuan Lee (ed.), *Voices of China: The Interplay of Politics and Journalism.* New York: Guilford Press.

Lee, Chin-Chuan (1997), "Media Structure and Regime Change in Hong Kong," in Ming K. Chan (ed.), *The Challenge of Hong Kong's Reintegration with China.* Hong Kong: Hong Kong University Press.

Lee, Chin-Chuan (2000a), "The Paradox of Political Economy: Media Structure, Press Freedom, and Regime Change in Hong Kong," in Chin-Chuan Lee (ed.), *Power, Money, and Media: Communication Patterns and Bureaucratic Control in Cultural China.* Evanston, Ill.: Northwestern University Press.

Lee, Chin-Chuan (2000b), "China's Journalism: The Emancipatory Potential of Social Theory," *Journalism Studies,* 1: 559–575.

Lee, Chin-Chuan (2000c), "State, Capital, and Media: The Case of Taiwan," in James Curran and Myung-Jin Park (eds.), *De-Westernizing Media Studies.* London: Routledge.

Lee, Chin-Chuan, and Junghye Yang (1995), "National Interest and Foreign News: Comparing U.S. and Japanese Coverage of a Chinese Student Movement," *Gazette,* 56: 1–18.

Lee, Chin-Chuan, Joseph Man Chan, Zhongdang Pan, and Clement Y. K. So (2000), "National Prisms of a Global Media Event," in James Curran and Michael Gurevitch (eds.), *Mass Media and Society.* 3rd edition. London: Arnold.

Lee, Chin-Chuan, Zhongdang Pan, Joseph Man Chan, and Clement Y. K. So (2001), "Through the Eyes of U.S. Media: Banging the Democracy Drum in Hong Kong," *Journal of Communication,* 51, 2: 345–365.

Leung, Kwong-hon (July 1997), "48 Hours Live Broadcast of Handover; Hong Kong Sets Web Broadcast Milestone," *Media Digest*, pp. 2–7.

Levi-Strauss, Claude (1966), *The Savage Mind*. Chicago: University of Chicago Press.

Liebes, Tamar (1998), "Television's Disaster Marathons: A Danger for Democratic Processes?" in Tamar Liebes and James Curran (eds.), *Media, Ritual and Identity*. London: Routledge.

Lincoln, Bruce (1989), *Discourse and the Configuration of Society*. New York: Oxford University Press.

Liu, Alan P. L. (1971), *Communication and National Integration in Communist China*. Berkeley, Calif.: University of California Press.

Luk, Bernard H. K. (1994), *The Implications for Canada of Hong Kong's Future*. York, Ontario: Joint Centre for Asia Pacific Studies, University of Toronto—York University.

MacAloon, John J. (1984), "Olympic Games and the Theory of Spectacle in Modern Societies," in John J. MacAloon (ed.), *Rite, Drama, Festival, Spectacle: Rehearsals Toward a Theory of Cultural Performance*. Philadelphia, Penn.: Institute for the Study of Human Issues.

MacBride, Sean (1980), *Many Voices, One World: Communication and Society Today and Tomorrow*. Paris: UNESCO.

Mackerras, Colin (1996), "Australia-China Relations: An Agenda," in Colin Mackerras (ed.), *Australia and China: Partners in Asia*. South Melbourne, Australia: MacMillan.

Mahlasela, Dumissani Glen (1990), *Mass Media and Social Movement Legitimation: A Comparison of South Korean and Chinese Movements*. Unpublished M.A. thesis, University of Minnesota.

Manning, Peter K. (1996), "Dramaturgy, Politics and the Axial Media Event," *Sociological Quarterly*, 37: 261–278.

Manoff, Robert, and Michael Schudson (eds.) (1986), *Reading the News*. New York: Pantheon.

Marshall, Peter J. (1996), "Introduction: The World Shaped by Empire," in Peter J. Marshall (ed.), *The Cambridge Illustrated History of the British Empire*. Cambridge: Cambridge University Press.

Martin, James (1999), "Holiness, Royalty, and Fame," in Kimberly N. Massey (ed.), *Readings in Mass Communication*. Mountain View, Calif.: Mayfield.

McAdam, Doug, John D. McCarthy, and Mayer N. Zald (eds.) (1996), *Comparative Perspectives on Social Movements: Political Opportunities, Mobilizing Structures, and Cultural Framing*. New York: Cambridge University Press.

McLuhan, Marshall (1967), *The Medium is the Message*. New York: Bantam Books.

Medhurst, Martin J. (1990), "Rhetoric and Cold War: A Strategic Approach," in Martin J. Medhurst, Robert L. Ivie, Philip Wander, and Robert L. Scott (eds.), *Cold War Rhetoric: Strategy, Metaphor, and Ideology*. New York: Greenwood.

Middleton, David, and Derek Edwards (1990), *Collective Remembering*. London: Sage.

Millerson, Gerald (1982), *Basic TV Staging*. London: Focal Press.

Molotch, Harvey, and Marilyn Lester (1974), "News as Purposive Behavior: On the Strategic Use of Routine Events, Accidents, and Scandals," *American Sociological Review*, 39: 101–112.

Mosco, Vincent (1996), *The Political Economy of Communication*. London: Sage.

Nelms, Henning (1958), *Play Production*. New York: Barnes and Noble.

Nimmo, Dan, and James E. Combs (1990), *Mediated Political Realities*. New York: Longman.

O'Connor, Michael (1995), "Mutual Security," in Greg Sheridan (ed.), *Living with Dragons: Australia Confronts its Asian Destiny*. St. Leonards, N.S.W.: Allen & Unwin.

Orwell, George (1954), *A Collection of Essays*. New York: Doubleday Anchor.

Osterhammel, Jurgen (1997), *Colonialism: A Theoretical Overview*. Translated by Shelly L. Frisch. Princeton, N.J.: Markus Wiener.

O'Sullivan, John L. (1976), "Our Manifest Destiny," in *The Annals of America*. Chicago: Encyclopedia Britainnica, 7: 288–292.

Ozaki, Robert S., and Walter Arnold (1985), *Japan's Foreign Relations: A Global Search for Economic Security*. Boulder, Colo.: Westview Press.

Page, Benjamin (1996), *Who Deliberates? Mass Media in Modern Democracy*. Chicago: University of Chicago Press.

Pan, Zhongdang (2000), "Improvising Reform Activities: The Changing Reality of Journalistic Practice in China," in Chin-Chuan Lee (ed.), *Power, Money, and Media: Communication Patterns and Bureaucratic Control in Cultural China*. Evanston, Ill.: Northwestern University Press.

Pan, Zhongdang, and Gerald M. Kosicki (1993), "Framing Analysis: An Approach to News Discourse," *Political Communication*, 10: 55–75.

Pan, Zhongdang, Chin-Chuan Lee, Joseph Man Chan, and Clement S. K. So (1999), "One Event, Three Stories: Media Narratives of the Handover of Hong Kong in Cultural China," *Gazette*, 61: 99–112.

Pan, Zhongdang, Chin-Chuan Lee, Joseph Man Chan, and Clement S. K. So (2001), "Orchestrating the Family-Nation Chorus: Chinese Media and Nationalism in the Hong Kong Handover," *Mass Communication and Society*, 4: 331–347.

Park, Robert E. (1940), "News as a Form of Knowledge," *American Journal of Sociology*, 45: 669–686.

Patten, Chris (1997), *Letters to Hong Kong*. Hong Kong: Government Printer.

Patten, Chris (1998), *East and West*. London: Macmillan.

Pharr, Susan J., and Ellis S. Krauss (eds.) (1996), *Media and Politics in Japan*. Honolulu: University Press of Hawaii.

Polumbaum, Judy (1990), "The Tribulations of China's Journalists after a Decade of Reform," in Chin-Chuan Lee (ed.), *Voices of China: The Interplay of Politics and Journalism*. New York: Guilford.

Pool, Ithiel de Sola (1952), *Prestige Papers*. Stanford, Calif.: Stanford University Press.

Ramaprasad, Jyotika (1983), "Media Diplomacy: In Search of a Definition," *Gazette*, 31: 69–75.

Real, Michael R. (1989), *Super Media: A Cultural Studies Approach*. Newbury Park, Calif.: Sage.

Reese, Stephen D. (1989), "The News Paradigm and the Ideology of Objectivity: A Socialist at the Wall Street Journal," *Critical Studies in Mass Communication*, 7: 390–409.

Robertson, Roland (1992), *Globalization*. Newbury Park, Calif.: Sage.

Robertson, Roland (1995), "Glocalization: Time-space and Homogeneity-heterogeneity," in Mike Featherstone, Scott Lash, and Roland Robertson (eds.), *Global Modernities*. London: Sage.

Robinson, Gertrude F., and Donald J. Theall (eds.) (1975), *Studies in Canadian Communication*. Montreal: McGill University Printing Service.

Said, Edward W. (1978), *Orientalism*. New York: Pantheon.

Said, Edward W. (1981). *Covering Islam*. New York: Pantheon

Said, Edward W. (1993), *Culture and Imperialism*. New York: Knopf.

Salisbury, Harrison E. (1990), "China Reporting: From *Red Star* to *Long March*," in Chin-Chuan Lee (ed.), *Voices of China: The Interplay of Politics and Journalism*. New York: Guilford Press.

Sanders, David (1990), *Losing an Empire, Finding a Role: British Foreign Policy Since 1945*. London: Macmillan.

Scannell, Paddy (1995), "Media Events," *Media, Culture & Society*, 17: 151–157.

Schlesinger, Peter (1978), *Putting 'Reality' Together*. Beverly Hills, Calif.: Sage.

Scholte, Jan (1996), "Beyond the Buzzword: Towards a Critical Theory of Globalization," in Eleonore Kofman and Gillian Youngs (eds.), *Globalization: Theory and Practice*. London: Pinter.

Schramm, Wilbur (1959), *One Day in the World's Press: Fourteen Great Newspapers on a Day of Crisis, November 2, 1956*. Stanford, Calif.: Stanford University Press.

Schudson, Michael (1978), *Discovering the News*. New York: Basic Books.

Scott, James C. (1988), *Weapons of the Weak: Everyday Forms of Peasant Resistance.* New Haven, Conn.: Yale University Press.

Shannon, Claude E., and Warren Weaver (1964), *The Mathematical Theory of Communication.* Urbana, Ill.: University of Illinois Press.

Sharkey, Jacqueline (1994), "Judgment Calls: O. J. Simpson Case," *American Journalism Review*, 16: 18–27.

Sigal, Leon V. (1973), *Reporters and Officials: The Organization and Politics of Newsmaking.* Lexington, Mass.: D. C. Heath.

Sigal, Leon V. (1986), "Who: Sources Make the News," in Robert Karl Manoff and Michael Schudson (eds.), *Reading the News*. New York: Pantheon.

Smythe, Dallas (1994), *Couterclockwise.* Edited by Thomas Guback. Boulder, Colo.: Westview.

Snow, David A., and Robert D. Benford (1992), "Master Frames and Cycles of Protest," in Aldon D. Morris and Carol M. Mueller (eds.), *Frontiers in Social Movement Theory.* New Haven, Conn.: Yale University Press.

Snyder, Jack, and Karen Ballentine (1997),"Nationalism and the Marketplace of Ideas," in Michael Brown, Owen Cote Jr., Sean M. Lynn-Jones, and Steven E. Miller (eds.), *Nationalism and Ethnic Conflict.* Cambridge, Mass.: MIT Press.

So, Clement Y. K., and Joseph Chan (eds.) (1999), *Press and Politics in Hong Kong: Case Studies from 1967 to 1997.* Hong Kong: Hong Kong Institute of Asia-Pacific Studies, Chinese University of Hong Kong.

Sreberny-Mohammadi, Annabelle (1991), "The Global and the Local in International Communication," in James Curran and Michael Gurevitch (eds.), *Mass Media and Society.* London: Arnold.

Sreberny-Mohammadi, Annabelle (1996), "Globalization, Communication and Transnational Civil Society: Introduction," in Sandra Braman and Annabelle Sreberny-Mohammadi (eds.), *Globalization, Communication and Transnational Civil Society.* Cresskill, N.J.: Hampton.

Sreberny-Mohammadi, Annabelle, Dwayen Winseck, Jim McKenna, and Oliver Boyd-Barrett (1997), "Editor's Introduction—Media in Global Context," in Annabelle Sreberny-Mohammadi, Dwayen Winseck, Jim McKenna, and Oliver Boyd-Barrett (eds.), *Media in Global Context: A Reader.* London: Arnold.

Strahan, Lachlan (1994), *Australia's China: Changing Perceptions from the 1930s to the 1990s.* Cambridge: Cambridge University Press.

Taneja, Pradeep (1994), "Hong Kong and Australia: Towards 1997 and Beyond," *Australia-Asia Papers No. 70.* Queensland, Australia: Centre for the Study of Australia-Asia Relations, Griffith University.

Thompson, John B. (1990), *Ideology and Modern Culture*. Stanford, Calif.: Stanford University Press.

Thompson, John B. (1995), *The Media and Modernity*. Stanford, Calif.: Stanford University Press.

Tolson, Andrew (1996), *Mediations: Text and Discourse in Media Studies*. London: Arnold.

Tomlinson, Alan (1996), "Olympic Spectacle: Opening Ceremonies and Some Paradoxes of Globalization," *Media, Culture & Society*, 18: 583–602.

Tomlinson, John (1991), *Cultural Imperialism*. Baltimore, Md.: Johns Hopkins University Press.

Tomlinson, John (1999), *Globalization and Culture*. Chicago: University of Chicago Press.

Touraine, Alain (1997), *What is Democracy?* Translated by Daivd Macey. Boulder, Colo.: Westview.

Tu, Weiming (1991), "Cultural China: The Periphery as the Center," *Daedalus*, 120, 2: 1–32.

Tuchman, Gaye (1973), "Making News by Doing Work: Routinizing the Unexpected," *American Journal of Sociology*, 79: 110–131.

Tuchman, Gaye (1978), *Making News: A Study in the Construction of Reality*. New York: Free Press.

Tunstall, Jeremy (1971), *Journalists at Work*. London: Constable.

Tunstall, Jeremy, and David Machin (1999), *The Anglo-American Media Connection*. New York: Oxford University Press.

Turner, Victor (1969), *The Ritual Process: Structure and Anti-structure*. New York: Aldine de Gruyter.

Turner, Victor (1982), "Social Dramas and Stories about Them," in W. J. T. Mitchell (ed.), *On Narrative*. Chicago: University of Chicago Press.

van Dijk, Tuen A. (1988), *News as Discourse*. Hillsdale, N.J.: Lawrence Urlbaum.

van Ginneken, Jaap (1998), *Understanding Global News*. London: Sage.

Vogel, Ezra F. (1979), *Japan as Number One: Lessons for America*. Cambridge, Mass.: Harvard University Press.

Volkmer, Ingrid (1999), *News in the Global Sphere: A Study of CNN and its Impact on Global Communication*. Luton, U.K.: Luton University Press.

Von Vorys, Karl (1990), *American National Interest: Virtue and Power in Foreign Policy*. New York: Praeger.

Wallerstein, Immanuel (1976), "Semi-Peripheral Countries and the Contemporary World Crisis," *Theory and Society*, 3: 461–484.

Wallerstein, Immanuel (1993), "Geopolitical Strategies of the U.S. in a Post-American World," in Kaarle Nordenstreng and Herbert I. Schiller (eds.), *Beyond National Sovereignty: International Communication in the 1990s*. Norwood, N.J.: Ablex.

Wang, Georgette, and Ivan Servaes (2000), "Introduction," in Georgette Wang, Jan Servaes, and Anura Goonasekera (eds.), *The New Communications Landscape: Demystifying Media Globalization*. London: Routledge.

Wasserstrom, Jeffrey N., and Elizabeth Perry (eds.) (1994), *Popular Protest and Political Culture in Modern China*. Boulder, Colo.: Westview.

Waters, Malcolm (1995), *Globalization*. London: Routledge.

Weaver, David (ed.) (1998), *The Global Journalist*. Cresskill, N.J.: Hampton.

Wilensky, Harold (1964), "Mass Society and Mass Culture: Interdependence or Dependence?" *American Sociological Review*, 29, 2: 173–197.

Wong, Anny (1991), *Japan's Comprehensive National Security Strategy and its Economic Cooperation with the ASEAN Countries*. Hong Kong: Hong Kong Institute of Asia-Pacific Studies, Chinese University of Hong Kong.

Wuthnow, Robert (1989), *Communities of Discourse*. Cambridge, Mass.: Harvard University Press.

Xu, Xingtang (1997), "Hong Kong's Return and the News War of the Century," in Gong Yu (ed.), *The Night of the Transfer of Political Administration*. Hainan, China: Haitian Press (in Chinese).

Yokoi, Yoichi (1996), "Major Developments in Japan-China Economic Interdependence in 1990–1994," in Christopher Howe (ed.), *China and Japan: History, Trends, and Prospects*. Oxford: Clarendon Press.

Zaller, John R. (1992), *The Nature and Origins of Mass Opinion*. New York: Cambridge University Press.

Zaller, John, and Dennis Chiu (1996), "Government's Little Helper: US Press Coverage of Foreign Policy Crisis, 1945–1991," *Political Communication*, 13: 385–405.

Zelizer, Barbie (1992), "CNN, the Gulf War, and Journalistic Practices," *Journal of Communication*, 42, 1: 66–81.

Zelizer, Barbie (1993), "Journalists as Interpretive Communities," *Critical Studies in Mass Communication*, 10: 219–237.

Zhao, Yuezhi (1998), *Media, Market, and Democracy in China*. Urbana, Ill.: University of Illinois Press.

Authors

Chin-Chuan Lee is a professor of journalism and mass communication and the director of the China Times Center for Media and Social Studies at the University of Minnesota, formerly visiting chair professor at the Chinese University of Hong Kong. Among his English publications are *Media Imperialism Reconsidered: The Homogenizing of Television Culture* (author); *Mass Media and Political Transition: The Hong Kong Press in China's Orbit* (coauthor); *Voices of China: The Interplay of Politics and Journalism* (editor); *China's Media, Media's China* (editor); *Power, Money, and Media: Communication Patterns and Bureaucratic Control in Cultural China* (editor). He is also an author or editor of eight books in Chinese.

Joseph Man Chan is a professor in the school of journalism and communication at the Chinese University of Hong Kong. Among his publications are *Mass Media and Political Transition: The Hong Kong Press in China's Orbit* (coauthor); *Hong Kong Journalists in Transition* (coauthor); *In Search of Boundaries: Communication, Nation-State and Cultural Identities* (coeditor); *Press and Politics in Hong Kong: Case Studies from 1967 to 1997* (coeditor); *Communication and Societal Development* (coeditor, in Chinese); *Mass Communication and Market Economy* (coeditor, in Chinese).

Zhongdang Pan, formerly associate professor at the Chinese University of Hong Kong, is an associate professor in the Department of Communication Arts at the University of Wisconsin-Madison. Among his publications are *To See Ourselves: Comparing Traditional Chinese and American Cultural Values* (coauthor); *Mass Communication and Market Economy* (coeditor, in Chinese); *Symbol and Society* (coeditor, in Chinese).

Clement Y. K. So is an associate professor of journalism and communication at the Chinese University of Hong Kong. Among his publications are *Press and Politics in Hong Kong: Case Studies from 1967 to 1997* (coeditor); *Television Program Appreciation Index: Hong Kong Experience* (coeditor, in Chinese); *Impact and Issues in New Media: Toward Intelligent Societies* (coeditor).

245

Index